THE WORLD OF MIRRORS

A Bridge to Knowing and Being Your "True" Self

Also by Valerieann J. Skinner

Returning to the Heart

Cashing in on the "Simple Magic" of Color

THE WORLD OF MIRRORS

A Bridge to Knowing and Being Your "True" Self

Valerieann J. Skinner

NOTE: This book reflects only the personal experiences and views of the author. The information contained herein is for educational purposes only. This book is not designed to diagnose, treat, or prescribe any illness or disease. The author accepts no responsibility for such use. Conditions requiring medical attention should be referred to a physician.

Grammar editor: Cynthia Ann Johnson
Content editor: Nancy Hendriks
Author Photograph: © Bob Kempe
Cover painting, illustrations and design: Valerieann J. Skinner

Inner Light Creations

Published by Inner Light Creations
P.O. Box 32 Georgetown, Idaho 83239
valerieann@valerieann.com
www.valerieann.com
208-847-3129

Library of Congress Control Number: 2002105614

ISBN 0-9715621-4-8 $17.95 USA

For the peacemakers

Acknowledgements

A gracious thanks to, Alan, my eternal friend and companion, for your love and support. I am grateful that you are happy living with a woman who is forever answering the call of the creative voice. Thank you for making it possible for me to be at home with the children and realize my dreams as an artist, author and creator. I am blessed to be married to you.

A warm and loving thanks to my precious children, Sophia, Phalecia, Robert, Valanna, Neliann and Maria Rose. You are my greatest teachers and most delightful friends. Thank you for all of your help taking care of the house, the laundry . . . and me, while I created this book. I couldn't have done it without each one of your contributions. Thank you for your unconditional love and for believing in my dreams with me. May each of you realize your own dreams as well.

My deep gratitude goes to my mother and dear friend, Anna Marie, for continually believing in me and my dreams. Thank you for your commitment to the inner life and for sharing the journey with me. You are forever there, helping me see the light in the darkness and the peace in the storms . . . strengthening me when I'm weak. Without your encouragement, this book may never have been.

I honor my father, Russell, as a noble man of integrity. Thank you for your love and support all of my life and for the years filled with sound advice. You have taught me so many things for which I am most grateful.

Thanks to my brothers, who mean so much to me. You are the musical notes in my life, helping me play my song more harmoniously. Albert, thank you for your willingness to help me with anything I ever ask of you and for your excellent example of love and leadership. Todd, thanks for the tools I needed for breaking out of the boxes I was in and for your unique perspective on life. Mario, thank you for the feedback you gave me as you read the rough drafts of this book. It helped me more accurately say what I meant. And thank you for your example of flowing with life and doing what you love.

Many, many thanks to Cynthia Johnson, for your thorough and masterful job of grammar editing. Thank you for blessing me with your skills. You are a joy to work with. Thanks also to Adrianna, for sharing your mom with me and for your "editorial marks."

Nancy Hendriks, my content editor . . . a heartfelt thanks for your loving, excellent, editorial touch. You were a God send!

A heartfelt thanks to Alan Higley for the many unselfish hours spent preparing this book for the printer—what a loving gift!

With all my heart, I thank my dear friend and mentor, Karol K. Truman. Thank you for the knowledge and wisdom you have so freely shared with me. You are the angel who opened many important doors and a mirror I enjoy looking in. Thank you for your heart of gold and for your healing work when I was at the very bottom. I will be forever grateful.

Thanks to Delmont Truman for being a pillar of strength behind the scenes and for sharing Karol with people like myself. Alan and I have thoroughly enjoyed our association with you and appreciate your good example in the loving way you live your life.

To Marcy Freestone, a loving friend from way back—thanks for your unending love and friendship and for being a constant reminder to "lighten up." Thanks for the beautiful clothes you have made for me using your wonderful gift as a seamstress. You are one in a million!

Thank you, Tiina, for your unique and stimulating perspective on everything. Our delightful conversations always bring balance to my views. Thank you for valuing my inner light paintings and writing when they were in their infancy—when others weren't quite sure how to respond to them.

Janet Pancoast, thank you so much for the joyful months in Taiwan and for your wonderful friendship. Thank you for adding your wisdom, insights and editorial help to the early edition of this book and for the many other times you have come to my rescue.

A warm thanks to LaDawn DeWitt, for your unique way of being the love that you are. Thank you for helping me check the final draft and for your love and support while I was bringing this book to completion. You are a delightful friend indeed.

Many, many thanks to Connie and Alan Higley, Vance Barrett and David Pattey, for believing in this book enough to help me publish it. What would I have done without you? Sure glad I didn't have to find out.

A special thanks to the art students I have taught over the years. Little do you know how much I have learned from you. I love and appreciate each one of you.

Thanks to the many other friends and associates who's names are too numerous to mention, for your love, encouragement and support.

A loving thanks to you, dear reader, for your interest in this book. With this thanks goes my hope that it helps you on your journey to knowing and BEing your "True" Self.

Most of all, I thank my Creator, for life, passion and a physical world in which to know my "True" Self and experience joy therein.

Contents

Introduction
YOUR TRUE SELF

Part I
THE "WORLD OF MIRRORS"

Part II
DREAMS

Part III
MANY MIRRORS

Part IV
HEALING NEGATIVE REFLECTIONS

Part V
INTERPRETING SYMBOLS MADE SIMPLE

Your "True" Self

This book was written to assist you on your journey to knowing and BEing your "True" Self. The ideas presented herein are intended to supplement your understanding of life and supply more tools for your journey, not replace any spiritual or religious beliefs that are already serving you well. Hopefully, they will expand your view to include parts of your Self you have not yet explored.

What does it mean to know your "True" Self? There are many definitions describing who you are and hundreds of books covering the subject. However, when it comes right down to it, knowing your "True" Self is a personal experience revealed in a unique way to you . . . and you alone.

What the "True" Self is, can be hinted at, alluded to, openly discussed or laid out on a silver platter—but until you walk the path of discovering who you are for yourself, other people's definitions are meaningless. You are the one who must open the door and discover that truth—a truth too often covered by layers of negative feelings and thoughts and false and limiting beliefs. What you need, more than a definition is a way to get there—a bridge that enables you to know which feelings, thoughts and beliefs are keeping you in the box labeled "less than who you are"—a way that helps you discover who you really are . . . for yourself. This book provides a powerful tool for doing just that—a tool called the "World of Mirrors."

If you are willing to take a look at yourself in the "World of Mirrors" with a sincere desire to know what is therein revealed, you will find yourself surrounded by the answers you seek, the guidance you are looking for and the healing you desire. They are staring you in the face day and night. By learning to use the "World of Mirrors," you will be able to walk the path of Self discovery and cross the bridge to knowing your "True" Self with greater ease and more surety.

The information in this book is put together as follows:

First, you will be introduced to the wonderful "World of Mirrors" and how it works.

Second, you will learn—step by step—how to tap the reflective and healing power of a rarely understood and yet very beneficial mirror—your "dreams." These steps include learning how to remember *and* interpret them.

Third, you will learn how to extract guidance, healing and vital information about yourself from the other mirrors available.

Fourth, you will learn about a painless way to resolve the negative feelings that surface as you begin seeing your reflection in the "World of Mirrors."

Fifth, you will learn how to hear and trust the voice within . . . a vital stepping stone on the path to knowing your "True" Self.

Sixth, you will read about the opposing elements of which you and your world are comprised and then learn how to balance them peacefully. You will also acquire a unique vantage point that will forever change the way you view your life, other people and the world.

Seventh, you will find hundreds of symbols and possible interpretations for each one, plus questions to help you find your own meanings for the symbols.

Eighth, there is a section for recording your own symbols and interpretations as you begin observing the *"reflections of yourself."* This section will become a valuable and helpful friend.

**Enjoy your journey to
Knowing and Being Your "True" Self!**

The "World of Mirrors"

One

Reflections

Every morning, to make sure you look your best, you probably get ready for the day using a mirror. Do you give equal attention to the appearance of your inner Self? Wouldn't it be wonderful if there was a mirror with the unique ability to reflect what's going on *inside*, a mirror that could reveal the solutions to your problems? Well . . . there is! It's called the "World of Mirrors." You may be able to walk away from the mirror of your outer appearance, but you can never escape the inner reflections found in this unique mirror. It constantly reveals the truth of your inside world to you, every detail, both desirable and undesirable—just as the outer mirror reflects your beauty or blemishes on the outside. As you learn how to use the "World of Mirrors," freedom will fly to your doorstep and reside within you.

The "World of Mirrors"

This is a tool you can use to see your reflection in virtually everything. It is unlimited in its ability to reflect things about you to yourself—good and bad. It reveals the things you need to change, the solutions to your problems, your path to healing and much more.

Are you happy with everything in your life right now? What are your desires and goals? Are there things that challenge you and your ability to realize your dreams? What would you like to change or improve? This is where the "World of Mirrors" can help. Gather the courage to really face yourself. Pick a mirror . . . any mirror . . . and take a look. Look with a real desire to see what's being reflected. Where can you find the "World of Mirrors?" Virtually everywhere.

Here are just a few of the mirrors from which you can choose . . .

- your dreams
- your life
- your home
- your car
- your spouse
- your surroundings

- your children
- your friends
- your business
- your job
- movies
- your memories

- world events
- your finances
- your thoughts
- your words
- scriptures
- books you're reading

All of these mirrors reflect you . . . believe it or not. You are connected to everything. What you do or don't do affects the entire planet. You have the power to change the world. You create your own destiny. It all begins inside. This book will help you master the art of seeing your reflection in the "World of Mirrors." It will teach you how to recognize and interpret the messages in these mirrors. It will enable you to successfully extract the guidance, healing and wisdom available—that which will help you uncover and get to know your "True" Self.

Acknowledging our less acceptable aspects is challenging, (none of us want to admit to undesirable/bad/evil tendencies). But . . . in order to find the truth of who we are, remedy our problems and bring peace and healing into our lives, we need to recognize these tendencies and change them.

It's one thing to look in the outer mirror to see if your hair is combed neatly, but quite another to look in the mirror of your dreams, other people and the world to see if there's something about you that needs repairing. Learning how to find the behaviors you don't like about others—*in yourself*—is especially challenging. The "World of Mirrors" is very accurate, however, in revealing what is really going on inside, whether you choose to believe what you see or not.

Sometimes the reflections are obvious and at other times more subtle, but still they reflect something about you. For example, the friend who stabbed you in the back may be reflecting that you are somehow doing the same to yourself or someone else . . . or perhaps the situation was there to help you learn to be more forgiving. The car that broke down may be warning you that you are about to have a break down . . . or perhaps it's reflecting that you need to take better care of yourself. The people who give you the most difficulty in life are also reflecting things about *you* to *yourself*—attitudes and parts of your Self you may not want to recognize—or perhaps reflecting your unresolved negative feelings.

If you have never heard this concept, you may want to reject it. It's sometimes hard to swallow until you have experienced it for yourself. I didn't want to believe it either. Most of us don't want to believe that the things we don't like about others are reflections of ourselves—especially when the reflections are undesirable. Because my husband was the main mirror in my life when I first heard this, I argued:

- "He's the one who doesn't understand."
- "He's the one who is stubborn and unwilling to change . . . not ME!"
- "How can finding 'his' undesirable characteristics in 'me,' and changing them there, have any affect on him? He still won't understand me. He will still be stubborn and unwilling to change!"
- "He's the one who needs to change!"

When I finally decided to give this idea a try—seeing my husband as a reflection of me—the results were astonishing! I began seeing how little "I" tried to be understanding and how stubborn and unwilling to change "I" had been. To my amazement, however, as I resolved the problems I saw in him, *inside myself*, I began noticing more desirable qualities in him. Why? Because I was improving *myself*. We see that which we are! As I improved, I saw the better side of myself reflected in him.

Once we see what the mirrors are showing us, if we change these reflections . . . from the *inside* out, we will experience more peace, joy and happiness.

As the awareness of "everything being your reflection" begins traveling with you, openness and honesty will become your companions. All the areas of your life (physical, mental, emotional and spiritual), as well as your attitudes and beliefs, will be in plain view, *reflected in everyone and everything*. Others with this same awareness, will likewise see you as you are. Honesty will become part of your daily life. You will no longer want or be able to hide behind the mask of pretense or a false identity. What a wonderful world . . . when we have all removed our masks and cleaned our mirrors . . . from within!

At first, the idea of being totally unmasked . . . open and honest . . . willing to see and be the real you, may seem a bit scary, but it's the only way to experience true freedom. This is a freedom which allows you to live according to that which you feel inside, without fear of other peoples judgements or expectations. Ask yourself, "Am I truly free right now?" "Do I ever do things because it's what *others* expect, instead of doing what I feel to do?"

In a class I was teaching, we were discussing the feelings that keep us from freely expressing ourselves. A woman, with beautiful auburn hair and a lovely smile, gave a concrete example of how we limit ourselves by yielding to the fear of what other people will think. She said, "Do you know what I'd really love to do but don't dare because I'm afraid of what others will think?" Everyone in the class leaned forward a little, eager to hear her secret desire. She continued, "I would love to go to used clothing stores and purchase all kinds of old ladies' hats with flowers and things on them and buy bright, colorful, strange clothes and wear them around town!" What would be the harm in her doing so? Everyone in the class agreed that it would add color and a spark of life everywhere she went. They felt it would be a positive experience for not only her but everyone who saw her. By resolving the fear of what others would think, she would be free to wear her colorful hats and clothes around town and be her True Self. By being true to herself, or in other words, by loving herself and acting accordingly, the energy emanating from her would be "love," and others would feel it. It's effect would be positive. The Self revealed after looking in the mirror of the world and resolving whatever negative, limiting feelings are reflected, is always beautiful and desirable. By sharing this with the class, this woman was also mirroring to everyone the need to face their own fear of how others would respond if they did the things they desired to do.

Go buy your colorful, outrageous hats or clothes and wear them! Give yourself permission to follow the desires of your heart. Be true to yourself. Face yourself in the "World of Mirrors" and break through the fears, negative feelings and limiting beliefs therein revealed. Get rid of everything that is keeping you in a box. Throw away the clothes that are hiding your true identity. Who else can set you free . . . but *you*?

Successfully interpreting the reflections you see in the many mirrors available includes being honest with yourself and being willing to break out of your box. It requires that you learn to be sensitive to how you feel and familiar with your inner world. As you begin honoring your true feelings and desires with your actions, it is important to remember your connection to everyone and everything. Living your life honestly does not mean living it as though it's "only about you." This is an attitude of separation psychology, which disregards your relationship with others. We would do well to follow the motto of the Three Musketeers: "All for one and one for all" because we *are* in this together!

It is important to pass your words and actions through your heart before you say or doing anything—considering yourself and your feelings, while still remembering your connection to everyone else. For example, when my three-year-old shows me a picture she has just drawn, I don't say, "What in the world is that? It looks like a bunch of scribbles," even though it may appear that way. Rather, I consult my feelings of love and my connection to her and respond with, "That's beautiful, Maria!" I then give the artwork a special place on the wall, honoring her and her ability to express herself on paper. This is coming from feeling connected to my daughter rather than feeling separate from her. It is listening to the wise sage within who will always prompt you to react lovingly and with consideration for everyone while still honoring how you feel and what is best for you.

As you see and heal the undesirable reflections in the world you're in, learn to live a life of honesty and be true to the deepest, most loving feelings you know . . . from feeling connected to all. How you respond is your choice. By learning to use the "World of Mirrors"—learning to see yourself in everything—you will see just how connected all of us really are.

The reflections in the many mirrors of your inner and outer world will provide you with the glasses to clearly see your path and the messages, wisdom and guidance along the way—a way to see the "Celestial Wings of Glory" that are already yours. This reflective process is a bridge to knowing and BEing your True Self.

A Mirror in Action

When I was twenty-one I had a strong desire to serve God by sharing His gospel as a missionary. I studied Mandarin Chinese for nine weeks, then flew to Taiwan, where I lived and served as a missionary for sixteen months. Little did I know when I left, that it would be "me" who would benefit the most.

As missionaries, we typically served in companionships of two, living in assigned areas for an undetermined number of months. When directed by the President of our mission area to do so, we moved to a new city and/or changed companions. My third companion was Sister Hsiao, a Chinese woman, who still wore the mandatory hair style for schoolgirls—cut straight below the ears. Her tapered bangs were the only indication that she was old enough to choose the way she wore it.

When we first met, we both had a premonition that we would be companions at some point. We were therefore excited when we finally experienced this. Being together, however, was not at all what either of us expected.

From 9:00 a.m. to 9:00 p.m. we knocked on one red door after another in Feng Shan, a city on the southern tip of Taiwan, searching for people who were interested in our message. I wasn't very fluent in Mandarin yet, which made it challenging for me to talk to people. Besides, I rationalized in my mind, people would surely prefer listening to a native, like Sister Hsiao, speak eloquently, than a foreigner making a mess of the language. I was also afraid of "not being accepted" and of "appearing stupid" if I revealed my inability to speak the language. Like most people, I wanted to be loved and accepted. The beliefs I internalized as a child however, caused me to believe this was achieved by "being smart, good and not making mistakes." While growing up, I had observed that people who knew a lot—those who spoke fluently and knowledgeably—were considered smart, were looked up to, approved of and generally more accepted. Therefore, I wanted to be smart, knowledgeable and speak fluently—so I could be looked up to, approved of and accepted too. At the time of this experience, however, I was completely unconscious of the underlying reasons for feeling afraid to speak.

For weeks, I refrained from speaking my true feelings, unless I could do so in English. I especially denied voice to any feelings which didn't fit into the "good" category, so as to appear as good as possible, banishing these feelings into oblivion . . . or so I thought. Even though I would have sworn on a stack of Bibles that I was "free"—in reality I was trapped in a self-created prison of negative feelings, a result of the false beliefs I internalized as a child. These feelings influenced my response to every situation. The "fear" of making a "mistake" and of "appearing stupid" kept me from speaking the feelings of my heart. The "fear" of not being "accepted" and not being "good enough" suppressed any desire to do things I thought would not be considered "good" or "acceptable" to others.

As time went on, the desire to freely express myself increased, but my fears kept me silent. As a result of not sharing how I felt in various situations with Sister Hsiao, I began perceiving her as someone who thought she was always right and whose opinions mattered more than mine. It *seemed* that whenever I did speak out on anything, my ideas were cast aside in favor of hers. We *always* did what *she* thought we ought to do . . . or so it appeared to *me*, reinforcing my feelings of being "stupid," "not good enough" and "not accepted." This caused me to bury even more feelings. I went along with her on the outside, while unconsciously "resenting" her on the inside. As long as I projected the cause of my unresolved feelings onto Sister Hsiao, making it "her fault," not mine, I created a false sense of "being good" which protected me from having to face the real problems inside myself—at least for awhile.

It's so amusing to me now, to think about the two of us going from door to door every day, preaching a gospel of love, when our lives were far from being good examples of it. We put on our "masks of perfection" as we went out the door each day, only to return to the truth of our lovelessness each night.

Week after week, the bad feelings piled up as we tried to make our conflicts invisible. I was miserable inside, however, feeling guilty for my ill feelings, knowing that I was preaching to others not to entertain such. My companion, on the other hand, was experiencing extreme headaches, which I later learned were a result of the negative feelings she was stuffing inside. The inner pressure was building for both of us.

Each month we received a letter in the mail from the president of our mission informing us which city we were to serve in and who our companion was going to be for the next month. I prayed continually to be removed from this situation by being transferred to another city and a new companion . . . but month after month I was left in the same spot. I began questioning whether or not my prayers were being heard. Why would God allow me to suffer so? Finally, my companion was down to the last month of her mission and **I did not want to spend it with her!**

When the letter came in the mail mandating that I remain with Sister Hsiao, it was more than I could bear. The pain inside was so great that the thought of having to endure it any longer finally forced me to face myself and my feelings. As I read the letter, all of the negative feelings I thought I had successfully avoided or permanently done away with, exploded to the surface. The long suppressed hate, anger and resentment were like hot lava in my throat. I immediately bolted down the hall and into the back room of our second story apartment. Slamming the door—I began venting. I cried and spoke horrible things out loud for what seemed like hours. Words I had denied myself the privilege of speaking spewed out of my mouth. The eruption of my emotional volcano revealed the folly of thinking I could do away with negative feelings by stuffing them inside. These feelings were much like the sewage in the canal that ran behind the back of our apartment and it felt good as I finally released them.

As the lava began cooling, I realized how helpless I felt in my ability to change the situation. I began praying for help. While doing so, what many of the other missionaries had said about my companion came to mind . . . that she was "chyang lye de." I didn't know what it meant and hadn't bothered finding out either, as there were many words I heard daily that I didn't understand. This reveals yet another example of being imprisoned by negative feelings. I acted as if I understood more Mandarin than I did for "fear" others would think I was "stupid." This only resulted in my being dishonest with myself.

As I pondered the situation with Sister Hsiao, I decided to find out what the words used to describe her meant, so I looked them up in a Chinese dictionary. To my amazement, I learned that the other missionaries had been saying she was "strong willed." Oh really! I immediately recalled my mission president saying the very same thing about *me*. The realization that I was just like her penetrated me to the core—I was just as strong willed as she was and that is what I hated about her. Prior to this experience, I had never recognized this about myself. With this new awareness, I was able to see that *all* of the things I didn't like about her were found in the mirror—reflections of me. *What a revelation . . .* yet, very difficult to face!

One of the other things I found so unacceptable about her was her need to be perfect in every way. She was always right, never making mistakes . . . or so it appeared to me. How interesting! I was probably more of a perfectionist than she was, having worked hard for years to avoid the very appearance of making a mistake. Now I recognized that I had made one of the biggest . . . denying myself and my feelings!

With this new understanding of the situation, how could I hate someone . . . who was just like me? That would mean I would have to hate myself! It was at this moment of looking in the "World of Mirrors" that I experienced my first real change of heart. I began understanding love in a new way. In order to truly love Sister Hsaio, it was necessary for me to accept both of us, with our imperfections included, which became easy once I recognized that we were so much alike. This realization actually made me laugh aloud, which also helped change the negative energy inside. This was the first of many experiences wherein I learned that being "good" has more to do with being true to and accepting yourself just as you are, than in pleasing others and seeking acceptance outside yourself.

The green grass and flowers that grew out of the lava were beautiful—unconditional love replaced the hard black hate, anger and resentment. By forgiving her and myself and accepting us as we were, both the good *and* the bad, I was relieved of a great burden.

> *"And why beholdest thou the mote that is in thy brother's eye, but considerest not the beam that is in thine own eye? Or how wilt thou say to thy brother, Let me pull out the mote out of thine eye; and, behold, a beam is in thine own eye?"* — Matthew 7:3-4 —

My experiences as a missionary were many and wonderful. Whether or not I helped any *Chinese* people better understand the love of God can only be known by those I came in contact with, however, I do know there was one person who began to understand love . . . **me!**

What transpired during the last month with this companion was no less than a miracle. I grew to love her with the same degree I had hated her and her love was returned. Most important, I began loving and accepting myself in a new way . . . uncovering and knowing more of my "true" characteristics . . . becoming more acquainted with my True Self.

Our parting was difficult. We both wished our time together could have been longer. What an amazing transformation, all because we were now coming from *love* . . . *unconditional love.*

As I prepared to board the plane for home at the end of my mission several months later, Sister Hsiao, who was now married and expecting her first child, came to see me off. It was a joyous reunion. I cried once more, but for a different reason. I didn't want to leave her!

Now that I had tasted the sweetness of unconditional love—a bit of my True Self—it was easy to understand why I had been left with this companion for so long. It's amazing how effective difficult and challenging experiences are as teachers.

Looking at your reflection in the mirror of other people may be like a constant slap in the face. But, if you use what is revealed in the "World of Mirrors" to become aware of the things you need to change within yourself, it will definitely be worth whatever you have to go through to reach the end results . . . the truth of who you are!

I challenge you to see the difficult people and circumstances in your life as your teachers. Ask what they are there to teach you about yourself. Be open and willing to see the things you need to change . . . and then change them. This is the bridge that will help you connect where you have been to where you desire being . . . to knowing your True Self.

Dreams

Three

Your Reflection Revealed in Dreams

Dreams are useful and powerful as mirrors. The most helpful method of interpretation available for using dreams to heal and give direction is by utilizing their reflective power and likening every element in your dreams "to yourself." The wise sage within, the part of you who knows everything about you, puts on graphic plays nightly, reflecting your truth, the truth that is so often buried deep inside. Dreams unfold the mystery of who you are.

Finding the *reflective* power in the symbols, rather than only seeing objects of reality allows your dream dramas to bring you to a greater and greater conscious awareness of yourself and your world. It allows the divine aspect of you to perform his/her magic. Let's look at a dream to see how this magic works.

— Chased by a Bull —

Over and over, as a child, I dreamed of a black bull chasing me. Around the corrals I ran, jumping over fences . . . scrambling to escape. At times I would stop and face the bull, my fear disappearing. Whenever I did so, the bull would stop chasing me and stand upright on his hind legs. Taking on human characteristics, he would lean on the fence, as you would with your elbow, and talk to me. Eventually, the fear would return and with it the chase.

As a child, because I took this dream objectively, I was always alert when I was around the bulls on the farm, not wanting to be chased. Finally, with the knowledge of the "World of Mirrors," I learned to ask what the bull represented about *me*. How did the nature of a bull represent something about my own nature?

A bull can represent many things, such as the following:

- strength
- force
- power
- fertility
- masculine characteristics

Running from the bull in my dream shows that I "feared" the attributes represented by the bull. And, what were these attributes? After contemplating the bull as a metaphor, I realized that I feared my own strength, power and masculine side.

I was being shown that I needed to face my fear of these attributes and embrace them. In the dream, as soon as fear left the scene, I was able to face the bull. Upon doing so he quit chasing me and began conversing with me instead—or in other words, I began interacting with the parts of myself, of which I had been unconscious. This indicates that there was a part of me that did have the courage to face and embrace the aspects of myself I was not integrating into my personality at the time. I would be able to "take the bull by the horn" so to speak . . . as soon as I faced my fear. By embodying the attributes of the bull—my own strength, power and masculine aspects—I would have nothing to run from.

In looking further into this dream, you recall that the color of the bull was black. What did black represent? I read many ideas about the meaning of black. After considering the possibilities, I could see that it represented the unknown parts of myself, my shadow or the mysteries of my subconscious mind. Black also means strength, therefore representing *my* strength. By identifying the meaning of each element in the dream (not only the meaning of the bull, but also the meaning of the color) it helped me more clearly identify what I was afraid of and the parts of me I needed to face and/or embrace in myself.

If identifying the meaning of the bull and the color had not been sufficient information to know the meaning of the dream, I could have asked more questions, like, "What was the breed of bull?" "Was it a breed that I was familiar with or not?" "Was it a young or old bull?" "Was it a sunny or cloudy day?" "How was I dressed?" Probing with questions always sheds more light on the symbols, opening up new possibilities for meaning—paving the way for an "aha." Ask questions until one of them sparks your inner knowing of what the symbol means to you.

There was another interesting aspect of this dream—the way I felt while the dream played out. Even though I was trying to get away from the bull, I recall enjoying the chase like a game. Therefore, the fear was also something good. What could possible be "good" about the fear? It was the *friend* that kept me in motion, motivating me to jump the fences. What did the fences represent? Fences can symbolize barriers. In my dream, they represented the structures and beliefs conditioning my view of the world, the views keeping me boxed in and unable to see a bigger picture. Strangely enough, the personal attributes I sought, which were represented by the bull, were also the very attributes my structures and beliefs caused me to fear. In turn, this fear motivated me to jump the belief barriers that were keeping me from embracing my power and strength. This dream showed *me,* trapped in a circle of contradictions. Yet, these conflicting metaphors helped me step into the truth of who I was . . . to acknowledge *me*, with all of my inherent strengths and characteristics. I have had many such dreams as I have walked my path, each one progressively helping me come to more fully know my True Self.

Often, the things which appear bad in one situation can be equally good in another, like the fear in my dream. Who wants fear hanging around? And yet, fear motivated me to jump the fences, which is what I needed to do in order to find my strengths. Life is full of contradictions, but are they really contradictions? Once you realize that *everything* can be either good *or* bad, depending on your perspective, seeming contradictions fade and with them the need to judge. You can then accept situations and people as they are "in the moment." There is more on this later in the book.

Your life's journey is dramatically acted out while you sleep. By uncovering the meaning of the dramas, you can avoid the longer route of hard knocks to becoming aware of the web you have woven with unresolved negative feelings—the fabric covering your True Self. Use your dreams to recognize what these negative feelings are and to help you resolve them. Take advantage of the "World of Mirrors" and harvest the healing and help there for you.

Steps for Interpreting Your Dreams

These steps do not need to be followed in order. Become familiar with them and use them as you feel best serves you.

1. PAUSE EACH MORNING TO RECALL YOUR DREAMS

As soon as you realize you are waking up, keep your body still and your eyes closed. You can still dream while your body is not moving. Focus on remembering your dreams. Locate key images and allow the story line to form. Notice your feelings and allow these feelings to generate images. See the dream, feel the feelings, and rehearse the dream to yourself silently so that all parts of the brain work together. Get the details in your mind before you open your eyes. You may want to begin making a gentler transition from dreaming to waking. Allow quiet time for this important rite of passage.

2. RECORD YOUR DREAMS

Writing down your dreams is one of the most important things you can do to help you remember and understand them! Keep paper (just a notebook will do) and pencil/pen by your bed. As soon as you wake up, write down everything you remember including all activities, colors, people, the setting and the feelings.

Even if you awaken in the middle of the night with a powerful impression on your mind or a dream you are sure you will never forget . . . write it down. If you don't . . . you *will* forget.

You may even want to have a recorder by your bed and speak into it instead of writing. It doesn't matter *how* you record your dreams. By keeping a record, you can refer back to what the various symbols represented in past dreams. You will begin recognizing repeating elements and will become more and more familiar with what they are saying to you.

3. GIVE YOUR DREAM A TITLE

Use a title that will help bring the details of the dream to mind when you refer back to it later. As you have similar dreams, you can compare their interpretations to learn what specific symbols more accurately mean to *you*.

4. RECORD THE DATE ON WHICH YOUR DREAM OCCURRED

Knowing the date of your dreams can sometimes help you better understand the symbols after time has passed. Look back at your dreams once in awhile. Notice when you had certain dreams and pay attention to their relationship to the events in your life surrounding the dream. You may get a few "aha's" that will help you better understand future dreams.

5. DRAW KEY IMAGES OR DOODLES

When a dream or image in a dream is too difficult to describe, draw a picture of it. Pictures always say more than words . . . even if they are poorly drawn. Quality doesn't count here. You may want to do a rough sketch of the images that come to mind or just doodle. Doodling keeps you out of your left, logical brain and in the right brain where your intuition has a chance to work. Sometimes while doodling, something seemingly out of the clear blue will come to mind. If and when it does, you can know it is connected to the meaning of your dream.

6. MAKE A LIST OF DREAM SYMBOLS

Refer to what you wrote in step 2, then list the objects, people, places, main events and colors of things. Leave space for writing ideas, information and interpretations by each one as you explore them in the following steps.

7. STUDY THE SYMBOLS AND APPLY THE "WORLD OF MIRRORS."

Dreams are filled with symbols. A symbol is defined as something that represents more than itself. We need to look at things associated with the symbol, things that are similar or even opposite in order to discover their meaning. Symbols bridge the gap between the outer and inner world, expressing what we have no words for. They're like puzzles. We find a piece at a time and eventually put them all together to see the whole picture.

Look at the symbols you listed in Step 6 and apply the "World of Mirrors"—looking for ways in which the symbols represent things about you. Look them up in Chapter 21, *"Symbols and Possible Interpretations."* Here you will find ideas and questions you can ask to help interpret the symbols. Remember, however, that the meanings may or may not apply to you and your dream specifically. It is imperative that you listen to the voice within to know which ideas are true for you. It may also be helpful to look up the central symbols in an encyclopedia or dictionary. Learn everything you can about each symbol and then go inside yourself and ask to know how the things you learn apply to you. Record your insights by each symbol.

Take the symbol of a baby for instance. It can mean a new responsibility, project, idea or attitude that you may have or will give birth to. What takes place in the dream in regard to the baby will give more clues about your new project or idea.

I have known several women who have dreamed of having a baby and have only seen the literal message of their dreams. One woman for instance, dreamed of a little girl. She already had seven children at the time, one girl and the rest boys. She therefore thought there was another girl for her. Three boys later, she began wondering if it meant something else. Even if the dream was literally about a girl waiting to be born, even now it would help her to look at what the new baby girl in her dream represents about herself. What new project, idea, or part of herself, of a feeling nature, was she putting off or avoiding? I say "feeling nature," because a female (the baby girl) represents female aspects which have to do with feelings. A male, on the other hand, represents male aspects which have to do with thinking or analytic characteristics.

If your dreams have a symbol not listed in Chapter 21, consult Chapter 15, *"Steps for Interpreting Any Symbol."* For future reference, record any symbols not already found in Chapter 21 in Chapter 22, *"My Personal List of Symbols."*

Remember: every aspect of a dream symbolizes something about *you*, even if it has a literal meaning or accurately portrays things about others!

8. USE FREE ASSOCIATION

Write down any thoughts that come to mind in regard to the activities, people, setting and emotional content of the dream. Use free association with the symbols identified in step 6. Ask yourself, "What else does this symbol bring to my mind?" Perhaps it will trigger a memory of an event years ago and/or something seemingly unrelated. If an event comes to mind, it probably has something to do with the meaning of your dream. Allow yourself to go with the thoughts that come to you and see where they take you. Don't be too hasty to dismiss ideas that don't seem related.

9. ANALYZE YOUR FEELINGS

Feelings are an important part of your dreams. Upon waking from a dream, there are usually many feelings. Allow yourself to feel them. Try to discover what they are associated with and let them run themselves out. Use your dreams as a tool to reveal negative feelings you may have stuffed—feelings you haven't yet resolved. Make a list of these feelings.

It is now becoming well known that unresolved negative feelings can cause illness and disease. If indeed this is true, changing these negative feelings to positive ones is very important. Try using the *"Painless Tool"* in Chapter 14 to help resolve any negative feelings you have identified.

10. Look at the Different Levels of Meaning

Dreams are like ancient temples with outer courts for the masses and inner sanctuaries for the initiated. Anyone with a little faith can enter the outer courts, but one must work and study before entering the center where the mysteries are revealed.

There is the outer more obvious story of the dream which is like the outer courts (the objective meaning), and an inner more mysterious meaning (the subjective meaning) which is found only by diligent searching. We have to look beyond the obvious to get to the deeper, more beneficial meanings.

To be more specific as to the meaning of **"objective"** and **"subjective,"** we will consult the *"American Heritage Dictionary"* which defines them as follows:

Objective 1. Of or having to do with a material object as distinguished from a mental concept, idea, or belief. 2. Having actual existence or reality. 3. a. Uninfluenced by emotion, surmise, or personal prejudice. b. Based on observable phenomena; presented factually.

Subjective 1. Pertaining to the real nature of something; essential. 2. a. Proceeding from or taking place within an individual's mind such as to be unaffected by the external world. b. Particular to a given individual; personal. 3. Existing only in the experiencer's mind and incapable of external verification.

When we dream of something or someone familiar to us, we need to focus on the question of whether the dream symbol should be analyzed on the objective or subjective level . . . or both. It's important to be balanced in our observations. Most of us have spent a lot more of our time viewing our dreams and life from an objective angle. We need to balance that by spending some time going within ourselves and looking at everything from an inward, subjective perspective. This is the part of us that is less explored and therefore most often reflected in dreams.

As you look at each dream, you may want to begin on the objective level. When analyzing objectively, ask whether the dream's message is *literally* telling you about a person, object or situation which exists in your waking life. Ask if it is telling you something about your friend or spouse (or whoever the person in the dream is), or your job (or whatever situation is being addressed), or your pet or clothes (or whatever familiar object appears in the dream). It is unusual for the dream to have it's most powerful meaning on this level, but one should examine the objective level to see what can be learned.

Sometimes people find warnings in their dreams on an objective level. A girl I know, dreamed that her uncle and grandfather were going to sell a particular cow at the auction. She had raised this cow and loved it dearly. The dream really upset her because she didn't want to lose her friend. She told her grandmother about the dream and her grandmother understood and valued her feelings. Being aware that this is exactly what the uncle and grandfather were going to do with the cow the next day, her grandmother was able to stop it from happening. So . . . in this situation, by paying attention to her dream and sharing it, the girl did not have to experience the actual event in waking life. These types of dreams are not as common . . . but they do happen.

Remember, as you begin interpreting your own dreams, it is more common for all elements in your dreams, even the familiar, to speak subjectively. Even in a dream of warning, there will also be subjective meaning. Therefore, every dream about the familiar should be looked at closely, not only on the objective but subjective level. This means, after you do associations with the familiar elements, you should then substitute those associations to find the dream story that is being told symbolically.

In other words, the girl could also ask questions like, "What does this cow mean or represent about me?" "What does it remind me of?" "Does the symbol have any cultural or other associations that are significant?" This is the process that should be applied to any familiar element as well as the unfamiliar in order to find the symbolic, subjective meaning of a dream.

The message of a dream can vary dramatically depending on whether you, the dreamer, pay attention to the objective or subjective level. Once again, it is my experience that the real richness is found on the subjective level.

Here are examples of questions you can ask for each level of meaning:

QUESTIONS TO ASK FOR OBJECTIVE MEANINGS.

- What is the image's function in the dream . . . its kind, color, shape, texture, age, condition, etc.?
- What is the image's function in waking life?
- What does it do?
- What is its main purpose?
- What is the literal message?

QUESTIONS TO ASK FOR SUBJECTIVE MEANINGS.

- What does this image mean to me?
- What does this image represent about me?
- What does it remind me of?
- What is it like?
- What are my personal associations with it?
- How am "I" like each person or object in the dream?

11. ASK QUESTIONS AND FISH FOR MEANING.

Use the 24 questions in Chapter 17 to further analyze your dream and its symbols. Not all questions will work equally well for every dream. Find the ones that apply and keep fishing. Ask questions and listen for the answers. Your inner wisdom will answer, but first . . . you must ask.

12. SUM IT UP.

After recording and analyzing your dream and its symbols in the above steps, take a minute to sum up your findings. In a sentence or two, write the main message of your dream.

Those Strange Dreams

Oh the horror! As you drop the bloody ax from your hand, it's unmistakable . . . your brother's body lies limp and lifeless on the cement floor. Later that same night, after making love with your neighbor, your chest tightens with the realization of your unfaithful act, guilt rushing through you like a lightening bolt. A hand softly touches your face and you open your eyes to see the smiling face of your spouse and hear, "What dream has caused you to tighten your body so?" Relieved beyond measure that it is only a dream, you take in a deep breath and let it go. "Oh, nothing," you answer, but inside, the desire to know why you dreamed such things haunts you. The experiences are so real that you continue feeling guilty until the events of the day take over your thoughts, banning the memory of the dream into oblivion . . . only to be replaced by new adventures and horrors the next night.

Many people have experienced similar kinds of dreams and if you're like most, you have also wondered *why*. These types of dreams stem from aspects of you that have been locked away in the dungeons of your psyche. Your natural inclination for balance and wholeness is constantly calling these parts forth, hoping to integrate them into the whole. When, for instance, you deny, fear, or avoid parts of yourself and bury them in the subconscious, they will appear in your dreams in an effort to break through the repression and gain access to consciousness. Your buried aspects may take on many forms to get your attention, and appear in frightening or dreadful ways, becoming the "monsters" or undesirable elements in your dreams. It is easy to mistake them for something bad or devilish, when in fact, they are parts of *you* asking to be set free by being consciously *understood* and *accepted*.

Parts of your repressed personality or feelings may show up as, not only *dreams* of illness, but actual *physical* illnesses. Thus, paying attention to your dreams may reveal disease and illness about to manifest in the flesh. As you face and resolve the fears and darkness of your subconscious, the negative processes going on in your life can be reversed and healing can begin taking place.

Going back to the disturbing dreams of murder and adultery, why would anyone dream such things? Remember, in the "World of Mirrors" . . . *everyone and everything in the dream represent something about you, the dreamer*. These dream dramas are trying to tell you something about *you*. If you murder someone, it may be bringing to you the awareness that you have just done away with an undesirable behavioral pattern or personality trait. Ask yourself what the person you murdered represents about you. What attitudes or beliefs are you letting go? Or, maybe it's trying to tell you that you *need* to do away with some of your present attitudes or beliefs. Ask yourself what you need to do away with, then listen to the first ideas that come to mind. These impressions are your intuition or inner wisdom speaking to you. Pay attention!

If you find yourself making love to someone in your dream, once again, look at what that person represents about *you*. What do you love about that person that you haven't recognized in yourself? Do you need to "love" yourself more? Do you need to be more passionate about something? It may also indicate that you are integrating the male/female side of yourself (opposite from your gender or if it is a homosexual dream, you may be integrating the aspects of your own gender) into your personality. On the other hand, perhaps you are not being true or faithful to yourself. Look at both sides of the coin. Most important, pay attention to the ideas that resonate with you. As soon as you have the slightest "aha" about the meaning of something in a dream, you can know that you have received the most accurate interpretation . . . the one from your inner Self. Trust it. The more you listen, the easier it will be to interpret your dreams.

There are as many versions of strange dreams as there are people. When the next one strikes you, remember to use the "World of Mirrors." No matter how "strange" or "bad" the dream seems, if you can step back and see every element as a symbol representing something about you and your life, you will be able to more easily find the meaning. Even though they may be very strange or scary, there really aren't any "bad" dreams. They are all working for your ultimate good. Be grateful for all your dreams.

Five

Only For "You"

There have been times when others have warned me with their dreams of doom and gloom. Observation and experience have taught me not to take the dreams of others as an authoritative voice for myself. Most often, their dreams were prophesying of *their* personal story of doom and gloom lying in wait, not mine or the worlds.

For instance, one woman dreamed of the dam breaking above her community, destroying everything in its path. Because she only interpreted the dream's message on an objective level, she and her family moved to another state thinking to avoid the catastrophe. As time passed, the dam broke "within her" and I watched as she swam through a flood of emotions. She tried to run from that which she could never escape . . . herself! Wherever you go . . . there you are!

There are many symbols which tempt us to interpret them only on a literal level—death for example. Having dreamed of many family members and friends dying over the years (people who are still alive today, by the way) it has been my experience that death has more to do with putting to rest either less than desirable aspects of our Self or traits that are no longer needed. These are represented by the dying person in the dream. Ask yourself how you are like the person in the dream. What does this person mirror about you?

There may be times when you are given information in your dreams for someone else, but this is *rare*. Your dreams are usually for *your* benefit and direction. Remember this when you are inclined to warn someone because of a dream you had which involved them. Your dreams will often reveal things about other people, but they are usually doing so to bring awareness to you about *you*! After all, wasn't it YOUR dream? Don't you think other people are given their own dreams with messages for them? There are always exceptions, but as a general rule, it is most effective to apply *your* dream imagery to *yourself*.

The time has come to quit projecting what you don't want to see about yourself, in your life and your dreams, onto others. Remember to look in the mirror the next time you think you need to warn someone else because of a dream you had which involved them! Be willing to confront yourself and make the changes necessary so you can walk into your unlimited Self and realize your full potential. Listen to and heed the messages given to you through your dreams with an awareness that . . . *they are for you*!

Six

How to Interpret Colors in Your Dreams

Color appears in dreams in many ways—as an image that is completely or partly in color or as an entire dream in natural color (meaning that everything is colored the way you normally see it). Some people say that most of their dreams are without color, or in other words, in black and white. These are cases where, perhaps, color was not a part of the dream experience. It may also represent the lack of living a life that is "colorful" (not living life with zest and joy).

Black, white or gray images in dreams can actually have color significance. Recalling a black object for example represents the visual image of "blackness" which is different from simply recalling the image in its usual color. The reason something is "black" in a dream is usually because it needs to be so in order to convey a message—its blackness has meaning.

Color is as much a symbol as any image in a dream. Color represents the emotional conditions that stimulated a dream segment or a particular image. Color combines with the imagery to form a more complete meaning for the image, giving it greater emotional significance. Color imagery can be derived from past associations, like something you saw in waking life that the dream is recalling, or from the affect that color has on your feelings. If you can determine the affect a particular color has, you can then understand its meaning in your dreams and life.

Sometimes dreams use color to directly represent feelings with little support from other imagery. This is particularly true when the color is by itself or when you dream of an object that is a solid color and the color is what the focus is on. The color generally relates to either feelings or situations that created the dream story or a condition that is needed to establish balance. Wholeness or balance can also be represented by a perfect geometrical grouping of four, such as four different colors found together. For example, if you dream of four objects, and each one is a different color—one red, one yellow, one blue and one green.

Learn about the individual colors and their meanings under Color in Chapter 21. For more in depth information about individual colors, read "*Cashing in on the 'Simple Magic' of Color,*" a free e-book at www.valerieann.com. (*see also* Bibliography)

Steps for Interpreting Colors

1. WRITE DOWN THE COLORS OF THE SYMBOL.

Select from your dream the images you feel are most important, those that you feel most drawn to or feel the greatest emotional reaction to. What color are they? In dreams, it is best to pick images that are not common colored objects like the blue sky, unless they stand out as being significant. Write them down.

2. EXPLORE THE MEANING OF EACH COLOR.

Read the definitions of each color under Color in Chapter 21. Pay attention to your emotional reaction to what is said about each color. The correct meaning will elicit the most feeling. Ask yourself what the color means to you. Does it bring any particular memory to mind? If the color of an image seems to be "missing" in a dream, it may have to do with something you are rejecting or not wanting to see, or something you are "missing" in your life. Write the meaning by the colors identified in step 1.

3. IDENTIFY ANY FEELINGS ASSOCIATED WITH THE COLOR/S.

Do you identify with one or more of the meanings for the color/s you explored in step 2? Do you have an emotional reaction to one or more of the things listed about each color in Chapter 21? Do any of the statements express a way you have felt recently? When you think of a color, what feeling comes to mind? Do you have a specific feeling that you associate with the color? Make a list of the feelings.

4. IDENTIFY A SITUATION IN LIFE WITH THE SAME FEELING ASSOCIATED WITH THE COLOR.

Close your eyes. Recall and describe a situation the day before or recently when you felt the same feeling/s as the one you identified with the color in Step 3. The dream may have stemmed from this situation or, the event you recall may simply bring more understanding to the meaning of the color in your dream. Often times, a dream will stem from unresolved feelings from past experiences. If a past situation comes to mind, it may indicate the importance of resolving the negative feelings associated with it. Use the *"Painless Tool"* in Chapter 14, or whatever method works for you, to change the negative feelings to positive.

5. EXPLORE HOW THE MEANINGS OF THE COLORS IN YOUR DREAM RELATE TO YOUR LIFE.

For instance . . . say you have not been speaking what you really feel in certain situations and then have a dream with blue as the main color. Blue is related to the *throat*, the part of the body which has to do with *speaking* your truth or what you really feel. This could be an indication of the need to resolve the fear that is keeping you from speaking what is in your heart. Once again, you may want to use the *"Painless Tool"* to resolve the negative feeling.

6. LISTEN FOR THE ANSWERS COMING FROM WITHIN.

Ponder the information you have identified about the colors of each image in the preceding steps. Now, go inside and ask to know the correct meaning in relation to your dream. It's likely that you have already received the answer as you have gone through the preceding steps. As soon as you do receive the answer, write it by the color. If the meaning you determine for a color is different than the ideas found in Chapter 21, record your interpretation in Chapter 22, *"My Personal List of Symbols"* for future reference. Remember to give thanks for the answer you received.

Seven

Remembering Your Dreams

　　We all dream. Some people remember every dream they have while others can't remember any. With the right techniques and practice however, virtually everyone can remember at least some of their dreams. Be playful, patient and persistent. Although most people start having success the first week or two, dream recall is a mental muscle which may require some time to get it back into shape. Maintain a relaxed and playful attitude of looking forward to your dreams while being willing to let them come all in good time. Trying too hard or being too serious can be limiting factors. Dream recall and the motivation to do so tend to come and go in natural cycles, depending upon what is going on in your life. Here are things you can do to help you remember your dreams.

Steps for Remembering Your Dreams

1. PAY ATTENTION TO YOUR DREAMS.

Once you decide you want to remember your dreams, stick with it for several days. As you do so, it is important to focus your attention on *remembering* them. Whatever you put your attention on will increase. If you find yourself thinking things like, "I know I won't remember my dreams," you're right! When these kinds of thoughts come to mind, say to yourself, "cancel and clear that thought," then replace it by saying something like "I am remembering my dreams." My friend, Karol Truman, shared this idea with me. I use it whenever I catch myself saying something negative about anything, always replacing the thought with a positive statement. It's very effective!

Putting your attention on *"remembering"* your dreams will eventually bring them into your awareness. Once again, if you put your attention on not remembering . . . you will create more of the same. Therefore, *visualize* yourself recalling your dreams and *feel* the excitement of being able to remember them. You *will* begin remembering them.

2. REVIEW YOUR DREAMS AND RECORD THEM.

Your best recall is when you wake up. As soon as you are conscious of waking, keep still with your eyes closed. Recall any hint of a dream and follow it wherever it takes you. Go over any images that you remember . . . even the smallest thought of a dream element . . . until you have it securely in your mind. Then open your eyes and write everything down. Talking about it to someone else can also be helpful.

3. ASSESS YOU PAST PATTERN OF DREAM RECALL.

What has been the frequency? Are there cycles of remembering and forgetting? What happened last night as you moved from dreaming toward waking? Remembering any patterns associated with the times when you recall dreams or when you don't may give you ideas for things you can do or not do in the future to increase your ability to retain them.

4. BEFORE GOING TO SLEEP, REVIEW THE EVENTS OF YOUR DAY.

When I say "review" the events of your day—do it briefly—you don't need to relive the day. Just recall the main events to help you be more conscious of them in relation to any dreaming you do. Don't judge what has happened, just be a witness. Were there events that were troubling or particularly pleasurable? Was there a question or puzzle you were pondering? Often, the events of your day will be what triggers your dreams. Ask to be given answers or insights in your dreams about any questions or problems you may have concerning things that have transpired during the day, then let your thoughts go and sleep.

5. USE THE POWER OF SUGGESTION.

Don't forget to use the power of "telling yourself to remember your dreams." It is extremely effective. State your intention to recall your dreams aloud if you want. Speak this intention clearly: "In the morning, when I awake, *I will* remember my dreams." Picture yourself waking up the next morning with your dreams still intact. Imagine yourself recording your dreams in your dream journal. Surround this picture with golden light and positive feelings. Say to yourself, "I am remembering my dreams." If you wake up and don't remember your dreams after doing this, don't give up, repeat this step again the next night.

6. MAKE IT EASY TO RECORD YOUR DREAMS.

Open your journal and have a pen or pencil handy or put a portable tape recorder by your bed. This is a physical affirmation that you "will remember something and write it down in the morning."

7. GET ENOUGH SLEEP.

Alarm clocks are dream-killers, so if you want to remember your dreams, it is best not to use one. It is helpful if you go to bed early so you don't need an alarm clock. You can still set the alarm clock, but make sure you have gone to bed so early that you wake up before the alarm clock goes off. You will even dream more if you sleep longer. When you wake up naturally, you will most likely wake up from REM (rapid eye movement) sleep. This is when you dream. After eight to nine hours of sleep, you will almost always have continual REM sleep. This means you will be dreaming and are more likely to remember them. Extra dreaming and deep sleep also allows you to cleanse the nervous system of stress.

8. EAT NUTRITIOUS FOODS, USE HERBS AND ESSENTIAL OILS TO HELP DREAM RECALL.

Foods. Eating raw fruits and vegetables increases your body's ability to function properly and will therefore help you recall your dreams.

Vitamins. Just before retiring, take the stress vitamins, B-complex and C. It is also important to have adequate levels of amino acids.

Herbs. Valerian, Licorice Root, Jasmine, Honeysuckle, Bee Pollen, Catnip, Hops, Scullcap, Lavender, Chamomile, Cardamom, Ginkgo Biloba, Rose, Cinnamon, Marigold, Nutmeg, Peppermint, Holly, Yarrow and Anise are just some of the herbs that may help you dream more.

Essential Oils. Using Lavender, Chamomile, Rose, Cinnamon, Nutmeg or Peppermint will help you remember your dreams. I like to put a little Lavender under my nose or on my pillow before I go to bed. Many people use Lavender to help alleviate insomnia. (*see* Appendix II)

9. USE A DREAM CATCHER.

Dream catchers are traditionally used to catch bad dreams, letting only good dreams through. In reality, once you learn to interpret your dreams correctly, you will see that *all* dreams are *good*. Therefore, this is how I suggest using a dream catcher. Hang one in your home with the intention of having it catch your dreams and help you remember them.

Doing this is an outward symbol that will help you keep your attention on *remembering* your dreams whenever you see the Dream Catcher during the day. Dream Catchers can also be used with the intention of helping you attain life's dreams and desires. (*see* Appendix III)

10. THINGS TO AVOID.

Using Tobacco, Alcohol or Coffee prohibits the absorption of necessary vitamins and amino acids. They also suppress REM sleep which is when you dream.

The wise sage within is eager for you to remember your dreams so he/she can help you interpret and understand them. Believe that you will remember them and you will!

Eight

Dream Interpretations

— Blue Sphere and Fawn —

On my left, I saw a blue sphere or world. In the center or where the equator would typically be, was a red band of waves wrapped around it. The sphere was floating in space and moving toward me. To my right, I saw a fawn (young deer). It moved towards me, hopping by my right side then out of view. As it moved quickly past me, I mostly saw a faint brown form and the white spots on its rump.

I then dreamed that I woke up, and was intent on finding C. G. Jung's book "Mandala Symbolism." I knew there was a painting of a similar sphere in this book and wanted to see how Jung interpreted it so I could better understand the one in my dream.

As my dream continued, my mother and children were trying to help me find the book in a house that was a combination of the house I grew up in and the house I lived in at the time of the dream. We looked in all the usual places but didn't find it. Finally, my mother remembered seeing a book under a blanket somewhere and sure enough, when we looked there, we found the book. I then looked intently through the pages to find the picture.

I painted this the day after I had the dream.

Upon waking from this dream, I quickly found the book *"Mandala Symbolism"* and thumbed through the pages looking for the picture highlighted in my dream. This part of my dream was very literal (objective). The rest of the dream contains symbols that have to be looked at symbolically (subjectively).

When I found the picture, I was amazed to see how closely the sphere in the book, painted from a dream in 1928, resembled the sphere in my dream. There was also an interpretation of the symbols by the author C. G. Jung, some of which I resonated with, feeling that they applied to my dream as well. From the impressions I received after reading these interpretations, I determined that the sphere represented a planet in the making, or in other words the birthing of the True Self which is often symbolized by a circle of some kind. The red band of waves around the center of the sphere represented the vibrations or frequencies that kept the sphere afloat, balancing the equal and opposite forces—or polarities. The blue color of the sphere was another indication that the sphere had to do with the inner kingdom of the soul. The dappling of the fawns coat also brought in the idea that both light and dark must be loved to create balance. Whenever there is balance, there is also peace. The transition into a peaceful world within, where the True Self resides, involves learning to love all opposites.

The fawn also represented the gentleness of spirit that heals all wounds and removes all fear of moving forward. It indicated that following my instincts and being sensitive like a fawn would enable me to maintain the vibration or frequency needed to keep afloat and stay balanced in a world of opposition.

Because Carl Jung studied dreams and their meanings, the focus on his book in my dream indicated that searching dreams and understanding their symbolism would help me come to know my True Self. My mother and children represented that in my search, I would need to use my older wiser aspects as well as my curious playful attributes.

Not finding the book in the usual places in the dream indicated that I would not find the knowledge I needed in the "usual" places in life either. Success in finding my True Self would also include balancing previous knowledge, attitudes and beliefs (the house I grew up in) with the ideas, attitudes and beliefs I learned in the present moment of each day (the house I lived in at the time of the dream). The knowledge of the world within was something I had to search for, just as I searched for the book in the dream. This would be found by remembering the knowledge and wisdom of my "mother" aspects under the security and warmth of the "blanket" of the outer physical world.

This dream previewed the path I have traveled to learn the principles shared in this book. At the time of this dream I was in the early stages of exploring my dreams, a "fawn" so to speak, still growing into myself and my mission in life. This dream indicated that knowledge and understanding (represented by the book) was something that would come to me little by little, just as the sphere slowly moved towards me in the dream. I knew I wanted to understand dreams but had no idea at the time just how much doing so would affect my life. Even though I understand this dream on a deeper level now, at the time of the dream, it gave me the assurance I needed that my life was on course.

Studying dreams has taught me how to see my reflection in everything, helping me more clearly see the things I need to change to improve my life. My dreams even led me to write this book. By the time you have finished reading it, you will see that this dream and the following one actually contain the entire contents of this book in symbolic language.

As I learned to interpret my dreams and the symbols in the many mirrors of life, a new world *was* revealed "within," just as my dream indicated would happen—a world wherein I am continually discovering more and more of my True Self. This world exists in a universe parallel to the one in which we live. It is a world anyone can enter and explore. One way to walk into it is to begin thinking beyond the box of physical limitations. Interpreting the symbols in dreams and life is an exercise that helps one to think outside this box, enabling a person to walk into this other world and live in the outer world simultaneously.

For fun, let's stretch our minds a little right now. When do dreams begin and when do they end? Are dreams and life one eternal round with no beginning and no end? Perhaps we only "think" our dreams begin and end because we go to sleep and wake up. Maybe they are really just one continuous "dream" . . . or are they one with life and therefore part of one continuous "life?" I am still exploring the dream of the *Sphere and Fawn*, finding that it is still in progress . . . connected to all of my other dreams . . . and every day of my life. What about your dreams and your life?

— Temple Reflections —

I was alone in a temple. Somehow I knew that I had been given unusual permission to enter one of the rooms where I would have a special experience. I entered the room which was very ordinary. It was about 20' x 24' in size and dimly lit. The only thing in it was a mirror on the east wall. I walked to the center of the room and looked into the mirror. As I looked at myself, I saw that I was wearing an ivory colored dress made of thin, flowing material. My reflection was repeated in smaller and smaller mirrors within the main mirror, going into what seemed like eternity, towards the center of the mirror. Each reflection reflected less and less of my body until the last mirror in the middle showed only my face. The reflection then changed. I saw in the mirror, a series of doorways going into the distance just as the previous reflection of me had done. There was light coming from behind each door, through the cracks around the edges, becoming brighter with each door until it was the brightest around the last door in the center. During the course of the experience, I felt like I was receiving a great revelation and then the dream ended.

This dream came about six weeks after the *Sphere and Fawn* dream. Both dreams focus on the path to the True Self.

The temple represents the body which houses the spirit. The thin flowing ivory dress represents being open and able to see what is beneath the exterior or physical world, into the purity of the Self within. The dimly lit room represents part of me that I was unfamiliar with. By going inside and looking at myself in the mirror, I would become more familiar with these unexplored areas.

This watercolor was painted right after the dream.
It represents the doorways that I saw as I looked in the mirror.

The numbers in the dimensions of the room (20' x 24') reduce down to eight (2 + 0 + 2 + 4 = 8) which has to do with balancing and integrating logical knowledge with knowledge learned through the Spirit. When they are in balance, they represent true power. Therefore, applying what I learned in the spirit, to the physical world, would bring me true power.

The mirror was reflecting me to myself, indicating the importance of seeing my reflection or really taking a look at myself. By looking at my Self "within" (inside the temple), I was taken to the center of myself. I was also taken through many doors and into many rooms within myself revealing more of my light and glory—more and more of my True Self—a "special experience" indeed. Because the mirror was on the east wall, the direction of the rising sun, it therefore symbolized the light rising inside of me as well.

As you can see, the central theme of this book is looking in the "World of Mirrors," an idea presented to me in this dream years ago. Little did I know at the time of this dream, how much I would learn by looking at myself in the unique "World of Mirrors." It was a path that has truly walked me through many doors. The fun part being that there continues to be more doors to open and more rooms to explore. We may have explored the outer world from top to bottom, but the worlds within are still largely unmapped. There are yet vast frontiers into which any modern day Columbus can set sail. All aboard!

Many Mirrors

Nine

Your Reflection in Life Events

Life is the dream we all remember. The steps for interpreting life are almost the same as for interpreting dreams. That's right! By looking at life the same way you look at dreams, you can respond to life events in a way that will make a positive and healing difference.

Get out the "World of Mirrors." Begin seeing everything and everyone as a symbol representing something about you. The people and circumstances that irritate you the most are your best mirrors and greatest teachers. They reflect the attitudes, beliefs and characteristics in which you are in the greatest denial. I hope you don't resist this idea at first, like I did. Even if you do, if you will apply it to your life, you will find out how accurately the mirror of "others" and "life events" reflect you.

My husband is one of my greatest teachers. Until I figured this out however, living with him was a challenge. Now, after learning how the "World of Mirrors" works, I am grateful when he reflects things I don't like; because I recognize there is something about me that needs to be looked at and resolved.

Try This!

This fun and enlightening exercise will be most effective if you carry out the instructions in the next paragraph *before* you read any further.

Get a piece of paper and a pencil/pen. Now ask yourself, "Who is it that irritates me the most?" "What person challenges me the most in my life?" Write the name of the person on the paper. Under their name, list all of the things that bother you about this person—all of the things you dislike. What is it about this person that challenges you? Be as descriptive as possible. If you can't think of one particular person, write down things that bug you about people in general. STOP READING and start writing NOW!

Come on, do the assignment *before* reading any further!
☺

Now that you have completed the assignment, erase or cross out the persons name and write *your* name in their place. That's right, this is the list of things *you* need to work on the most . . . the major clues as to what *you* are in denial about. It is a reflection of you. How could you see it in another person if it didn't first exist within you? This person or other people is/are actually your greatest teacher/s in this life. Be grateful for the gift of reflection in the "World of Mirrors!"

You may not see the resemblance of yourself in this other person or in people in general right now, but as you begin looking at your enemies and things you don't like about anything or anyone with this idea in mind, you will begin to see its truth. When you begin to recognize how it works, ask yourself, "How can I dislike someone who is so much like me without disliking myself as well?" The "World of Mirrors" is a very effective tool to use when dealing with perceived enemies. You can never change the other person, but you can change yourself and how you feel! The story of my mission companion and me in Chapter 2 is a good illustration of how to see yourself in other people.

Changing *in yourself*, the things you don't like in others, will do more to heal your relationships and life than anything else you can do.

Just for fun, look at your life as if it were a dream for the next week. See what you can learn about yourself. What is the most difficult situation in your life right now? Is there a person who is a thorn in your side? A job you hate? Physical or emotional abuse? Addiction? Overwhelming debt? Illness? Obesity? Would you like to change whatever is keeping you from experiencing peace, joy, health, wealth or happiness?

No matter how deeply you feel that you are buried in your undesirable experiences, *there is a way out*! Recognizing the problem is the obvious first step. Seeing it from a new perspective is the next step. This new perspective is seen by looking in the "World of Mirrors." Use the mirrors to learn how the difficult and challenging people in your life are your teachers and friends. "Yeah, right!" I can hear you say. This statement may seem ridiculous at first, but if you will give the following ideas a try, you will have an eye opening experience.

Go through a week following the steps below. If you can't do it for a week, at least do it for a day.

Steps for Effectively Using Your Life as a Mirror

1. KEEP A JOURNAL.

Record daily or as often as you feel, the events happening in your life. This helps you see yourself and your relationship to what is happening more clearly. A simple notebook works great unless you prefer something fancier. Add the date and give the day a title.

2. IDENTIFY THE DIFFICULT SITUATIONS OR PROBLEMS IN YOUR LIFE.

Record your challenges and problems in your notebook, leaving space after each one for recording more information in step 6.

3. LIST THE PEOPLE YOU CAME IN CONTACT WITH DURING THE DAY.

After each name, write down a brief description of that person and what they were doing in your life that day. Leave space for your interpretation of each one later.

4. LIST OTHER SYMBOLS IN YOUR DAY.

Write down any numbers, colors or unique objects. The most simple things can reveal much, like the car you drove to work, the rain you drove through, the deer you saw on the side of the road, the mess your three year old made, the piles of laundry, the broken water pipe, the business deal at work, the sale you closed and the one you didn't. Look at the list of symbols you have written down. Which ones take your attention more than the others? Underline them or some how indicate their importance. Once again, leave some space after each symbol.

5. APPLY THE "WORLD OF MIRRORS."

Look up each of the symbols identified in steps 2 through 4 in Chapter 21. Read the suggested meanings for each of them. Do you resonate with any of the meanings listed for each symbol? How is the symbol a metaphor for you? What does it represent about you, your attributes, attitudes, beliefs or characteristics? Write down the things that feel right to you in your notebook by the corresponding symbols. Use free association to help you identify the meanings of symbols if needed. What does the symbol cause you to think about? If the symbol isn't listed in Chapter 21, use the *"Steps for Interpreting 'Any' Symbol"* in Chapter 15. Look at the symbols both objectively and subjectively. For more help, refer to step number 10 under *"Steps for Interpreting Your Dreams."*

6. IDENTIFY AND RESOLVE ANY NEGATIVE FEELINGS.

Referring back to what you wrote in step 2, write down the way the challenges and problems of the day made you feel. Are there any negative feelings that need to be resolved? If so, you may want to use the *"Painless Tool"* in Chapter 14 to resolve them.

7. USE THE *"QUESTIONS FOR FINDING THE MEANING IN YOUR REFLECTIONS"* IN CHAPTER *17*.

These questions will help to further identify the symbols and understand what the events of the day mean to you.

8. SUM IT UP.

Read what you have written about your day and what you have learned in the steps above. What message jumps out? What do you see about yourself that you didn't see before? Write a sentence or two summing it up. Express gratitude for any new awareness you receive.

The next time a situation or person in your life causes you to feel negative feelings, give thanks for the opportunity to see things about yourself that you need to recognize and change . . . then change them.

Your Reflection in World Events

On September 11, 2001, terrorist hijackers deliberately used four passenger jets, each carrying full tanks of fuel and large numbers of passengers, to cause death and destruction in an unthinkable way. It's a day not soon forgotten. It has impacted the world and each of our lives.

Within hours, two of the airplanes crashed into the World Trade Center in New York City and a third airplane flew into the Pentagon in Arlington, Virginia, next to Washington, D.C., the capital of the United States. A fourth plane was kept from hitting its intended target of Camp David, the Presidential Retreat in Maryland, by heroic passengers, crashing instead into a field near Shanksville, Pennsylvania.

Many of us were stunned as we watched these events unfold before our eyes on television. The dramatic scenes of the twin towers totally collapsing, ending thousands of lives, are etched in our minds forever. Feelings of all kinds were stirred. Many people lost loved ones, friends and colleagues. The lives of thousands were forever changed. Regardless of how intimately these events affected us or how distanced we were from them, still, they reflect something about each of us.

We could analyze every detail of this event as symbols of ourselves, just as we would a dream and learn mountains, but it would involve writing a book within a book. Therefore, I will reduce it to some of the basic elements, zeroing in on the collapse of the twin towers. I suggest that you analyze it further on your own to see what more you can learn about yourself.

The twin towers of the World Trade Center were the second tallest buildings in the world, housing approximately 50,000 office workers on a normal weekday. This is where the "world" traded. It was the largest office complex in existence. The structures were made of enormous amounts of concrete and more than 200,000 tons of steel, appearing to be sound, secure and unshakable . . . yet, they crumbled to the dust. Because of these terrorist acts, thousands were killed in a totally unexpected and unthinkable way, leaving the rest of us to ask, "Why?"

What does this event reflect about me? What does it reflect about you? Let me approach it by asking questions so you can answer for yourself. Are there structures in your life that the twin towers are perhaps mirroring? What structures do you rely on to make you feel safe, secure, valuable or important? Are there structures you feel will never fail or let you down, structures that are solid and indestructible? Your job? Your family? Your marriage? Your religion? The government? Could the disaster at the World Trade Center be warning you of similar events that could possibly happen in your own life if you don't learn from this occurrence? Have you already experienced a devastating event in your life? Is this event a reflection to help you better understand or resolve something that has already happened? Do you think the events on September 11th could be a reminder that all temporal things can crumble to the dust?

When major events occur in our lives or in the world, they have messages for us, the same as dreams. If we fail to pay attention to these messages, ignoring them instead, they will be sent again on a bigger scale. If we don't listen to the whisperings of the voice within—we get a tap on the shoulder. If we don't pay attention to the tap—we get a bump on the head. If a bump isn't sufficient—we get knocked to the ground. The longer we avoid the messages, the more intense the delivery methods can be . . . until (hopefully) we get the message . . . until we wake up and see what we need to do and/or change in our lives.

Have you ignored any of the subtle messages from within? Do you need to go within and examine your own structure? Upon what is the knowledge of who you are, built? Could something attack the structures of your life without causing you to crumble to the dust—without causing you to lose your identity? What if one, two or all of the structures you rely on in your life disintegrate tomorrow . . . just like the twin towers? Without them, who are you? Does who you are depend on the titles associated with your name? Do you identify who you are with the roles you play within the structures in your life? Do you really know the person behind the role of father, mother, doctor, secretary, teacher, artist, priest, engineer?

What does the extreme height of these buildings say about us? Have we become high and mighty? Do we need to be knocked down where we can get another view of ourselves? Do we need to be more humble? Do we have high and lofty ideas that need to be more down to earth? What is this event reflecting to us about the things, people or organizations we have looked up to or exalted in our lives? What can we learn about ourselves from this event?

What about the deaths of so many people? What does this reflect? Perhaps we have done away with the things that matter most in our lives in pursuit of worldly goals. Do the choices we make each day reflect the things that are most valuable to us? Do we need to be reminded to value people over things?

On and on the questions could go. When we look at any world event using the "World of Mirrors," *everything* becomes a symbol of us and our life. Asking questions can help us identify the messages reflected. *We* are the twin towers, the airplanes, the passengers and the hijackers. *We* are the firemen, the survivors and even the media. There are multiple ways to look at this and all are valuable in helping us more clearly see wherein we can improve the quality or our life experiences.

Remember to use the "World of Mirrors" the next time an event happens in the world that grabs your attention. Your emotional reaction indicates that it does indeed have a message—a reflection specific to you. Pay attention to the "taps on your shoulder.

Steps for Effectively Using
World Events as a Mirror

1. RECORD THE EVENT.

Write down everything you know about the event. Your description of it is more helpful than the one you see on TV or read in the newspaper because it contains your feelings and the elements that stand out *to you*. Add the date and give it a title.

2. LIST THE SYMBOLS.

Read your description from step 1. List the people, places, things, colors, numbers and any other symbols found in the event. Leave space for your interpretation of each one later.

3. APPLY THE "WORLD OF MIRRORS."

Look up each of the symbols identified in step 2 in Chapter 21. Read the suggested meanings for each one. Write down the things that feel right to you by the corresponding symbols. Use free association to help you identify the meanings if needed. What does the symbol cause you to think about? Pay particular attention to the symbols that stand out. If the symbol isn't listed in Chapter 21, use the *"Steps for Interpreting 'Any' Symbol"* in Chapter 15.

4. IDENTIFY THE FEELINGS ASSOCIATED WITH THE EVENT.

What was your emotional reaction to the event? How did it cause you to feel? List the feelings. What are the other situations, events or experiences in your life that have caused you to feel these same feelings? Often times, the experiences of today which elicit feelings associated with past experiences, do so because we have failed to resolve them in the past. An event causing us to feel them again is a *gift*, helping us know what they are so we can now resolve them.

5. RESOLVE THE NEGATIVE FEELINGS.

Use the *"Painless Tool"* in Chapter 14, or any method that works for you, to change the negative feelings identified in step 4 to positive feelings.

6. PROBE WITH QUESTIONS.

Use the 25 "Questions for finding the meaning in your reflections" in Chapter 17. Answering these questions and any others that come to your mind, will help you further understand what each symbol means.

7. LOOK WITHIN.

Take time to be silent and listen to the voice within as you ponder the event. What can you learn that will help you improve your life? What is it reflecting about you? Refer to Chapter 18 for help in hearing the messages.

8. SUM IT UP.

Read what you have written in the other steps, then write a sentence or two that sums up the events main message to you.

By identifying your negative feelings—those associated with the world events you connect with emotionally—and changing them *inside* . . . you will uncover more and more of who you really are. By doing so, you will be less and less adversely affected by world events . . . and you will feel more and more peaceful inside.

Your Reflection in Your Surroundings

Feng Shui, the ancient Chinese Art of placement is a helpful tool you can use to see yourself in your surroundings. Most of us are familiar with the Chinese yin and yang symbol. It represents the movement of energy. These two energies emerge as opposites that compliment each other, creating balance. They flow from one to the other. I like the way Suzan Hilton talks about these energies in her book, *"The Feng Shui of Abundance:"*

"In the West we call them polar opposites. Yet nothing is truly totally the opposite. The Eastern approach recognizes this with the dot of the opposite within the main body of each. Each is found within the other, interdependent and interrelated. And when they are balanced they easily create flow."

Feng Shui is the art of arranging things in your house or environment in a way that creates harmony. It teaches how to create a positive flow of energy that will enhance every aspect of your life. It also includes the idea of the "World of Mirrors". . . everything in your house or environment reflecting your inner Self. Everything becomes a symbol of you. Therefore, you can change your outer environment and it will help you change your inner environment and vice versa. By paying attention to your inner and outer Self and changing things in both places, you can create more balance and more of the things you desire to experience in your life.

When I decided to apply what I learned about Feng Shui to my own home, it was a very eye opening experience. I saw just how accurately my home reflected my inner world. Feng Shui divides your physical environment and life into nine areas which are:

- Wealth and Abundance
- Fame and Reputation
- Marriage and Relationships
- Creativity and Children
- Helpful People and Travel
- Career and Life Path
- Self-Knowledge , Skills and Wisdom
- Family
- Health

Each part of your house fits into one of these areas. I will use the Wealth and Abundance area of Feng Shui to illustrate how to see your reflection in your surroundings. To find this area in your home, stand inside the main front doorway facing towards the inside of the house. The Wealth

and Abundance area will be the room or area on the farthest
back corner of the house to your left as illustrated below.

| Wealth and Abundance Area | |

Main Front Door

When I first walked into this area of my house to take
a look using the "World of Mirrors," I didn't know whether to
laugh or cry. It just happened to be the master bathroom
where everything was constantly "going down the drain." (two
sinks, a bathtub, a shower and a toilet) In *"The Feng Shui of
Abundance"* it suggests that you always keep the toilet lid
closed if this part of your house happens to be the bathroom,
which I have done ever since I read it.

Water sometimes symbolizes money, which in this case
amplified the flow of "money going down the drain." In *"The
Feng Shui of Abundance,"* Suzan Hilton also suggests putting
a mirror on the outside of the bathroom door and keeping the
door shut to reflect the energy that flows toward this area back
into the house, keeping it from all going down the drain. I did
that too. It was true . . . money always left as fast as it came.
And what did that reflect about me? I recognized that I usually
"spent money as fast or faster than I made it." Right there and
then, I began to pay more attention to how I spent my money.
It also reflected that I gave of myself too freely. Giving is good,
but not to the point of giving at the expense of yourself.

As I looked at the many plants surrounding my bathtub,
I noticed many dead and dusty leaves mingled with the green

ones. In order for the growing, expanding energy of the plants to be most effective, I cleaned them and removed the dead leaves and their lifeless energy. The healthy leaves reflected the growth I had made and was currently experiencing in this area of my life. The dead and dusty leaves reflected that I had a little work to do. I needed to clean up my act a bit and get rid of the things that were no longer adding a spark of life.

Then there was the closet. This, I realized, was a source of stuck, old, stale energy . . . a place where I stored a lot of "stuff." Many things hadn't been used for years . . . things I no longer payed any attention to. I immediately went through the entire contents of the closet, filling six large trash sacks with items to send to a second hand store. This created positive space . . . more room into which an abundance of "more needed items" and "money" could flow. And, what did the closet reveal about me? It represented all of the old beliefs I had about money which hadn't served me very well. They were keeping me stuck and in old ineffective patterns. There were also items collecting dust that were obviously not as important as I thought they were when I bought them. I realized that by using more wisdom in choosing what I purchased in the future, money wouldn't go down the drain uselessly.

Next, I looked in the drawers and cupboards. They were cluttered and needed a thorough cleaning. Clutter and dirt are always negative energies that need to be taken care of in order to create a good flow of positive energy. I suppose I had a little clutter to clear inside of me too. ☺

I was also amazed when I found a few broken items that I had intended to fix . . . for years. "If there are broken items in this area," says Karen Carter in her book, *"Move Your Stuff, Change Your Life,"* "you're broke." I threw all of these things away with a smile on my face having no desire to be "broke" any more.

I cleaned and organized my bathroom from top to bottom. I then added some purple accents and a few items that represented abundance to me and began giving this room a little extra attention and honor. Interestingly enough, doing this changed the way I felt inside. "Now," every time I go into this room, it is a "positive" reminder of "Wealth and Abundance" in my life.

Hopefully you see how helpful it can be to look at your reflection in your surroundings. It has been amazing to see how doing so, and changing the undesirable things I saw reflected, has positively affected my life!

What does your Wealth and Abundance area look like? Is it clean or cluttered? Does it give you a sense of satisfaction? Is this a place of honor in your home? What does this area reflect about you?

It isn't necessary to use Feng Shui to see your reflection in your surroundings, it's just one way. All you need to do is walk through your house and look at every room with your eyes focused on seeing and understanding more about yourself and your current attitudes. In what ways would change benefit you? What could you do to bring more of what you truly desire into your life and less of what you don't like? You may be tempted to blame some of the undesirable things you see in your house on the "other people" living with you and perhaps rightly so, however, regardless of what you see and who "seems" to be the cause of it . . . it is still reflecting something about YOU. The best thing you can do to help others is be an example of that which you would have them do. Actions *still* speak louder than words. If you desire to change the undesirable reflections in your surroundings, begin by changing the things *you* can change. The "others" living with you will be affected by your changes and they may even change as well.

Steps for Effectively Using
Your Surroundings as a Mirror

1. TAKE INVENTORY.

Walk through your home, business, yard or whatever part of your daily surroundings (Self) you would like to evaluate. Focus on one area at a time.

2. RECORD YOUR FINDINGS.

Write about everything you see. What do you like about the things you see? What don't you like? What do you enjoy about the room, yard, or office? Is it clean, neat organized—messy, dirty or cluttered? Be specific. What would you like to change? Are there drab colors anywhere? Write it all down. Add the date and name it something specific to the area like—"My Office."

3. LIST THE SYMBOLS.

Read your description from step 2. List the symbols found in your surroundings. Remember to include colors. Leave space for your interpretation of each one.

4. APPLY THE "WORLD OF MIRRORS."

Look up each of the symbols identified in step 3 in Chapter 21. Read the suggested meanings for each one. Write down the ideas that resonate with you by the corresponding symbols. Use free association to help you identify the meanings of symbols if needed. If the symbol isn't listed in

Chapter 21, use the *"Steps for Interpreting 'Any' Symbol"* in Chapter 15.

5. IDENTIFY THE FEELINGS.

What is your emotional reaction to what you see in each area surrounding you in your life? Do you feel peaceful or appalled? What feelings are evoked? Do you feel comfortable here or not? Really pay attention to the way each area causes you to feel. List the feelings. Are there things you could change that would improve the way you feel when you are in an area? What you see is reflecting to you the way you have been feeling deep inside, good or bad. If you don't like what is being reflected, it can all be changed. Resolving any negative feelings is a good place to start.

6. RESOLVE THE NEGATIVE FEELINGS.

Use the *"Painless Tool"* in Chapter 14, or any method that works for you, to change the negative feelings that came up for you as you looked at yourself in the reflection of your surroundings. For example: if the room is dirty and you feel dirty inside, use the *"Painless Tool,"* to transform "feeling dirty" to "feeling clean and good about yourself." Do this with each negative feeling you identified. (*See* Appendix I for examples of negative feelings and positive replacements.)

7. PROBE WITH QUESTIONS.

Use the 25 "Questions for finding the meaning in your reflections" in Chapter 17. Answering these questions and any others that come to your mind will help you dig further into the meanings and messages reflected in your surroundings.

8. LOOK WITHIN.

Take time to be silent and listen to the voice within as you look at your surroundings and ponder what they are reflecting about you. What can you learn from them? Refer to Chapter 18 for help in hearing the messages.

9. LIST THE DESIRED CHANGES, THEN BEGIN MAKING THEM.

Make a list of the things you can do to change your surroundings to better reflect what you desire. List everything from dusting to changing the carpet. Choose the simplest things from your list and do all that you can now. Keep the list where you can see it every day. Make the rest of the changes as soon as time and money will allow. Do a little each day and consistently work toward your desired end. This is better than trying to do everything at once and perhaps not accomplishing anything—feeling overwhelmed by it.

Change your surroundings
to match who you really are
and it will be easier to
BE the real you.

Be who you really are
and your surroundings
will reflect you.

May your surroundings
quickly reflect
your True Self.

Twelve

Your Reflection in Your Words

The words we say are much more powerful and revealing than we realize. Too often, we are unconscious slaves to our words because we don't pay attention to what we are "really" saying. Regardless of whether or not we consciously pay attention to the actual meaning of the words we use or not, our bodies respond literally to their meaning. Words have the power to kill or cure, create or destroy.

What do you say during your day? What words do you use? What do they really mean? Think about the following expressions and ask yourself if you would truly desire the results of what these phrases actually mean. I'm sure you have used at least one of them some time in your life . . . and perhaps *many* of them.

I'm scared to death
I'm dying to meet you
I'm afraid
I'm broke
I'll never make it
You're spoiled rotten
It's weighing me down
I feel like I'm going around in circles
It blew my mind
That's sick
My mind went blank
That costs an arm and a leg
I'm so irritated
I've had enough
I'm so tired of . . .
I'm sick and tired
My heart aches for you
I'm really pissed off
My heart goes out to you
It nearly killed me
He's a pain in the butt
I was scared stiff
I don't care
That was brainless
We can't afford that
That really cramps my style
What a pain in the neck

Use the "World of Mirrors" to see yourself in the words you say. Can you see situations in which the words you have used created your experiences? What have you created with the words you have used? Words are literally charged with energy and you can consciously decide which energy to create. Choose life! Choose health! Choose love! Choose peace! *Every* word you speak is recorded in your body, your word becoming your flesh. Choose thoughtfully what you eat! By using carefully chosen words, your body can be energized and renewed. The energies can be changed and a transformation take place. Every word you speak is helping create the world you live in. Create the world you desire. Create it with care.

In order for our words to be most effective when we consciously speak of things we desire, it is important to use present time terminology. The *common* way to affirm something we desire is by using words like, "I want . . .," or "I would like . . .." These words create the things we are desiring *in the future* and always out of our grasp. We continue" to "want" because that is what we have said, "that we are *wanting.*" For example: "I want to be loved" is declaring a desire to always be "wanting" love—love never being a present time reality. By saying, "I *am* loved," we bring it into to the present moment so we can experience it in the now, the only place where anything can truly exist. Another example is when we say things like, "I need some money." This says we are "needy." Using this word creates the experience of always being in "need" of money. Affirm your true desire by saying, "I have plenty of money," or "there's plenty and more."

Think of how you word your prayers and all your desires in whatever forms you use. Do you ever *hope* something you desire *might* happen? Pay attention to your words. What are you saying to yourself and others during the course of your day? It takes a conscious effort to change a habitual, negative, doubting way of speaking, to one that is more positive and productive, but it's well worth the time and effort. Instead of *hoping* something *might* happen, exercise faith and *see it as though it already exists right now.* After holding the positive energy of seeing your desire realized and speaking of it in that way—*in the present time*—long enough, it will literally be your reality in the flesh—right here and now—for that is where you created it to be . . . with your words.

You may feel to argue that this is being unrealistic. How can you see yourself as rich or healed when you know you are not? All I can say is, I know it works. *Whatever* you put your attention on *increases*. Did you get that? Whatever, and I mean *whatever*, you put your attention on INCREASES! So . . . if you continue "seeing" and "speaking" about being "broke" or about "*your* illnesses" (claiming them as "yours"), feeding them more and more energy, they will obey your command and increase in your life. On the other hand, seeing yourself "wealthy" or "whole" will likewise enlarge "wealth" and "wholeness" in your life. So . . . affirm your desires each day as though they are already so.

By using conscious language, speaking accurately of your desires, you tap the power of the creative process. On the other hand, not being conscious of your words and speaking the way you probably have all your life, may be the very thing that is sabotaging the realization of your dreams. Start listening to the words you say. They may be reflecting the negative feelings that are disabling you. What you say reveals what is really in your heart. Speak the words that truly reflect your desires. In addition to your words, in your minds eye, *see* your desires. What do they look like? *Hear* your desires realized. What do they sound like? What do you hear yourself or others say (in your minds eye) when you see your desires realized? *Feel* what it feels like to realize your desires. *Smell* what they smell like, *taste* what they taste like. Involve all of your senses to experience your desires right here and now, in the moment, as though they already exist. This is creative power in action . . . speaking accurately about your desires in each moment.

Steps for Effectively Using Your Words as a Mirror

1. TAKE INVENTORY OF YOUR WORDS.

Begin paying attention to the words you say each day. Do it for at least one day to start with. Listen . . . I mean *really* listen to what you are saying.

2. RECORD YOUR FINDINGS.

Write down the phrases that have a literal meaning that is undesirable . . . a meaning that is contrary to what you *meant* to say or truly felt.

Notice any negative words you use, particularly when you are talking about other people. The way you describe other people and events, reflects much about you. For example, if in conversation, you tell someone that the man you work with is "critical of you," begin observing yourself to see if perhaps you are in any way guilty of being "critical of others."

Sometimes the reflections in our words are less obvious. For instance, the "being critical" example could also reflect that you feel like "you aren't good enough." In this case, you may be *noticing* other's criticism because it validates your negative feelings and beliefs about your Self. If you change how you "feel," you will not be so apt to notice or care when others are critical.

Write down any negative words you hear yourself say, no matter at whom or what they are directed.

3. APPLY THE "WORLD OF MIRRORS."

What have you created with the words you have used in the past? Do you see any connection with your past words and present experiences? As you listen to the words you say, ask questions to find how they are reflecting attitudes, thoughts or beliefs that are less than glorious—things you would like to change. Write them down so you can remember to change them.

4. CHANGE THE NEGATIVE WORDS TO POSITIVE WORDS.

Whenever you catch yourself saying things that you don't want to experience "literally" . . . like, *I'm sick and tired of . . .* or *I'd just die if such and such happened*, recognize what you have said and change your words right there and then. Try using an idea I shared earlier. Whenever you say something you wish you hadn't, say to yourself, "cancel and clear those words," then replace them by stating more accurately what you were trying to say in the first place . . . like, *I wouldn't like to experience such and such any more* or *I wouldn't like it if such and such happened*. Who would consciously choose to be *sick*, *tired*, or *dead*?

If you hear yourself repeating words like "afraid," "can't"or any other negative feeling words, more than likely, you are speaking of negative feelings which exist inside you, feelings that you need to resolve. Use the *"Painless Tool"* in Chapter 14, or any method that works for you, to change the negative feelings you identify to positive feelings.

As you recognize your less than accurate use of words, change them to positive, honorable and beautiful words.

Begin speaking your truth . . .
express your true desires precisely
and you will create a world
reflecting who you really are.

Speak the words of a King or Queen
and you will feel like one . . .

or perhaps become like one . . .

or perhaps discover
that you already are one!

Your Reflection in Your Body

Many books now claim that negative feelings are one of the main cause of illness, disease and the discomforts of life. If indeed this is true, and you want to heal by finding and resolving the negative feelings associated with the part/s of the body causing you discomfort . . . you need to know how to determine which feelings are associated with each illness and/or disease? Our most obvious signal is simply noticing the negative feelings we experience each day. Often, however, we are not even aware that we are experiencing negative feelings. We have become so used to feeling awful, we don't remember what it's like to feel good. The most effective way to find out what these feelings are is to look at the *physical illnesses* and *discomforts* we are experiencing using the "World of Mirrors."

Lets pull out the "World of Mirrors" and look at our physical and emotional bodies. Our physical body mirrors our emotional body and vice versa. We can therefore look at the part of the physical body in pain or discomfort and discover what is wrong in our emotional body—what feeling is causing the problem. Begin by paying attention to the part of the body that is bothering you the most. This is where you will find your clues. Mentally scan your body. Where are the discomforts located? (Unfortunately, it is too easy for most of us to identify a problem area.) Next, you need to determine the feelings associated with the part of the body in question. This is a bit more difficult to do. A comprehensive list of illnesses and feelings causing them would be wonderful, but there are so-o-o-o many illnesses, diseases and ailments that it would be impossible to list all of them and make the list specific to each person. Therefore, I will teach you how to figure it out for yourself.

Following is a list of the main areas of the body and the conflicts and feelings that are possibly causing the illnesses associated with these parts of the body. Look at the ideas listed below under the general area where your illness, disease or discomfort is located. As you read through the list, notice your response to what you are reading. Do you resonate with anything? Does reading it trigger any thoughts or feelings? Maybe it will bring back a memory of something that has happened to you. If it does, immediately go to that memory and locate any feelings associated with it. Even though the event may not "seem" related, more than likely it is.

There are questions under each area of the body in the list below to help you explore the feelings connected with it. Use these to assist in finding the feelings causing your problems. You can determine the negative feelings associated with each part of the body much the same as determining the meaning of any symbol. It's the "World of Mirrors" concept again. Ask what that part of the body is typically used for. How is it mirroring your emotional body? For example, you

How is it mirroring your emotional body? For example, you "see" with your eyes. If your vision is "not good," ask what you are not "seeing," or what you are "afraid" to "see." What is it in your life that you would rather not see? What are the underling feelings associated with not seeing? Keep asking questions like this until you find the feeling at the core of your physical discomfort. Hopefully, the suggestions below will give enough ideas to help you determine the feelings causing your illnesses and discomforts.

Parts of the Body
and the Associated Feelings

Some of the ideas shared below for possible feelings causing illnesses, come from a list found in *"Feelings Buried Alive Never Die . . ."* by Karol K. Truman (*see* Bibliography). I hope you will avail yourself of the life changing information and help found in her book.

HEAD

• The HEAD is where one experiences conflict between centering oneself with a genuine awareness of who they are as opposed to ego-tripping. Where are you centering yourself? Are you more worried about what the world thinks of you or about who you really are?

One thing most of us have experienced in this area of our body is a HEADACHE. A pain in your head indicates a conflict of some kind that is keeping you from experiencing harmony. Ask yourself, (speaking to the part of you that knows) what that conflict is, what the inharmonious feelings are. Ask yourself,

"What do I do with my head?" Well, that's where your brain is located and where you think. Ask yourself what you have been thinking about. Have you been mulling something over in your mind which has put a lot of pressure on you? Are you feeling anxious about something that has been on your mind? Maybe you have not been able to express the things you have been thinking about, just going over and over them in your mind. Maybe you feel unable to be in control of what is happening to you. How have you been using your head? Are you afraid of something? Many times, fear crops up as the culprit. Does your head feel tight and tense? Maybe your headache reflects your uptightness or tenseness about something. You can also look at the individual parts of your head to gain more insights into the feelings causing your headache.

• If the discomfort in your head has more to do with your **FACE**, you might ask, "What is it I am unable to face?"

• Then there is your **MOUTH**. What has been coming forth in words or song? Have you been speaking negatively, such as speaking ill of others, or have you been silent, unable to express what is going on inside? What are the feelings coming to your mind as you ask these questions? Maybe you have felt restrained for some reason, unable to express joy, sing or laugh. If so, perhaps you would benefit by giving yourself permission to do so.

• What about the **NOSE**? What if your nose bleeds? A good question to ask when this happens is, "What am I feeling right now?" Pay attention to what is going on at the time. What is happening around you? A little neighbor boy used to spend time alone after school because his parents were working. He often came to my house to wait for them to return home. Every once in a while he got a nose bleed. I suspect his nose bleed had to do with "feeling overlooked." Or, perhaps you have been unduly sticking your *nose* into someone's business. (This falls under the first thing mentioned about the head, being more centered in ego than your heart/True Self.)

• What about **TEETH**? I have had several root canals and have gone through much pain with them. I have noticed a pattern associated with this experience. Every time I have had problems with my teeth, I have also been indecisive about something. Have you been "chewing" on a situation in your mind?

NECK

• The **NECK** has to do with willfulness. A bullnecked personality exemplifies this quality. The conflict expressed is whether or not you are being willfully constructive or not. We benefit greatly by doing the will of God. It does no good to be stiff-necked about things, not turning your head from side to side to see other possibilities.

• Because we use our **THROAT** to speak, the feelings involved with this part of the body usually have to do with what we have or haven't been saying. Ask questions like, "Have I felt confused as I have struggled with doing or not doing the will of God?" "Have I restrained my anger and not expressed it?"

"Have I ever 'swallowed an emotion' that was unpleasant?" "What are the feelings causing my sore throat?" "Do I have a fear of speaking my truth? Not speaking what you are feeling often results in a sore throat.

• The **THYROID** gland, which is associated with willfulness, is located in the throat area. Negative Feelings more specific to the **THYROID** are:
> • Feeling conflict between the conscious and subconscious
> • Feeling afraid to express myself
> • Feeling a deep sense of frustration/anxiety
> • Feeling a lack of discernment

SHOULDERS, ARMS & HANDS

• **SHOULDERS, ARMS** and **HANDS** symbolize changing thoughts and are associated at times with the trouble we have making up our minds.

• **SHOULDERS** are our expressive part of the body. It is also where we carry our burdens and stressful responsibilities. Are you carrying burdens? Are you burdened with heavy responsibility?

• **ARMS** are what we hold, carry or embrace with. Are you holding on to something or carrying something that is not yours to hold or carry. Do you need to embrace something? An idea? A person?

• **HANDS** are what we use to do things in the world outside ourselves. Thoughts are what we use to do things inside ourselves. Hands express outside what we decide to do inside. Are there opportunities for you to do what you love with your hands? Maybe you fear not having enough opportunities to do what you would like. With our hands, we hold others or push them away, we hit or caress. If you exhibit any of these behaviors and are afflicted in one or both hands, consider the feelings that cause you to do what you do.

If you have arthritis in your hands, you may be feeling rigid. You have probably been this way for a long time. Perfectionists are rigid, maybe you exhibit this behavior. Maybe you feel to criticize yourself or others. Because your fingers are inflexible, it may be mirroring the inflexible feelings you have kept inside. Your hands can also be sweaty or have cramps. Consider each element of what is going on.

• You may also consider each **FINGER** individually. Below are suggested feelings which may be associated with the individual **FINGERS**. Also included are the associate parts of the body. If the finger in question is on the right hand, the feelings may have more to do with your masculine side or characteristics. It the hand with the problem is the left hand, it has to do with your feminine side.

> **THUMB:** worry, spleen, stomach
> **INDEX:** fear, kidney, bladder
> **MIDDLE:** anger, liver, gall bladder
> **RING:** grief, lungs, large intestine
> **LITTLE:** pretense, heart, small intestine

STOMACH & BREASTS

• The **STOMACH** and **BREASTS** relate to giving and receiving. They represent an awareness of the needs of others as well as our own. They show the conflict between giving out nourishment and taking it in.

• Many **STOMACH** disorders such as ulcers arise from a conflict between these two needs. What are your needs? Are they to be loved, taken care of, happy and so on? In what way are your needs being compromised? Do you fear they will not be met? Are you receiving the love and affection you need? Do you fear you won't have your needs met or does your security feel threatened?

• **BREASTS** specifically relate to feelings of worthiness, individual worth or a conflict in your nurturing ability.

HEART & BACKBONE

• The **HEART** and **BACKBONE** are where the conflict between love and the pride of misdirected will is waged. To be small-hearted is to not have the courage to face an issue.

• The **HEART** relates to feelings as the stomach relates to needs. To be big-hearted is to help others by giving of ourselves. We love from our heart. We use a heart to symbolize love on Valentines Day. In what ways do we violate the laws of love? What are the matters of the heart? Do we feel loved? Do we love ourselves? Do we feel approved of by others? Do we feel hurt because of something that has happened in our relationships? Did this cause us to feel hurt or feel resentment? What are our family relationships like?

• And the **BACKBONE**? A spineless individual does not have the foundation in his personality to deal with the issue at hand.

• Feelings having to do with the **SPINE** are:
  • Feeling shy
  • Feeling inferior
  • Your ego being carried away with pride

BACK & KIDNEYS

• The **BACK** and **KIDNEYS** have to do with how we deal with friendships. They are the seat of affection. When this area has problems, it may be showing the conflict that arises when our tendency to be open and loving is inhibited by being too self-centered. Very often backaches arise in these types of situations. It is false pride that builds the ego at the expense of others by saying, "I am better than so and so." On the other hand, our True Self sees that we are all working together, using our attributes and abilities to help everyone.

• The **BACK** has a lot to do with whether or not we feel supported in our relationships, with our finances or even in our feelings. Do we feel a lack of support in these things? Are we fearful where our relationships or money are concerned? Maybe we would like to back out of something. Are we carrying burdens on our back? Are we able to feel confident in being able to support our self? What feelings do you need to become aware of?

• The **KIDNEYS** can have to do with being over-judgmental, feeling emotional confusion or having deep subconscious resentment toward people and experiences of the past.

BOWELS

• **BOWELS** are related to giving and withholding. They are also the area which symbolizes our feelings about how our giving is received and, as a result, oddly enough have a lot to say about love. Consider what the **BOWELS** are used for and then relate the same to the feelings. In what way are you failing to utilize that which is there for you? What is it you fear releasing? Are there old things you need to let go? What attitudes or beliefs are you not willing to eliminate? Are you unwilling to relinquish control? Are you resisting the flow of life? Are there problems that you are determined to keep?

GENITALS

• **GENITALS** symbolize a willful desire and the conflicts generated by sexual frustration. The lesson is to begin learning that pleasure is just another sensation. As we learn this lesson, we are then not so driven by sexual and other frustrations. When we are not feeling sexually fulfilled we may be feeling separated from our partner or even from our spiritual Self. This area can also have to do with feelings of apathy or feeling separated in other ways.

THIGHS & KNEES

• The **THIGHS** are the mainspring for independent movement. They emphasize our out-going, or on-going nature, either physically or socially. The **THIGHS** are also used to form a lap. The conflict which centers in this area is between being out-going and needing to hold back. It symbolizes the balanced control of a rider on a powerful steed. Because the thighs represent moving forward, you may ask yourself what feelings are keeping you from doing so. What are you afraid of? Are you afraid of moving forward on your own? Are you holding back?

• The **KNEES** are the flexible joints in our support and they represent using our material existence to climb to higher levels (spiritually). The coordination between support and the flexibility that enables one to climb resolves itself here with prudence and well thought out actions. We need to learn not to be so over-burdened by our attachment to worldly possessions that our knees can't bend properly. We need to be flexible. Sometimes, we bend to authority or someone else's will in a way that isn't for our highest good.

CALVES, ANKLES & FEET

• This area has to do with choosing. The conflict is between being inventive and conventional, as if at some level we know the way but have to choose to turn to it. In our **CALVES** and **ANKLES** are the muscles which turn our feet from side to side as we direct our path.

• The **FEET** are our foundation. They represent the understanding of our own nature and the nature of each situation and person we meet. If the feet become mired in material concerns, they are slow to take the steps necessary for growth. We must have down-to-earth contacts to support our work. They implement our purpose and symbolize the understanding, knowledge and faith necessary to do what we are here to do.

Hopefully, as you looked at the preceding list, you were able to relate to some of the feelings as having to do with some of your illnesses or discomforts. More than likely, however, either now or in the future, you will be tempted to blame your discomforts on something or someone else. For instance, if your main problem is a bad back that was the result of a car accident, you may blame the accident. Granted, the accident happened and now your back is bad, but . . . you must go deeper if you are to resolve the real problem. Start asking your self questions. "What was I feeling at the time of the accident?" "What are the events that were taking place in my life at that time?" "How was I feeling about this, or that?" Keep probing until you get to the underlying cause. Ask questions and listen for the answers. It is important to listen to your "inner knowing!" Remember, even though you may have remedied physical problems with outward treatments, if the inner healing has not been done, and the faulty belief system or negative feelings not changed, the illness will manifest in the physical body again. Therefore, after you identify the feelings associated with the body parts in question, it is important to resolve them.

Steps for Effectively Using Your Body as a Mirror

1. IDENTIFY THE LOCATION OF PHYSICAL PAIN, ILLNESS OR DISCOMFORT.

Where is the most intense pain or discomfort in your body located? This is probably the area of first priority for healing—the place reflecting the most imbalance.

2. USE THE "WORLD OF MIRRORS" TO IDENTIFY ASSOCIATED FEELINGS.

A. Look under the section for the area of the body in question in this chapter. Read the suggestions for associated feelings. Which ideas feel right to you?

B. Look the body part up in Chapter 21 and use the "World of Mirrors" to identify the associated feelings. Write the feelings down.

3. SCAN PAST EXPERIENCES.

Does the part of the body which is ill, in pain or discomfort bring to mind any past experiences? Have you had problems in this area before? Can you see any pattern with the events of your life and when this part of the body hurts? Does it bring any other memories to mind? When you think of past events that seem to be associated with this part of the body being in pain or discomfort, try to identify what you were feeling at the time. Your present experiences of discomfort in your body may be directly related to these feelings. Write down any feelings that surface.

4. RESOLVE THE FEELINGS.

Use the *"Painless Tool"* in the next chapter, or any method that works for you, to change the negative feelings you identified, to positive feelings.

In the Appendix I, you will find two examples of negative and positive feelings for physical problems. These lists illustrate the negative feelings that can cause **HEADACHES** and **NECK** problems and their appropriate replacements stated in the way you would say them if you were using the *"Painless Tool"* found in Chapter 14 to resolve them. This is the kind of list you may want to make for the feelings associated with any part of the body that is bothering you if you choose to use this tool to assist in healing.

By changing the feelings causing pain, illness, disease or discomfort in your body, to those of love, forgiveness, gratitude, peace and harmony . . . healing will begin and your body will reflect these changes, revealing more and more of the beauty of your True Self.

Healing Negative Reflections

Fourteen

Resolving Negative Feelings

     We all have a book of life that contains a complete and faithful record of our feelings, thoughts and actions. We have been creating it since the day we were born. We are not only the author writing the story, we are the artist painting the cover. How it looks is up to us. If we look in the mirror of our cover, we will see either a reflection of our True Self, or a mask created to suit the expectations of the world. If we don't like what we see, only we can do something about it. But, how do we change the undesirable reflections?

     Several years ago, when I was wading through deep physical, mental and emotional difficulties, I read *Feelings Buried Alive Never Die . . .* by Karol K. Truman. It was an answer to prayer. By using the tool in her book, my life improved dramatically. Until I read this book I was unaware of the many masks I had painted on my self-portrait. I had no idea that the real me was in hiding. This book was like food after a long fast. It was delicious and satisfying and I ate it in two days. I had received some hard blows and was looking for help, and here it was.

I had been doing what I thought I should in order to meet others expectations of what it meant to be an ideal wife, mother, and citizen—when I suddenly had a rug pulled out from under me, causing me to take a fresh look at my life. I had reached a point where I knew deep inside there was more to life than playing the roles others "expected." I began to realize that I had to find my own answers to the questions I had and that life must be lived honestly, and from my inner feelings. I began using the tool mentioned above to deal with the intense feelings of resentment, hate and anger that I was experiencing. To my amazement, these feelings diminished immediately. By using this tool—which I refer to as the *"Painless Tool"*—I was able to revise my self-portrait until my heart reappeared on the canvas. It was exciting when I came to the realization one day, that my feelings had really changed. There was no more anger inside for the things that had caused me discomfort for so long. I also discovered that I had truly forgiven others for things that had transpired. Most of all I had forgiven myself. What a joyous feeling to be released from old negative feelings!

A powerful lesson was learned . . . "I" was the author of my book and "I" had the power to change anything recorded on the pages.

The *"Painless Tool"* enables you to change your feelings at the level of the DNA. It works by employing the part of you that remembers and knows everything there is to know about you. According to Dr. Deepak Chopra, MD, the DNA contains a memory of our perfection which cannot be lost. It can be covered over, however, which is what happens when we deviate from the perfect blueprint—the truth of who we are. How does this occur? Our blueprint is distorted by the way we internalize our experiences. For example, if we incorrectly perceive the value of our Self in response to the negative things other people say, we buy into a belief that "we are less than who we truly are, less than our perfect blueprint." If we live our life according to this false belief, it will eventually manifest itself in some way in the physical body. We can then use all kinds of methods to remedy our ills but until we resolve them at the deepest level, they will continue to manifest in the flesh. Using the *"Painless Tool"* is a powerful way to resolve negative feelings and beliefs where they originated.

I have used it successfully for years and therefore offer it to you to use if you so choose. Give it a try and see what happens. If you would like to know more about this tool and how it works, read *Feelings Buried Alive Never Die . . . (See* Bibliography)

When you begin the *"Painless Tool,"* or *"Script"* as Karol refers to it in her book, you are talking to the part of you that remembers and knows everything about you. You can address it by whatever name feels comfortable to you. It is not intended to replace prayer or other spiritual practices, even though there are people who use it as a prayer. It is shared as a supplement to whatever methods you already use to heal and improve the quality of your life. There's no right or wrong way to use it . . . just *your way.* Feel free to change any part of it to better suit your needs and/or beliefs. There are many other ways to resolve negative feelings; use whatever method feels good to you . . . **use what works!**

Note: There is an earlier version of the *"Script"* or *"Painless Tool"* in *"Feelings Buried Alive Never Die . . ."* © 1991. *See* Bibliography. The version in *The World of Mirrors-A Bridge to Knowing and Being Your "True" Self* is a revised edition by Valerieann J. Skinner and Karol K. Truman. Revised April 22, 2002.

"Painless Tool"

Spirit/Super-Conscious/Intelligence or Higher Self
(whichever you choose), please locate the origin of my feeling(s)/thought(s)
of _____.
(Insert negative feelings or thoughts.)
Take each and every level, layer, area and aspect of my Being to this origin.
Analyze and resolve it perfectly with God's truth.

Bring this feeling/thought through every generation of time, and eternity,
healing each incident and it's appendages based on it's origin. Do it according
to God's will until I am at the present . . . filled with light & truth, God's
peace and love, forgiveness of myself for my incorrect perceptions, forgiveness
of every person, place, circumstance and event which contributed to
this/these feeling(s)/thought(s).

With total forgiveness and unconditional love I allow every physical, mental,
emotional, and spiritual problem and inappropriate behavior based on the
negative origin recorded in my DNA, to transform.

I choose Be-ing_____.

I feel_____.

I AM_____.

(Replace old negative feelings with appropriate positive feelings
by placing the feeling in each of the three blanks. For example:
I choose Be-ing forgiving. I feel forgiving. I AM forgiving.)

It is done. It is healed. It is accomplished now!

Thank you, Spirit (or whatever word/s you choose using), for coming to my
aid and helping me attain the full measure of my creation. Thank you, thank
you, thank you! I love you and praise God from whom all blessings flow.

(If you like, you can do this in the name of Jesus Christ)

Whenever you see a negative reflection in the "World of Mirrors," use the *"Painless Tool"* to resolve the negative feelings that are present. For example, every time I wasn't true to my own feelings and yielded to someone else and their feelings, my fear of not being right and my inability to stand up for what I really felt caused me to experience constant conflict and disharmony within.

Here is how I would use the *"Painless Tool"* to address the "fear of not being right" to return to a place of peace and harmony. The words I would insert in the places for negative feelings and their positive replacements are underlined.

Spirit, please locate the origin of my feeling of <u>the fear of not being right</u>. Take each and every level, layer, area and aspect of my Being to this origin. Analyze and resolve it perfectly with God's truth.

Bring this feeling through every generation of time, and eternity, healing each incident and it's appendages based on it's origin. Do it according to God's will until I am at the present . . . filled with light & truth, God's peace and love, forgiveness of myself for my incorrect perceptions, forgiveness of every person, place, circumstance and event which contributed to this feeling.

With total forgiveness and unconditional love I allow every physical, mental, emotional, and spiritual problem and inappropriate behavior based on the negative origin recorded in my DNA, to transform.

I choose Be-ing <u>confident and right according to my knowledge and understanding</u>.

I feel <u>confident, I feel faith and trust in myself and my thoughts, feelings and ideas</u>.

I AM <u>confident. I AM right according to my knowledge and understanding. I allow others to see things from their perspective and I from mine. It's okay!</u>

It is done. It is healed. It is accomplished now!

"Thank you, Spirit, for coming to my aid and helping me attain the full measure of my creation. Thank you, thank you, thank you! I love you and praise God from whom all blessings flow."

Quite often, one use of this tool is sufficient to resolve a negative feeling completely. However, using it doesn't mean you will never experience that negative feeling again. It will be contingent on the way you live your life afterwards. It is important to live the principles that bring the desired results. If you keep tripping over the same stone, you're going to keep hitting the same dirt. See what I mean?

There are also other factors to consider. If you find that using the *"Painless Tool"* doesn't completely resolve your negative feelings after one time, there are either more layers of the same feeling that need to be changed, something you still need to learn by experiencing it further or something else you need to recognize about yourself (something the negative feeling/s is/are there to teach you). Often negative feelings or experiences play an important role in bringing us to an awareness of things that are for our ultimate good. Therefore, they will remain until the good is accomplished.

You can process several feelings in one reading of the *"Painless Tool."* To do so, it may be helpful to write down a list of the negative and positive feelings first and then use the "Tool" to process them all at once. (*see* Appendix I for example) This will save time and is just as effective. This will make it easier for you to process the same feelings once a day if necessary, until the way you feel makes a shift. I also suggest memorizing the *"Painless Tool."* It is very helpful to have it in your mind so you can use it whenever a negative feeling surfaces.

There may be times when you will *not* be able to put a label on what you are feeling. When this happens to me, I simply ask my *Spirit* (or whatever word your choose) to locate and identify the feeling(s)/thought(s) causing my discomfort or illness, and then I go on with the *"Painless Tool."* Your Spirit or Higher Self *knows* what the feeling is, even if you don't consciously know!

I do the same when I have a difficult time knowing the appropriate positive replacements. Sometimes you *just don't know* which words to use. Once again, ask your *Spirit* to identify the appropriate positive feelings and to replace the negative feelings with them. It works! You can also consult a Thesaurus to find the antonym or opposite word to use for replacing a negative feeling.

The power of this *"Painless Tool"* to assist in changing negative feelings is incredible and wonderful! Use it faithfully for a week and notice the difference in how you feel. Pay attention to everything you're feeling. As soon as you notice a negative feeling or thought of any kind, big or little, use the *"Painless Tool"* to change it to a positive feeling/thought. It is helpful to state the positive statements in different ways—coming at the same issue from different angles. As you are inserting the positive, open your heart and listen for inspiration as to what to say. You may be surprised at the many words and ideas that will come to you for replacing the negative. You may experience the same feeling several times a day for a while, but if you keep using the *"Painless Tool"* you will eventually notice it diminishing until it is completely gone.

Even though the *"Painless Tool"* is simple to use, don't underestimate it's power for assisting you in changing your negative programming. Literally thousands and thousands of people use it successfully!

The *"Painless Tool"* is just what its name implies . . . a "tool." Our Creator desires joy, peace and happiness for each one of us, the same as we do and will assist us whenever we use this, or any other tool, to achieve our desires.

(Another tool I have found to be very helpful in changing the energy of negative feelings is Essential Oils. See Appendix II for more information.)

Interpreting Symbols
Made Simple

Fifteen

Steps for Interpreting "Any" Symbol

Quite often, symbols will show up in your dreams or life for which no meaning is written in a book. The following steps will help you find the meanings for *any* symbol. As you go through these steps, keep asking what the symbol is revealing about you and your life. Continue with the steps until you get an "aha."

1. KEEP A "SYMBOL DESCRIPTION" NOTEBOOK.

Write down the symbol and everything that is revealed to you as you go through the following steps. Writing helps bring the knowing from within to the surface.

2. WRITE DOWN WHAT YOU ALREADY KNOW ABOUT THE SYMBOL.

Describe the symbol as if you are telling someone about it for the first time. What memories are triggered by the symbol? Recall any experiences you have had in relation to it, recently or in the past. Write these in your notebook.

3. CONSULT OTHER SOURCES FOR MORE INFORMATION.

Look it up in a dictionary and/or encyclopedia. As you read about it, ask yourself what it is trying to tell you about you and your life. It may also be helpful to find books with more information on the symbol in question. Write down any helpful information you gather.

4. ANALYZE THE COLOR.

Look up the meaning of the color of the symbol under *Colors* in *Chapter 21*. What light does this shed on the meaning of the symbol? What does it represent to you? Record the ideas that resonate with you in your notebook.

5. ASK OTHERS.

Ask people around you to tell you what the symbol means to them. This may trigger your own knowing.

6. ASK A FRIEND TO TELL YOU HOW THEY THINK YOU OR YOUR LIFE ARE LIKE THE SYMBOL.

You may be surprised at others' ability to see things about you that you may have a more difficult time seeing. Be open to their ideas.

7. USE THE "WORLD OF MIRRORS."

Read the things you have written down from doing the previous steps. Use the "World of Mirrors" to see yourself in the symbol. What do the things you have learned about the symbol say about you? How is the symbol like you or you like the symbol? Do you need to *be* more like the symbol? Use the 25 *"Questions for Finding the Meaning in Your Reflections"* in the next chapter to help you better see your reflection in the symbol.

8. PRAY.

Now that you have gathered all the information you can about the symbol, ask God for further understanding and insights about what the symbol represents, then listen . . . listen . . . listen. What ideas stand out in your mind? What new thoughts come to mind?

9. RECORD YOUR FINDINGS.

Record the new symbol and its meaning for future reference in Chapter 22, *"My Personal List of Symbols,"* which is specifically for this purpose. This part of the book will become a valuable and helpful friend.

10. EXPRESS GRATITUDE FOR THE INTERPRETATION YOU HAVE RECEIVED.

Feeling and expressing gratitude will increase your ability to know the meaning of new symbols in the future, because it helps energy/spirit flow through your body more readily.

Just So You Know

Possible Limitations

    It is important to note that interpretations by others are always distorted by their assumptions and complexes. This is why it is so important to learn how to interpret your own reflections. You are the only one who fully understands what the symbols mean to you. A good interpretation leaves the door to the unknown open . . . open to the inherent mystery within each dream or life experience. Just as paintings or music cannot be fully captured or reflected in words, not all dreams or experiences in life can be fully understood by a verbal or written interpretation.

    If after using all of the steps and ideas found in this book, you still don't know what certain reflections or symbols mean, let them go! Don't dwell on them and feel like you have failed. Know that the messages will come again in different ways. It's okay. Remember, it's alright if you don't fully understand or even interpret all of your reflections in the "World of Mirrors." The magical part of you will still work his/her magic. Perhaps some messages are only intended to be understood on other levels, not on the conscious physical level. I still have dreams and life experiences that I don't take time to analyze or interpret. The main thing is to enjoy the process no matter what happens.

The Ultimate Interpretation

If you desire to understand the meanings of your reflections in any mirror, trust that you will and keep on trying. You will be directed on the path to your desired goal.

Included in Chapter 21 of this book is an extensive list of symbols and *possible* interpretations. These are included to give you *ideas* for how to see your reflection in the symbols surrounding you, but most important, they are given to trigger *your own inner knowing* as to the correct interpretations for you. Your interpretation of any symbol is the ultimate.

The meanings given in Chapter 21 are general ideas and can only partially reflect your connection to the symbols. For example, the suggested meanings for Ice Skating are as follows:

> • There may be feelings inside in a stagnant or inaccessible form. You may be functioning in your daily life without paying attention to larger issues which you are in denial about. (Skating on top of the frozen feelings within.)

• Take a look at those parts of your life that you are most reluctant to address.

If you are a professional ice skater, the meanings associated with ice skating will more than likely be different. It may have more to do with "the way you express yourself creatively."

An object in your dream which you use daily will mean something different to you than it would to someone who only uses the object in a dream.

It may be helpful to talk out the reflections of the many mirrors with a family member or friend who has a similar understanding about interpreting them. Often, something another person says will trigger an "aha" for you, but ultimately, you are the one with the correct answers for you. Hopefully you understand the value of listening to *your* inner knowing.

The interpretations given to you from within are the ultimate! **No one else can know of your life's experiences. The symbols are there because of what they represent to YOU.**

Everything you have learned about seeing your reflection in dreams, life, world events, surroundings and words can be applied to any and everything you experience. Use *all* the mirrors available to see yourself. See your entire world as a sea of glass reflecting YOU. Doing so will quicken your journey to knowing your True Self.

May you enjoy the rewards of
cleaning your many mirrors!

Seventeen

Questions for Finding the Meaning in Your Reflections

To find the meaning in any symbol, whether in your dreams, your life, world events or other mirrors, it is helpful to ask questions. Here is a list of questions you can ask about any situation to help you determine what it is reflecting to you about yourself. Asking questions will help you tap into the part of you that holds the answers. Ask with faith, believing that you will receive the answers and you will. Take time to be silent, listen and then trust the ideas that come to you.

Some questions may seem to be the same, but they are worded just different enough to perhaps bring ideas to mind that the other questions may not.

1. WHAT ARE THE MAJOR SYMBOLS?

Are they a person, place or thing? On what was the attention focused in the dream or life situation?

2. WHO ARE THE CHARACTERS?

List the main characters as well as others in the background. They all symbolize aspects of you, your attitudes, beliefs, attributes etc.

3. HOW WELL LIT WAS THE DREAM OR LIFE SITUATION?

If it was well lit, you are probably more familiar with whatever was going on. Or, perhaps you are becoming more aware of something. If it was dark, you may be "in the dark" about this part of yourself. Perhaps it represents the subconscious or less developed areas of yourself. Explore the many possibilities.

4. WHAT IS THE SETTING?

Did it take place indoors or outdoors? In a city or in the country? In the kitchen or bedroom? Was it close to home, a place you are familiar with, or in uncharted territory? Regardless of the location, once again it was reflecting something about you. For example, a busy part of the city with heavy traffic going here and there may symbolize all of the busy thoughts filling your head or the confusion inside you.

5. WHERE DID IT TAKE PLACE?

Were you in a foreign country or a neighboring city? If it was in a place that is familiar to you, it may represent something of which you are more aware. If it was in a foreign country or a land you are unfamiliar with, the contrary is true.

6. WHAT WAS THE TIME FRAME?

This question applies more to dreams than to life. Was it in present time or ancient? When did it happen? Maybe it took place in the house you lived in as a child. Perhaps it represents the ideas or attitudes you had at the time the dream took place. Maybe your attitudes are similar to the people of that time and place. Once again, ask and listen.

7. WHAT ARE THE SURROUNDINGS?

Were you in a crowd or on a city street? In a dirty room or a castle? Was there a lake or stream? If you were out in the woods, pay attention to the terrain. Were there hills, or mountains? Climbing a hill or mountain often represents an aspiration you are working toward. The mountain may represent a spiritual quest and how you are doing will be represented by what is happening in the dream on the mountain.

8. WHAT WAS THE WEATHER LIKE?

Weather has a lot to do with what you are *feeling* on the inside. Was it raining? Maybe you are depressed or being cleansed and renewed. Perhaps there is a "solution" arriving for your problem. Was the sun shining? Or, was there a rainbow . . . a promise of new beginnings or hope? Look up the specific types of weather in Chapter 21 of this book for more ideas.

9. WHAT KIND OF BUILDINGS WERE THERE?

These usually represent your physical body. The upper level of a building represents the mental or spiritual aspects. The center of the home, or main floor represents your heart or center within. The basement can represent your legs or feet, the part of you used to walk about in life. To better understand the meanings of the specific parts of the body and how they relate to the part of the building found in your dream, read the suggested meanings for specific body parts in Chapter 21.

10. WHAT WAS YOUR METHOD OF TRANSPORTATION?

Airplanes can represent plans or ideas because they fly in the sky —the sky representing the highest part of the body or head, where your plans and ideas originate. Was the airplane on the ground, taking off or in flight? This may represent how your plans are going right now.

What about a car as opposed to a taxi? A car can symbolize your spiritual or physical body and how you are getting yourself through life. You have to pay others to get to your destination when you ride in a taxi. Are you dependant on others to get through life? Trucks are what one uses to do work or haul heavy loads. Are you carrying a heavy load in your life? Ask yourself what you use *your* truck or car for to ascertain the meaning.

Trains or buses have more to do with how you are traveling through life with others. What about riding a horse or another animal? Look at everything and ponder how it is used in the outer world to help you discover clues to the inward meaning. With *all* of these, look at what the form of transportation represents to you. It may be a particular car with a specific meaning to you and you alone. You will know what it means if you listen to the voice within.

11. WERE THERE ANIMALS?

Each animal has a specific meaning. You may want to go to the library and find books about the animals that show up in your dreams or life situations. Pay attention to the characteristics of the animals and ask what they are teaching you about yourself. How could you benefit by acquiring these same attributes? Notice if the animal was tame or wild, free or controlled. See specific animals and their meanings in Chapter 21.

12. WHAT KIND OF CLOTHING WERE YOU OR OTHERS WEARING?

Clothing may have to do with the part of yourself you show to the world or how you are protecting yourself from your environment and others. Other people and their clothing also represent your attitudes and beliefs. Was there a uniform of a particular occupation? What does it represent about you? Maybe you were naked and therefore open, not holding anything back . . . perhaps living from your honest Self, or maybe you were feeling vulnerable.

13. WHAT WERE THE COLORS OF EVERYTHING?

Was there a color that stood out in your dream or life situation? Was there something that was an unusual color? Each color has its own meaning. Red, for example, can mean force, vigor, passion or energy. Like everything else, each color has both positive and negative connotations. The meaning depends on how it was found in your dream or life situation and on the particular shade of the color. Was it bright and clear, muddy or dull?

Several meanings for each color are listed under *Colors* in Chapter 21. Chapter 6 also has ideas and steps for interpreting colors in dreams. The ideas listed for each color are only that . . . ideas. Once again, remember that your own connection to each color and what it means to *you* is the most important!

14. WHAT NUMBERS WERE PRESENT?

How many of this or that were there? Was there a specific number mentioned? Was the same number repeated as in seeing 11:11 on a clock? In Chapter 21 of this book under *"Numbers,"* you will find meanings for each number. Read the suggested meanings then go inside and ask what each number means to you. Pay attention to your first impressions.

15. DOES THE DREAM, LIFE SITUATION OR WORLD EVENT ADDRESS A LARGER ISSUE?

What is it that you are dealing with right now? The "World of Mirrors" usually reflects the main issues we are experiencing.

16. WAS IT SPIRITUAL IN NATURE?

Did the events address a spiritual issue at hand?

17. WAS IT PROPHETIC IN ANY WAY?

Perhaps the events were showing the future. Was there a warning for or help for the future?

18. WHAT ASPECT OF THE EVENTS IN YOUR DREAMS OR LIFE WERE MOST INTERESTING, SCARY, BOTHERSOME OR FASCINATING?

Several years ago, I dreamed I was cutting one of my brothers in half with the front part of him on one side of the cut and the back on the other. Needless to say, when I woke up, I was quite disturbed.

When I finally let go of viewing it as a literal event, I saw that I needed to quit worrying about the future (represented by the front of him) and quit worrying about the past (represented by the back half of him) and live in the present, which is in between the future and the past.

There were many other symbols in this dream. For example, we were standing in water which usually has to do with feelings or that which is within. When I considered this in relation to cutting my brother in half, I realized that cutting him in half had to do with "feelings" I was experiencing as a result of worrying about the past and future rather than simply living in present time. By relating the meaning of water and other symbols in the dream to the most bothersome symbol (cutting my brother in half) I was able to understand the true message of the dream and not be disturbed by it anymore.

19. WHAT DID YOU FEEL?

What feelings were associated with each action? Be specific. What feelings were resolved or unresolved? Identifying negative feelings and resolving them is always a healing salve for your life.

Referring to the dream mentioned above, with regard to how I felt, cutting my brother in half was something I would *never* do in real life, therefore, it disturbed me greatly. Because of the way it made me *feel*, I pondered the dream more and the message of the dream made a difference in how I lived my life afterwards. It was beyond the realm of "normal" or "acceptable," helping me realize the importance of letting go of and not worrying about the past or future. At the time of the dream, focusing on the present was as difficult for me as doing something I would have considered bad or wrong, like cutting my brother in half.

20. WHAT WERE THE MAJOR PATTERNS?

Were there similarities, contrasts or repetitions? How do these patterns relate to your waking life? Perhaps you dream the same dream over and over or find yourself going down the same road night after night. Ask yourself if there is some behavior in your life that has become habitual that you need to be aware of and perhaps change.

Are you in the same house repeatedly or do you see the same color time and time again? Do you see a pattern in the dreams that occur in the same night? Noticing repetition and patterns will often be the key to unlocking deeper meanings. Your dreams may also repeat things because you have not been getting the message. What is it in your life that you are not seeing? Are you repeating things in your life? What are the patterns? Do you need to break out of an old mold?

21. WHAT WOULD YOU MOST LIKE TO CHANGE IN THE DREAM OR LIFE?

Why would you like to change it? Whatever you would like to change may indicate something you need to change or accept in your life. Once you identify things you need to change, know that the way to change it also exists . . . within you.

22. WAS THERE SOMETHING YOU WOULD LIKE TO HAVE AVOIDED?

Why would you like to have avoided it? If it was in a dream, does it represent something you are avoiding in your life? Do you *need* to avoid something or face up to something?

23. WAS THERE INFORMATION THAT WAS MISSING?

Were there feelings not resolved or expressed? Were there choices that were limited? Perhaps there was a person in your dream without a name, or a person in your life whose name you didn't know. What is this telling you about yourself? What are you missing? Are there things you need to say that are going unexpressed?

24. WAS THE DREAM COMPENSATING FOR SOMETHING?

Sometimes dreams compensate for that which you have either too much or not enough of in your daily life. For example: If you are ultra conservative in real life, you may find yourself experiencing extreme freedom in your dreams and doing things you would never allow yourself to do normally. This is a way of keeping you in balance . . . like a built in safety valve.

25. KEEP ASKING QUESTIONS.

Think about additional questions you can ask regarding your dreams and life. then, listen to the wisdom coming from within for the answers. Keep the "World of Mirrors" in mind as you do so.

Pick one of your dreams or a day of your life and apply these questions to it. As you do so, listen to the ideas and thoughts that come to mind. You will begin to better understand what is really going on in your life and will find resolutions to your problems as well.

Your dreams and your life are
messages from you to yourself.
You write the script, direct the play
and act out all the parts.
You also have the interpretations
because you and the wise sage within, are one.

Hearing and Trusting the Voice Within

Seventeen

Hearing the Messages

You have written down your dream, life experience, world event or other reflections. You know what the symbols are and you are asking questions to help unearth the meaning . . . now . . . *how* do you hear the answers—how do you hear the messages?

LEARN TO BE SILENT

Being silent means learning to shut off the inner dialog long enough to "hear" the messages. It means letting go of your thoughts of the outside world and clearing the clutter in your mind. How do you do that?

1. FIND A PLACE WHERE YOU WON'T BE DISTURBED.

(If you have children like I do, finding a place where you won't be disturbed may be a challenge. ☺) Find a comfortable place to sit.

2. RELAX, CLOSE YOUR EYES AND BREATHE CONSCIOUSLY.

Take a deep breath slowly in through your nose and let it go through your mouth. Take a second breath slowly through your nose, holding it for three counts at the top of the breath, then release it slowly through your mouth. This engages both sides of your brain. Relax! Let go of all that is on your mind. Now, put your attention on your breathing. Observe your breath as it goes in and out.

3. CATCH YOURSELF "THINKING."

As soon as you catch yourself thinking, let go of the thought and put your attention back on breathing. Granted, you are still thinking about "breathing," but it helps you let go of the chatter in your mind. Remember that thoughts are only real when YOU give them your energy or in other words, when you give them your attention. As soon as you shift your attention to something else, like breathing, the thought and whatever the thought was about no longer exists. So . . . catch yourself thinking and let your thoughts go, catch yourself thinking and let your thoughts go, refocusing on your breath each time.

4. "PRACTICE" NOT THINKING.

The more you practice "not thinking," the easier it will be. All you need is "an instant" of not thinking. That instant will gradually increase as you continue practicing. Even if you just practice doing it for a few minutes, you have succeeded.

LIVE IN THE "PRESENT"

Another way to hear the answers or messages is by being totally present in each moment . . . fully experiencing the "now." This means being there with your thoughts, feelings and actions . . . not thinking about the past or future, focused only on the present moment.

Do I take the time to Be,
The time to really truly see,
Looking deep within the mysteries
Of the world surrounding me?

Seems a pity not to do so,
Every moment, every hour,
For the joys of life are planted
In every tree and every flower.

"Present Time" Peas

It was a beautiful summer day in August. I had just miscarried twins. Having never experienced this before, I was surprised at the deep loss I felt. I had already given birth to five children with no problems, therefore, my heart was heavy with the question, *"Why* did this happen?"

Days passed and the question lingered. One afternoon, Neliann, who was two years old at the time, asked me to go with her to the pea patch in the garden. It was late afternoon and the sun was hanging low in the sky . . . one of those warm, wonderful evenings when everything is saturated with a golden glow.

Neliann toddled down the rows, picking peas and bringing them to me grinning with delight. To me, there is nothing quite like watching the bubbly spirit of one of my children . . . and nothing like eating fresh, juicy peas from my garden. A delightful combination!

While eating peas, my question entirely left my mind. I was filled with the smells of the garden, the taste of the peas, the warmth of the sun and Neliann's smile. It was then, while eating peas, that a light came on in my mind . . . an 'aha' arrived. As I opened one pod after another, I noticed that there were always one, two or three peas in each pod that hadn't fully matured. I then asked the question, "Could a pod be found in which ALL of the peas were mature?" With enthusiasm and anticipation, I opened and ate peas, checking each one to see if they were *all* big and round. Guess what? I didn't find any that day! Every pod had at least one pea that had not matured. In that moment of silence, I heard my answer, "Each one (pea or person) fills the measure of their creation." I understood in my heart that my babies had filled the measure of their creation, that the amount of time we spend here on earth has nothing to do with whether or not we accomplish our purpose. It's just the way it is! One *moment* of life is as valuable as one hundred *years* of life. The miscarriage was perfect in every way. My body filled with joy and excitement as I came to this realization and accepted the situation as it was. I then felt a strong desire to express what I was feeling by painting a picture of the peas. (As an artist, this is how I often process my experiences.) I decided to paint first thing the following day so I would have enough time to complete the painting in one sitting without a break in the flow of energy.

The next morning, I hurried to the pea patch and began searching for the perfect pod. The sun was just coming up and everything was covered with dew. Interestingly enough, the first pod I picked was perfect, with peas in many stages of development. I had found my desired treasure and was leaving the garden when a blossom caught my eye. I think it was the only one left in the patch. The sun shining on the dew drops caused it to sparkle as though it were covered with tiny diamonds, igniting my passion to paint even more. As I admired it, I heard it say, "Paint me!" I was surprised, because I had not thought about including a blossom. I obediently took it with me into the house to include it in the painting. The next five hours were spent in ecstasy as I put paint to canvas.

Upon completing the painting, I was amazed to "hear" words
of poetry ringing in my ears. I grabbed a piece of paper and
began writing . . .

The Mysteries of Life, In the Pod of a Pea

In the moments of silence, great truth's abound.
The mysteries of all things are there to be found.
In such a moment was revealed to me,
The mysteries of life, in the pod of a pea.

There are pods of all sizes, shapes, and forms,
Contained within each are peas newly born.
Some carry on 'til they're plump and round.
Some remain tiny and can barely be found.

Each has a measure of creation to fill,
That of knowing and doing the Father's will.
Each plays it's role as only it should,
Filling it's measure, God calling it, " Good."

The time that it takes doesn't matter a bit.
'Cause when in the Present, time doesn't exist.
In that moment of silence, I was able to see,
The source of all life, energy, light,
. . . and me!

This poem was an unexpected gift in many ways, for you see, when I was in the ninth grade, I took a creative writing class. No matter what I wrote, pleasing the teacher seemed to be impossible. I therefore assumed that I was incapable of writing anything worth reading and quit. After writing this poem and sharing it with others, I was surprised when they responded favorably and with excitement. It was then that I began to think "Maybe I *can* write."

After this experience, I began hearing poetry upon completing some of my paintings. I have since created my own line of greeting cards with these paintings and the subsequent poems. It is amazing what messages you can hear once you *"Learn to be Silent"* and *"Live in the Present Moment."* Somewhere I heard . . .

> *The past is history,*
> *the future is a mystery,*
> *but this moment is a "gift,"*
> *that's why they call it "the present."*
> —Author Unknown—

DISCOVER "YOUR" WAY

There are many ways messages can be received. The most effective way is the way that works for you! Here are some of the ways to know when you have received guidance.

- A peaceful feeling comes over you while contemplating a course of action.
- You experience coincidence or synchronicity.
- An insight or 'aha' comes quickly to mind.
- You get a glimpse of a larger picture.
- You are drawn to a book, or hear someone say something that feels like it was meant for you.
- You have an overwhelming feeling of compassion, gratitude, forgiveness or appreciation for life.

• You hear the lyrics of a song and have the "knowing" that the message of the song was meant for you.
• You hear the answer in your mind and heart.
• You experience a feeling of comfort or assurance in your heart.
• You feel a chill or surge of heat go through your body when you hear something.

Have you ever experienced a time when all of a sudden, something came flashing into your mind, like a reminder that you needed to do something or be somewhere? These messages are different than the constant thoughts that fill your mind all the time, like; "What shall I wear?" "I wonder what she thinks about me." "What am I going to do today?" and so on. It is often the voice that breaks into the middle of the minds useless chatter. This voice will answer you whenever you ask him/her a question. It will usually be the first thing that comes to your mind.

Because many are not used to listening to the voice within, and are hesitant to trust it when they do hear it, it may be helpful to use the following ideas at first.

1. LISTEN TO YOUR BODY'S WISDOM, AS IT IS EXPRESSED THROUGH THE SIGNALS OF COMFORT AND DISCOMFORT.

After asking a question, listen for the first thing that pops into your head. If you are unsure whether or not it is the correct answer, ask your body, "How do you feel about this answer?" Notice the slightest sensations.

• If your body responds with joy and comfort (or you may feel warmth in your heart area, chills somewhere in your body, peace or other similarly good feelings) you can know it is the correct answer.

• If your body sends a signal of physical or emotional distress (either you may feel an obvious pain somewhere or more subtle feelings of distress) then it isn't the correct answer.

Pay attention to the particular way *your* body responds to your thoughts or the things other people say. Your body has its own way of communicating messages to you. Once you are aware of the method your body uses, you will be better able to trust yourself and the answers you receive.

2. LISTEN TO YOUR BODY'S WISDOM AS IT SWAYS WITH THE ANSWER.

The following is an interesting thing to try. It works like Kinesiology or muscle testing (as it is often called). (For more information, read *Your Body Doesn't Lie* by John Diamond, M. D. *See* Bibliography) If you are unfamiliar with the way energy works in your body, this may seem a little strange at first, nevertheless, it is something that can benefit you if you are struggling with hearing the messages from within.

First, stand with your feet about one foot apart. Make a *statement* about something you are wondering about, or anything in life, and see how your body responds. If the statement is true, your body will sway forward, if not, it will sway backward. If the answer is neutral, meaning it doesn't matter one way or the other, it won't move at all. It is helpful to try this with a simple statement that you know the answer to at first. For example, "My name is (state your name)." If this is a method that will work for you, your body will sway forward. Next say, "My name is (state a name different from your own)." Your body will sway backward.

Here's an idea for using it to better understand your dreams. If, for instance, you are wondering if Aunt Cindy (in your dream) represents an aspect of you, you might make a statement like this, "My Aunt Cindy represents something about me in my dream." (This is a "statement" rather than a "question")

Perhaps your Aunt Cindy is a very successful woman in what she does in real life. This may represent something about your own success in what you are doing. Depending on the role Aunt Cindy played in your dream, it may be showing you what you need to do or not do in order to assure your own success. You could then make a statement like "My Aunt Cindy represents my ability to succeed with what I am doing." If this is true, your body will sway forward. If not, it will sway backward.

You can use this method to learn the truth of many things, for instance, if you are wondering if taking a particular vitamin is good for you, hold it to your chest. Make the statement, "Taking this vitamin is good for me." Then see what results you get. Does your body move forward, backward or not at all? (I was told by one person that you need to face north when doing this. For me, it works regardless of the direction I am facing. Try it both ways to see if doing it makes a difference to you one way or the other.)

Eventually, if you pay attention to how you feel, or how your body responds as soon as you make a statement, you will begin knowing the answer immediately and won't need to use other methods. Practice being sensitive to your heart or body's immediate response.

An **important awareness** to have when using the method above is to **"be in a *neutral* place with your feelings,"** allowing the answer to be *whatever* it is, having no need to force it one way or the other. This is vital if you want a correct answer.

The most effective way to receive direction . . .
is the way that works for you!

Ninteen

The "Value of "Your" Truth

While studying the world in school, I never thought about how the maps were laid out. I'll never forget my astonishment when looking at a map displayed on the wall of a grade school classroom in Taiwan. Instead of seeing *America* displayed in the center, as I was used to seeing it, mainland *China* and *Taiwan* occupied that space. It stunned me. Until that moment, I had never considered the possibility of the world being mapped out differently than how I had always seen it. I then realized that I had assumed, because of how I saw it while growing up, that *everyone* saw America as the center of the world. Even though I had never been conscious of it, that assumption included the mistaken idea that America was also the most important country. A round world all of a sudden took on new meaning. There is actually no place more important than another. The only way a person, place or thing is given more importance is by the attention and elevated definition an individual or group gives it. How we see the world is according to *our* particular point of view and ours alone. Unfortunately most of us don't realize that it is "only our view." There are as many ways of looking at the world as there are people. So . . . whose perspective is correct? Whose beliefs are right and whose are wrong? Is there an absolute right and wrong?

The more people I know, the more aware I become of the various contradicting views and beliefs existing in the world. In the midst of these seeming contradictions, I find one thing quite amazing. Each person is certain that their views or beliefs are correct. So . . . time and time again, you have two people with different views, each feeling that theirs are right and the other persons views are wrong. What is the truth in the matter?

In seminars, I use the following exercise to illustrate the importance of each person's perspective. First, I ask everyone to draw a *fast* line across their paper. When they have completed it, I ask them to draw a similar line on the same piece of paper, only this time they are to draw it *slowly*. As they do so, no one ends at the same time and no two lines are alike. I then ask who felt like they followed the instructions correctly. Of course everyone feels like they did. Everyone then holds up their lines so all can see and compare. The obvious differences become apparent. So, who was right and who was wrong in the way they drew the lines? Because everyone finished their lines at a different time and none were the same, they couldn't *all* be right . . . or could they? The truth is, *everyone* drew their lines correct according to *their truth*, to *their* understanding and interpretation of what it meant to draw a fast and slow line. "I" am actually the only one who could have drawn the lines correct according to "*my*" idea of doing so.

Think about how many words there are in the English language. How many do you think we understand exactly the same? When it comes right down to it, we live our lives *assuming* in many instances that everyone sees and understands things the same way we do, but they don't! Consider the beliefs of any given group or society. There may be general similarities in their understanding of their beliefs, but if you interview individuals within the group, you will always come up with different definitions for the same topics. So, why do we judge and condemn others for the things they believe, do or say just because they see things differently than we do? Aren't we judging them only by the way *we* see, according to *our* truth? Do we believe our truth is absolute to the exclusion of all else? Perhaps, if we saw and understood the world as others do, we would discover that the same things we see and judge as wrong, evil or bad can actually be *good* if understood from other points of view. We are unique in the way we see and experience the world. Each person's view is equally important and valuable.

"There are truths but no Truth. I can perfectly well assert two completely contradictory things, and be right in both cases. One ought not to weigh one's insights against one another . . . each is a life for itself."
— Tagebucher, Aphorismen, Essays und Reden, 1955 —

When you really come to understand this principle, you will find it much easier to be forgiving and allowing of others as well as forgiving and allowing of yourself. You will also know the value of hearing and heeding the voice within.

Going back to the maps—our natural instinct to put ourselves in the center of the world is really quite accurate. While there is no center point on the globe, there *is* only one point of reference for each of us . . . where we are standing. That is the center point of *our* world. How can anyone else know what is "right" for *us*? Others will always be seeing from their perspective, not ours. So it is when we interpret our dreams or life situations. Others can *help* us interpret them but their interpretations will always pass through their filter, not ours. The final interpretation has to come from us if we want it to be accurate.

As you learn how to interpret symbols and begin exercising faith and trust in your inner knowing, you will most likely experience opposition. It comes to you as a disguised friend—the strength training part of the journey. Resistence of some kind is necessary to strengthen all muscles and that includes spiritual muscles. The more you "know" and "understand," the more challenging life can be. In *The Millionaires of Genesis,* Catherine Ponder explains one of the reasons for this.

> *"If you know people who have developed a knowledge of the power of thought, yet are faced with human relations problems, your first reaction may be, 'If they are so knowledgeable in this way of thinking, why are they having these problem?' It is because they are so advanced mentally that they have those problems! They are having to do their*

emotional homework, so that their mind power can be balanced by love."

She goes on to say, *"Your growth and expansion come in phases of normality. First you gain knowledge of the creative power of thought and begin to use it mentally. Then human relations problems often arise so that you may prove it in the heart, emotionally. Indeed, there is no balance in your consciousness until love and wisdom are united in you, and reflected in your life."*

There was a time, while learning to more fully trust my inner guidance, when other people told me I was listening to "the wrong voice," the voice of "Satan." This pointed accusation really made me stop and think about what I was doing, which ultimately benefitted me greatly. It caused me to listen intently to make sure I was truly hearing the right voice from within. This helped me gain a stronger assurance of that which was true for me . . . knowing *my* correct path. For this reason, I'm grateful for those who constantly challenge my views, recognizing that their way of seeing is as valuable as mine. We challenge and strengthen each other knowingly or not.

A situation like this, in which someone is challenging your ability to receive correct guidance or anything else, is also an excellent time to look in the "World of Mirrors." Ask how the *person challenging you* is reflecting something about *you*. For example, in this instance, those who said these things to me were reflecting the insecure feelings I had at the time about my ability to hear correct guidance. The doubts existed in me before I experienced them on the outside with others. And yet, the outward experiences provided the resistance needed to help me become aware of my own doubts and more sure of myself in listening to the voice within.

You have probably experienced times when others have been bothered by the things you did and/or said and challenged you. One reason this happens is because they need to validate themselves in being "right"when their opinions and beliefs are at a variance with yours. They feel there has to be a right and a wrong. If they concede that "you" are "right," that means "they" are "wrong" and most of us don't like to be "wrong" . . . right? Therefore, when others challenge your ability to hear correct guidance because your views or direction differs from theirs, look in the "World of Mirrors," and *let go* of any need *you* have to be "right." Choose instead to be at peace, understanding the principle that has just been illustrated: *there can be two completely contradictory things and both can be right at the same time. "One ought not to weigh one's insights against one another . . . each is a life for itself."* There are many ways of seeing and as many truths as there are people. Nobody has to be right and nobody has to be wrong. By being understanding and allowing of opposite views, we enable ourselves to live in peace. It's a choice.

Sometimes, the consequences of following our guidance are not pleasant and we may think our answers were wrong, that indeed, we *have* listened to the "wrong" voice. Regardless of how it sometimes appears, following the voice within and living according to that guidance is your quickest path to your True Self—to God. It is also the quickest path to experiencing lasting joy, peace and happiness. Don't judge your experiences prematurely and harshly, God's not finished with the masterpiece. Besides, quite often the more difficult challenges teach the most valuable lessons.

Over the years, I have learned many things while wearing my "artist hat." During the process of each painting, it has been my experience that I nearly always arrive at a point of "no hope," a point where it looks awful, a place where I get stuck and have no clue what to do next. Because I have reached this point many times, I have learned not to judge the painting as awful and quit. Quite the opposite! I now get excited when I arrive at the edge of this painting cliff because I have discovered the power in letting go and jumping into the unknown. I just start wiping or scraping paint off the canvas with reckless abandon. As soon as I do this, I get an 'aha.' All of a sudden, I see the painting in an entirely new way and know exactly what to do next. More often than not, this part of the painting ends up being the most interesting and beautiful.

What would happen if I was in the habit of judging my paintings prematurely, of thinking I had the wrong idea to start with and quitting? I would never experience the beauty of the completed creation. I think it is the same with each one of us. We need to trust the guidance from within, act upon it and then refrain from judging the experiences that result "too soon"—just because they may appear undesirable at first—and trust the process of life.

Let Go and Trust The Power Within

A few years ago, I was in southern Utah teaching art classes. Some friends of mine were planning a hike to the bottom of the Grand Canyon where the Havasupai Indian tribe lives. Two people, who planned to go, canceled at the last minute and my husband, Alan, and I were offered an opportunity to go in their place. Even though Alan was still in Idaho at the time, he drove eight hours so he could go with us. We had talked of seeing the Grand Canyon for a long time and were eager for the experience.

It was not an easy hike, however, because we had not been able to prepare ourselves physically. My right knee reflected this fact with pain during the last few miles. The scenery was delightful though, having its special way of minimizing my discomfort.

The next day we hiked to the waterfalls beyond the village. Before reaching the last one however, my knee began hurting so much that I had to stop and give it a rest. I remained at Havasupai Falls to wait while the others went to the third waterfall.

As I bathed in the warm afternoon sun,
sketching the waterfall and surrounding area,
my full attention was eventually captured
by the awesome power
of the water
plunging
over the cliffs
into the pool below.
As it did so,
the water spoke . . .

The Water Fall

I am the water rolling down the stream
paying no attention to the objects of rigidity in my path,
flowing without resistance around them all,
knowing only this since emerging
form the depths of Mother Earth.

Yet now, something is different—what is it?

Nothingness? Destruction?

I let go . . .

flying into the air,

embracing the space and the sunbeams—

I fall . . . into my Self,

generating power . . . Divine power.

Reflecting . . .

I see that I did not really know my Self

while flowing as the stream, but now . . .

having gone over the edge into uncertainty,

into the unknown,

facing the fear of falling,

I find my Self and the power from within,

further knowledge of who I am.

With this knowing, I travel downstream again

flowing effortlessly and with more joy than before . . .

knowing more what it means to be the water.

I am not only flowing through the stream of life . . .

I am the stream of life.

There is no separateness.

I AM the source from whence I came.

The image of intense, beautiful power, generated from within, resulting from the action of letting go and submitting to the flow of nature—as with the waterfall—will remain with me always. The awesome power of the universe is experienced by letting go of the ego's need to control what is happening. Let go and trust the power within!

The morning of our departure from the Grand Canyon, my knee was still painful when I walked. I therefore debated as to what I should do—desiring to hike out, but knowing I might not be able to make it. Finally . . .
I let go of my original plan to hike and took a helicopter ride instead. This turned out to be an unexpected joy, as I had never flown in a helicopter before . . . and it was much easier than going out the way I had planned.

A week after arriving home, I discovered that I had been four weeks pregnant with my sixth child when I hiked the Canyon. It was a good thing I did let go and trust what I was feeling, flying out instead of hiking. Quite often, this is exactly what happens in other situations in life. As soon as we let go and submit to "what is," we find that we can fly out of our canyons rather than hike.

All of us have a Grand Canyon inside. If we follow the stream, letting go and trusting the voice within—taking the plunge—we will fall into ourselves—into the truth of who we are. By so doing, we will come to know the beautiful Divine Being that we are . . . and will be able to take flight, using our "Celestial Wings of Glory."

Until we come to know that we are okay just because we *exist*—because we are Divine and are a unique expression of that divinity—most of us fall into the trap of pleasing others to feel accepted and loved. We concern ourselves more with what others think and feel than what we think and feel—ignoring the voice within. We seek outside ourselves that which we haven't yet located inside. Traveling the path within and taping into our dreams and life by using the "World of Mirrors" will help us remedy this.

When you live according to your truth, you are in harmony with your True Self, the universe and God.

"And what is truth?
A difficult question: but I have solved it for myself
by saying that it is what the voice within tells you."
— Mahatma Gandhi —

Playing "Harmony with the Universe" is the most melodic, peaceful, soothing song you can play. Play it often! Fall into yourself and trust the wisdom within. It is the one friend that will never let you down. The more you trust the voice within, in the face of opposition, the stronger you will be. The resulting experiences, even though they may sometimes be challenging, will prove to you the correctness of following that voice. Eventually, you will find the courage to always follow and trust the wisdom within . . . your truth as it is given to you from your wise sage within. And when you do . . . look out! You will be the source of great things!

If, instead, you fear your truth and run from it, you will fall off the edge of the flat world you create with your resistance, onto a more difficult path. This alternative path will also provide the necessary experiences to help you awaken to who you really are, but your experiences will be more intense. The good news is that you are created to succeed in uncovering the Divine Being that you are. The spiritual path provides powerful help as you travel it. Let me warn you, however, of a trap that is also hidden along the way, so you won't fall into it. "Sometimes" the spiritual path works "against" people *because of the way they travel it.* I will use the words of Hugh Prather from his book, *The Little Book of Letting Go,* to explain.

> *"Everyone is on a path,' many openly devout people say. But what they seem to be thinking is, 'I, however, am on a <u>spiritual</u> path.' In other words, 'Now that I believe in oneness, I see that you and I are not one.*
>
> *From having repeatedly fallen into this trap myself, I now realize that nothing is more selfish or separating than thinking that you, personally, have a higher approach to life than other people. It's ironic that individuals with strong spiritual beliefs often have larger egos, are more rigid, are more unconsciously judgmental, and are more uncomfortable to be around than people who have little interest in pursuing mystical, religious, or metaphysical teachings. Those who assume the mantle of oneness often lack the desire to experience oneness with anyone."*
>
> Hugh also says, *"How could one person's way possibly be superior to another person's way if God is leading us all?"*

As you travel the spiritual path, it is important to stay grounded and connected to all . . . not above or below anyone . . . coming from love in all you think, say and do . . . giving yourself permission to live your truth while allowing others the same privilege. As you listen to the wisdom within and learn from the symbols in the "World of Mirrors," you will be empowered in your ability to extract the meaning and messages they contain.

Returning to Myself

The things I saw first
When I arrived in this sphere,
Were the beautiful colors
And the love that was here.

It was fun to explore
The world all around,
To experience it fully,
Enjoying what I found.

But as time went on,
There were others who'd say,
"Color inside the lines,
You mustn't do it that way."

"You see, this is black
And this here is white,
These things are all wrong,
And these things here are right."

Sometimes when they'd tell me
I wasn't correct,
It didn't match up
With the feelings I'd get.

It became quite confusing,
This world I was in.
The things I was feeling
Just didn't fit in.

I had learned all the boundaries,
Obeyed all the rules,
Discounting the things
I'd desired to do.

The joy I was promised
By living this way,
Just couldn't be found,
And there was no time to play.

The fear of men
Had me locked in a box,
'Til an angel gave me
The key that unlocks.

I learned that within
Was the power to change,
The truth of all things
Were therein contained.

As I went deep within,
Unlocking the doors,
I uncovered the joys
Experienced before.

I broke out of the boundaries
Others set before me,
And found that my soul
Was now joyful and free.

The beautiful colors
That once I had seen,
Were not only outside,
But were deep inside me.

Now that I've uncovered
The truth of my Being,
I'm once more enjoying
The world I am seeing!

—Valerieann J. Skinner ©1997—

Balancing the Reflection
of Opposition

Twenty

The Balancing Act

Opposition

Now that we have learned how to look at ourselves in the "World of Mirrors," it is essential to understand the act of balancing the array of desirable and undesirable reflections we will inevitably see—learning how to respond in a way that creates peace and balance. We live in a world with negative and positive, day and night, up and down, black and white, hot and cold, sweet and sour, good and bad—opposition in ALL things. Most of us probably wouldn't sign on as tight rope walkers in a circus, but it's about that challenging to maintain balance in the midst of the many opposing forces in our lives.

Fortunately for all of us, there's a big net to catch us when we fall. So what if we look like clowns in a circus while we learn to keep our balance—everybody loves clowns.

Have you ever wished you could do away with some of the negative things you experience, like sickness or pain? Have you ever considered what your life would be like without opposites—without contrasts? Could a physical world exist without them? If you took away the darkness, would there be light? If you experienced no pain, would you know joy? How exciting would it be to look at an oil painting that was painted using only white paint? About as exciting as looking at a white piece of paper. On the other hand, if you were to mix white and black paint together, varying the amounts of each, you could create an illusion of anything you wanted—something fun or interesting to look at.

The World Within is the World We're In
Original acrylic painting, 16" x 20" © 1995

Perhaps life works the same way, providing each of us with the necessary elements to create and experience our life in any way we choose. Have you ever wondered why you are here experiencing what you experience? Have you ever questioned the need for opposites or how you could live in their midst and experience peace at the same time? One day I was pondering these very questions and the following analogy came to mind.

72°

All of our lives we encounter a constant stream of what we term "good" and "bad," "right" and "wrong." At an early age we begin deciding which things we like to experience and which things we don't. We tend to avoid the unpleasant whenever possible and seek to experience that which is agreeable to us. Even though we become quite efficient at avoiding most of the undesirable things, it never fails that things "just happen". . . things that are painful, heartbreaking and difficult to deal with. Because these things are usually perceived as totally unfair and undeserved, we tend to ask the question, "Why me?" But it may be helpful to pose a different question, "Why are we here having *any* experiences, good *or* bad?" To answer this, let's go back to childhood.

When a child is first born, does she know what "warm" is? She experiences warmth as she is snuggled in a blanket in her mother's arms, but the concept of temperature has no meaning for her. Eventually, as she begins to toddle, she is told not to touch something because "it is hot." But what does *that* mean? She figures it's "bad," if the tone of her mother's voice is anything to go by, but until she actually experiences "hot," that's all she knows.

Can you recall your first experience of hot, or did you totally avoid it because your mother told you to? It's not likely. Being blessed with a healthy dose of curiosity, the child in our story eventually "experiences" hot by either touching something hot with her fingers or by experiencing it in some other way. Now that the child has experienced hot, does this teach her what "warm" is? I don't think so.

For the purpose of this story, let us now say that she has always lived in an environment of 72° in warmth. This, and having burned her finger, is all she knows of temperature. But because she has been warm (72°) all of her life, she takes warmth for granted. It still has no real meaning for her . . . not the way "hot" does after her experience of it.

Winter arrives and the child is now old enough to go out and play in the snow. Her mother bundles her up and out she goes. After a period of time her fingers and toes begin tingling and feel quite uncomfortable . . . she has discovered cold! She comes in the house to get warm because she realizes that she would prefer a temperature closer to the hot side of things. Now she knows hot and cold, and that there is something in between . . . warm.

She is also learning about "good" and "bad," and that sometimes the same thing can be either. As she sits in front of the hot stove to get warm, what at first seemed "bad" about "hot" is now starting to feel pretty "good." As she gets older she learns that, just as warm fits somewhere between hot and cold, there is a wide range of things between the extremes of good and bad. She would have learned none of these things if she had spent her entire life in the house in a constant state of warmth, protected from all experiences of opposites.

We all don't have to burn our fingers in order to know what hot is. Many times we are able to avoid experiencing extreme opposites simply by observing the experiences of others. For example, It was not I who touched a hot stove as a child, it was my brother. Even though I have avoided many undesirable experiences by heeding the warnings of my parents and others, experiencing opposites is unavoidable in this physical world. I have certainly had my share of "good" and "bad" experiences, as I'm sure you have.

Having now explored something that is familiar to us all, allow me to take it a step further. It is my understanding that love is the essence of who we are. If we were *love* before we came to earth, living in total peace, and that was all we had ever experienced, could we, anymore than the child did of warmth, know what love or our true nature really was? Wouldn't we take it for granted? Would we ever have a full knowledge or understanding of love without something to compare it to? Could this possibly have something to do with why we are here experiencing all that we are experiencing? Could it be that this is the very purpose of our existence . . . coming to know our True Self, our true nature, gaining knowledge and wisdom that we could not gain in our pre-mortal state?

What if we divided the light from the dark, the good from the bad, the love from the fear? What if we divided our totality, the whole essence of our being (love), into all of its various parts and pieces . . . into opposites? Would the experience of hate, pain, war and misery give us something with which to measure love, pleasure, peace and joy? Would we then be able to *consciously* and fully experience love, peace, joy or who we really are?

Assuming we were whole in the beginning, or in other words, all *One* (love), could we now be experiencing a separation of the whole—a separation that has created the various parts of our love or (whole) Self. This would mean that even what we perceive as *evil* and *negative* is as much a part of us as *love* and *goodness*. If indeed this is so, why should we fear our negative elements and try to avoid, run from or abolish them? In doing so, aren't we then running away from our Self, a part of the whole us? Aren't we trying to abolish a part of our Self? Perhaps there's a better way to deal with our negative parts—especially if they are there to help us come to know ourselves, to know what love is.

Albert Einstein's equation $E=MC^2$ tells us that all matter is energy, including our bodies and our feelings. By isolating and observing the smallest particles of energy in sealed chambers, physicists have discovered that energy *does not die*, it can only *transform*. Therefore, it is impossible to abolish negative elements. The only effective thing we can really do with negative or "dark" energy is change or transform it into positive or "light" energy. This is why it is important to recognize all parts of ourselves being reflected in the "World of Mirrors." We need to see and recognize energy of all kinds— then somehow change the negative, destructive energy to positive, creative energy. (The tool in Chapter 14 is effective in helping you do this.)

So . . . what things do you fear? What parts of yourself are you running from? According to Einstein's equation, fear is a negative feeling or energy that can be changed into something positive. Once we face what we have been fearing and change it rather than try to accomplish the impossible of doing away with it, we transform our experience—changing the "boogie man" into a "blessing." For example, I consider being able to freely read books on any subject of my choosing a wonderful blessing, but there was a time when I was afraid to do so. For years, when it came to spiritual topics, I was careful to read only those books written by members of the church I was raised in, for fear *others* would lead me astray. I ran, so to speak, from these other books—my fear chasing me. (Ironically, some of the books I feared were those about dreams and many of the other things I am now writing about.)

For years, therefore, I missed out on the beautiful truths that were available—things which are now so joyful to me.

Encompassed within this experience was a fear of perhaps finding out that some of the beliefs I had embraced while growing up were *wrong*, which would mean that some of the things I based my actions on in life might crumble to the dust and leave me with little or nothing to stand on. Therefore, for a period of time . . . rather than face my fear of finding out the truth in the matter, it was easier to project *wrongness* onto *other books and other people.*

During the process of working through this fear, I even hid the books I was reading so those around me wouldn't condemn me for reading them. This revealed yet another fear . . . how I perceived others would judge me. I eventually discovered wherein lay the real problem. I was projecting the problem and opposition "out there," when in reality, the only problem or opposition of any significance was the fear "within me." I was projecting what I didn't want to see in myself onto the church and others. Whether or not anyone else was to blame doesn't even matter. The only way anything could be changed for me was by looking inside myself—through the reflection of everyone and everything "out there"—and by also resolving what I saw "out there" . . . "inside myself." Eventually, my desire to know things for myself became greater than my fear of reading the books I felt drawn to read. Instead of relying on the voice of others as a guide for what I should read and for what I should believe, I did as Paul admonished the Thessalonians, *"Prove all things; hold fast that which is good."*

Perfect love casteth out fear. When we fear examining or contemplating another aspect of truth . . . regardless of where it comes from . . . we are not assured in our own convictions.

After changing fear to faith and trusting my ability to discern the truth of what I read for myself, I began openly reading the books I desired to read. The books I feared the most became stepping stones of love on the path to discovering my true identity. And yes, I did have to rebuild a few places with rocks when parts of my foundation crumbled to the dust, but I am grateful to be rid of the sand.

We often project "badness" or "wrongness" onto others or things outside ourselves, making them out to be the "enemy" in order to avoid looking at the real causes of our problems inside ourselves. This brings us to the question of what to do with these perceived enemies. In Matthew 5:44-45, Jesus says,

> ". . . *love your enemies, bless them that curse you, do good to them that hate you, and pray for them which despitefully use you, and persecute you; that ye may be the children of your Father which is in heaven . . .*"

What if we were to take this advice to heart, loving not only the enemies "out there," but the "enemies within," knowing now that without the enemy, we would never know the true essence of our being? How would we then view what we saw . . . the good and bad, the right and wrong, the peace and war, the love and fear? As the hot and cold illustration points out, could we *know* the love that we are—like the child with temperature—if we weren't brought to an awareness of love's essential elements? Would I have valued being able to search for and find truth for myself had I not experienced a feeling of being restricted to established beliefs? Would I have even searched? As I see it, experiencing opposites is the way we have of coming to *consciously* know ourselves, the love that we are . . . to knowing God . . . which includes knowing and then balancing *all elements* of creation—within ourselves.

I will now share a way to balance opposites that allows us to experience peace while living in the midst of them.

Balancing Opposites

Balancing opposition is challenging, as it is not always easy to know how to deal with difficult experiences. Take for example, instances of physical abuse. In these cases, there are perceived enemies because of the physical control they have exerted over our bodies. In these situations, however, others *only* have power over "who we truly are" as *we* allow ourselves to *feel negative feelings* about what they have done—in which case, our only real enemy is within us. It's the negative feelings inside that take us out of balance—not the "bad" acts of others. They may be able to hurt the body, but no one except us has control over the essence of who we are and the part of us that is eternal. We can still choose how we respond and how we feel. As long as we harbor anger, thinking we are hurting the person who abused us, we err—for the only person we are hurting is our self.

All experiences are God's way of helping us return to the love that we are . . . to our sacred heart . . . to knowing and BEing our True Self! The more difficult our physical challenges, or the more extreme our opposition, the more opportunity we have to exercise ourselves in being love. Does the enemy truly have any power over us when we love and forgive him/her? Christ was the ultimate example of this as he suffered all he did, never deviating once from love.

*"To forgive is to set the prisoner free
and then discover . . .
the prisoner was you."*
—Author Unknown—

There is much unrest in our world and for the most part, it is a result of the overall way we have chosen to respond to our experiences—to opposition. It's one thing to recognize things for what they are, the positive and negative, the good and bad. We don't want to call evil, good and good, evil. However, when we do experience things that are less than desirable, it's important to respond in a way that creates peace, balance and harmony—to respond as Christ did. Even while they nailed him on the cross, he never accused them of evil. He continually saw the the ultimate "good" that would come out of the seeming "bad"—remaining balanced and peaceful throughout.

When faced with opposition, it is often difficult to see that there could possibly be anything good come out of it. We all prefer pleasure over pain, health over sickness, joy over sadness, and would rather not experience the negative, but think about the things you have learned in your life and the things that give you great joy. Would you have these without some kind of pain, sickness or difficulty? For example, giving birth usually includes much pain and discomfort, but when you get through it and hold your newborn in your arms, the feeling of joy is unequaled. *Perhaps* part of the reason becoming a mother is so incredibly joyful *is* because you have just experienced extreme opposites . . . having come to the ultimate place of balance, wherein resides the ultimate joy.

There may be times when you want to argue in favor of standing exclusively on the "white" or "good" side of things, and that's perfectly wonderful. If in doing so, however, you simultaneously *deny* your negative feelings and stuff them inside, thinking you can deny them and by so doing, cause them to go away—you are only fooling yourself. By responding in this way, these "black" or "bad" characteristics increase in energy . . . becoming the demons and monsters in your dreams, the things you fear in your daily life, the dreaded things in your world and the culprits causing the "mid-life crisis." Trying to live a life of one sided goodness, by thinking to deny and hide any "badness" looks something like this:

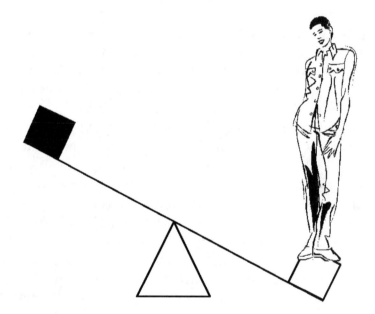

How do we remain in balance and in peace without tipping the scales from one side to the other? When extreme opposition strikes, or in other words, when all hell breaks loose around us in our life or in the world, can we remain peaceful inside? Can we stay in balance? Or, do we get caught up in what is happening and allow ourselves to become upset? When enough people are able to remain peaceful in these kinds of challenging situations, the outer world will reflect their balance and inner peace. This can only happen by each of us doing our part—by each of us striving to remain peaceful in the midst of the difficult situations in our daily lives.

Most of us are blessed with healthy doses of opportunity every day in which to practice our balancing act . . . to maintain peace in the midst of chaos. One of the keys for doing so is in how we view any opposition or perceived enemies. As long as we see them as separate from us, and resist or fight against them, we will remain in unrest and chaos ourselves. The "World of Mirrors" is a powerful tool for seeing what we need to change inside in order to establish lasting balance and peace within . . . the only place we can change the world . . . one heart at a time. Be grateful for the unique people and situations in your life who reflect the things you have yet to work on. Recognize what is being reflected and resolve any feelings that result when your feathers get ruffled. When you are no longer disturbed or bothered by what the people right around you say or do, you will know you have mastered your feelings and tight rope walking abilities. No one will mistake you for a clown any more.

There *is* a way to avoid negative feelings in the first place. This is done by walking out of judgement and blame, and by learning to "accept what is." When I suggest making no judgements, I do not mean that you never make any judgements at all. There are judgements of all kinds, judgements that have to be made every day, like what to do in any given situation. What I am suggesting is that you choose non-judgement and non-blame whenever you are faced with a situation in which judging or blaming someone else, or an event, will create undesirable feelings inside you, taking you out of peace or balance. Peace comes when we learn to see the light in the darkness, the joy in the sorrows, the spot of black in the white and the spot of white in the black . . . *accepting "what is."*

Perfect balance is like entering a city of peace in the center of your heart . . . a place where you can see the world of opposites through eyes of pure love, where judgement and blame no longer exist because you recognize the Divine in all things, seeing and accepting everything as being part of one great whole . . . the Kingdom of God within . . . where you are love.

Once you realize that *everything* and *everyone* can be either good *or* bad, depending on your perspective, seeming contradictions fade and with them the need to judge. You can then accept situations and people as they are "in the moment." Just like the story about 72°, a hot stove is *not* what you would judge as "good" when touching it with your fingers, but it *does* feel pretty "good" when you stand by it after being outside on a cold winter day. So . . . is a hot stove "good" or "bad?" It obviously depends on *your* point of view. In reality, a hot stove *is just* "a hot stove." The goodness or badness of anything only exists because of the way *you* choose to view (judge) or use it. The next time you're tempted to label something or someone "bad," out of habit or because of beliefs, you may want to stop and consider how it or they may be serving the good in another, less obvious way. Whether or not you *find* how the "bad" may be serving the "good," walk out of judgement and into balance and peace. The pastures on the compassionate side of the fence, which are found within your heart, are much greener and the flowers more beautiful. And yes . . . there's even gold there. Pick up your "compassionate nugget," and claim it.

If you ever find yourself feeling upset or are in some way feeling less than peaceful inside, ask yourself what has really caused you to be upset. What judgements have you made of a person or situation to cause you to react with negative feelings? What comparisons have you made? Why can't you accept "what is" in the moment? What expectations did you have? Were you blaming someone for how you chose to feel? Remember, you can respond in whatever way you choose. What if you chose to be understanding of the person or situation? Do you think negative situations could reach positive solutions more easily if you remained balanced, peaceful and understanding, rather than being upset, closed minded and out of balance?

Seek to be understanding, in balance and peaceful rather than being right at all cost. You will have greater influence for good if you respond with love . . . from a peaceful place inside. It's infectious. It's much more powerful than any negative feeling there is, besides . . . you'll feel better.

Accept people and situations as they are in the moment (that includes yourself), without needing to put them on the black or white side of the scales. By so doing, you are also loving and accepting yourself "as you are." (Remember *your* potential to be both good *and* bad as well.) Doesn't it feel wonderful when someone else refrains from judging or blaming you . . . when someone takes the time to really understand you . . . when someone accepts you as you are? Doing so creates an environment in which positive and beautiful things can be created . . . like a peaceful world in which to live.

Have you ever practiced putting your attention on seeing the good in the seeming bad or finding beauty in unlikely places? Give it a try. You may be amazed at how much better your world appears.

Present Time Poppies

There is a little town by a beautiful lake wherein resides one of the most delightful and refreshing souls I know. When you visit her in early summer, not only are you greeted by her warm smile but also by a field painted with red-orange poppies. As you walk through the gate and into her yard, you are welcomed with a spectacular display of yellow, blue, red and orange bursting forth from inviting plants and flowers which tuck in the white country cottage in which she lives. The aroma from cut wood stacked inside her porch fills the air as you pass through the screen door. Once inside, you are soothed by the down to earth, simple beauty of all that occupies the space. You immediately feel no need to be anything but who you really are . . . a place with an air of acceptance . . . a place void of pretense.

It is common to see remnants of her most recent activities draped creatively around the house on tables, chairs and bookshelves. Unlike the disarray that many people leave in their wake, there always seems to be an underlying order and deeper meaning to everything in the house. I'm always eager to see what I will experience when I visit her. Her surroundings lend themselves well to divine communication, opening up the heart to that sacred space inside.

On such a day in August of 1996, I enjoyed one of these memorable and rewarding visits. Having already chatted about many topics over tea, we walked through her yard as I prepared to leave. The sun was warm and a gentle breeze was blowing, which may be why the poppy pods caught my eye . . . for all of a sudden, I was seeing them as if for the first time. The soft, brown velvet shapes of star-flowers on top of each pod aroused a sense of awe, for they were beautiful, each one unique. I had never seen them as I saw them in that moment—I became the poppies and they became me.

I immediately pointed out my discovery of the beauty of the poppy pods to my friend who joined me as we picked pods, one by one, marveling at the different designs and patterns they exhibited. I was amazed to discover that each one was completely different. Finally, with my hands filled with treasures, I ended a perfect visit.

Whenever I experience a connection of this kind to the spirit of another of God's creations, I often desire to express that oneness with a paint brush on canvas. So it was on this day as I headed home, basking in the joyful anticipation of the painting I would do.

A few days later, when I prepared to paint, the feelings I had experienced with the poppies dictated the need for a large 36" x 24" canvas. The pods, which averaged one inch in diameter, were now shouting to be represented in sizes many times bigger. As I moved through the painting with my brush, I wondered what to use as a backdrop for the pods. The idea of suggesting poppy *petals* came to mind. The irony of a role reversal with the pods and petals seemed interesting—the pods taking center stage instead of the petals. How often is it that once the petals have fallen to the ground, we take time to enjoy the beauty that remains?

By taking the time to really *see*, with no preconceived ideas or judgements, we can discover beauty in all things and in all seasons. In order to do so, however, we need to truly "be" where we are at any given moment. It requires our "full" presence! We can't be worrying about the past or fretting over the future. Walking into the beauty of the moment, into "present time," without carrying judgement or blame with us, most always rewards us with divine communication and insights to help us live a balanced life, filled with peace and harmony.

We all are created uniquely, just as each poppy—with our petals and our pods. By accepting and not judging the various parts of our Self, we are also accepting and not judging our Creator. Following is the poem I wrote after completing this painting.

Embrace Your Creator

As one observes the poppy,
one sees how securely grounded they are.
Secure with their place in the Universe,
abundantly increasing.

Their great pleasure
in their connectedness to the Universe
is apparent in their radiant beauty each summer.
Their healthy glow abounds, as they
completely accept their measure of creation.

Embrace the message of the poppy.
Accept yourself
and your measure of creation.
Embrace Your Creator!

Practice putting your attention on what "is" and see its fullness and beauty in every moment. Accept totally and completely that this present moment is as it should be. Think about it . . . this moment is the way it is because everything in the universe is the way it is . . . which is what has created this moment. So, to resist what is happening is to struggle against the universe. The world will never be the kind of "perfect" that is flawless—having no bad or negative elements—because they are half of what it is. The only perfection you will ever find in this world is in accepting "what is" as being "perfect." By so doing, you are creating a peaceful world to experience in the moments that follow. This is the only way to change the undesirable. If, on the other hand, you keep putting your attention on the bad and negative in each moment, you will only create more of the same.

Once we *see* a peaceful world, we will *live* in a peaceful world—*we create the world we're in from our world within.*

The following illustration is my version of what it looks like to accept "what is"—not judging and not blaming. Once we learn how to do this, we will be able to maintain balance . . . and life will become an enjoyable dance. (All aspects of the illustration represent parts of one individual. Also notice that there is no gray area—it is black and white because we're balancing what is, not mixing paint.)

Balance . . . Dancing With Life

The line that divides good and evil . . . even all opposites . . . cuts through every human heart. Who is willing to do away with a piece of his own heart? Are you? May we live as wholly as we can . . . balancing the earth and the sky, the inner world and the outer . . . mind, body and spirit. May we laugh and cry, feel pleasure and pain, know joys and sorrows and experience life freely. May we celebrate life by accepting each moment as it is . . . without judgement or blame . . . living it with grace and humility, wonder and peace . . . living it with love . . . because love is who we are.

We create the world we're in . . . from our world within!

Let's create peace.

Returning

*The Dove of Peace and Love
Is now come forth
From the heart of the earth
With her colors of joy,
Gathering all who are returning
To the heart,
Bringing them back
To oneness,
Wholeness,
The Divine Self,
And the Love of God,
To the truth of who they are.*

(This poem was written to go with the cover painting.
See Appendix IV to learn the story behind this painting.)

Symbols

Symbols and Possible Interpretations

The following lists are found inside this list:

- Colors
- Letters of the Alphabet
- Numbers

A

Abandoned
- Feeling left out or not included in some area of your life
- Do you need to let go of or release something?

• Is there a part of yourself that you need to accept?
• Do you need to enter a state of abandonment . . . living without feeling inhibited?
• Signs of abandonment can sometimes occur just before you become more independent.
• The unconscious attempts to compensate for imbalances in the conscious, therefore, if you are overly attached to someone in daily life, in the dream state you may be abandoned by him/her. This is an attempt by the unconscious to make you aware of your dependency.

Abdominal area

• This area is associated with emotions such as: disharmony in relationships, being bound up in fears, tension or anxiety
• May have to do with sexual feelings. What are your recent experiences and how do you feel about them? Are you feeling possessive of someone?
• Are you digesting life's lessons, absorbing what you need, releasing the rest?
• If you are feeling pain or discomfort in this area? Consider how well that part of your body is functioning.
• Are you identifying with possessions as a source of worth instead of having a true sense of self?

Abort/Abortion

• The loss of new potential in your life, a new project, or idea
• Are you prepared for sudden changes in your life or plans?
• Take note of the feelings you have about the word *abortion*. It may represent your unresolved issues about it.

• If you are a woman who has experienced this, you may have many dreams about it. Even though the dream may be disturbing it is usually a healing dream. In your dream state you may be working toward accepting and resolving any unconscious feelings.

• It may indicate that you are feeling significant anxiety about current endeavors.

• Perhaps you are anticipating failure of some kind.

• Is there a project or idea you need to abort?

Above

• If there are things above you in your dream, this could represent inspiration or the Higher Self.

• Are there things hanging over you?

• If you are above somebody or something in your dream, perhaps you have risen above whatever the person or thing represents about you.

• Do you need to rise above it all?

Accident

• Do you need to pay more attention to the details in you life?

• Do you feel like a victim?

• If it is the result of going too fast, in what way do you need to slow down?

• Feeling stressed, tense or worried

• Are you punishing yourself? Do you feel you deserve to be punished for something?

Ace

• Excelling in something

• Hidden talents

• "Ace in the hole"

Achilles tendon

• Vulnerability

Acne
- Denial of what is happening in your life
- What is it you don't want to face?
- Self rejection/dislike
- Unexpressed anger
- Unwillingness to face up to issues

Acorn
- From small beginnings come great power/your great potential

Actor/Actress
- Are you putting up a false front?
- The roles you are playing in life
- Act now

Addictions
- Giving your power away to something or someone
- Inability to see clearly & correctly or to think rationally
- Avoiding your feelings

Adolescent
- A time of great change and turmoil
- A time to find direction in life
- Youth

Adultery
- Conflict between your duties and desires
- What quality in another are you being drawn to which you haven't been recognizing in yourself? Love that part of yourself.
- How is your relationship with the opposite aspect of yourself (male/female)?

Airplane
- Your ideas or plans
- Striving toward higher consciousness or spiritual ideals
- Soaring to new heights

• Liberation; release; freedom; expansion

Airplane crash

• A bad outcome to your plans

• Falling from great heights

• Perhaps you need to let go of the idea or plan you are working on for now.

Alarm

• Warning . . . pay attention

• What do you need to be more aware of?

• Notice the type of alarm it is. Alarm clocks awaken us into consciousness. Fire alarms awaken us to the fire or the spirit within.

• Are you unduly alarmed?

Alien

• A part of yourself you aren't acknowledging or are unfamiliar with

• The meaning greatly depends on your personal view of them. How do you regard them?

• Space aliens represent an unknown part of yourself. Pay attention to how you feel about them. Do you need to open up to messages from the unknown aspects of yourself? Maybe you are fearing an unknown part of yourself. Face the fear.

Allergy

• Sensitive to the external environment

• Are you having difficulty either resisting or assimilating something in your life?

Alley

• What kind of alley is it?

• That which lies behind what you show to the world, the place where you keep your secrets . . . behind everything else, within.

Alligator

• Vicious speech

• Destructive feelings rising from the depths of the unconscious

Alphabet, Letters of the (*see* **Letters of the Alphabet**)

Altar

• Sacrifice

• Having to do with honoring the spiritual aspects of life

• Are you sacrificing something or do you need to honor a part of yourself?

Amputation

• Giving up a part of yourself associated with the body part that was amputated and what it represents about you. (*see* specific body parts)

• Releasing a part of yourself that you may now be identifying with which isn't an integral part of your true being.

• Perhaps you are cutting off situations, people or parts of yourself that *should* be integrated.

Anchor

• Strength and security

• Do you need to ground yourself?

Ancient History

• Your own early days or past

• Characteristics or attitudes which you have inherited

• Is there something from the past you need to learn from?

Anesthesia

• Numb to your senses

• Inability to perceive what is going on around you

• Avoiding your feelings

Angel

• Messenger from God

• Pure love
• Spiritual ideals
• A divine aspect of yourself you need to become more aware of

Anger

• Subconscious anger
• Can provide vital energy to make needed changes in your life
• An unresolved feeling that has been stuffed inside

Animals (*see* specific animal names)

• Animals usually refer to an aspect of the instinctive side of your nature. If they are wild and free, they can represent your connection to nature or the natural way of doing things. If they are ferocious, they can represent your more primitive, aggressive side. Tame animals represent the controlled expression of your instinctual nature.

Ankles

• What you use to turn your feet to choose your path
• Which direction should you choose?
• Mobility. Are you feeling mobile or immobile in your life?

Another state (location)

• Another "state" of mind
• Somewhere beyond where you are currently located relating to either your physical, mental, emotional or spiritual aspects.

Ant

• Patience
• Working for the good of the whole
• Perhaps it is time to show trust and patience in some aspect of your life.

Antenna
- Transmitting and receiving ideas and energy
- An antenna expands your awareness of the world around you

Antique
- A relic from the past
- Belief system or old pattern that may no longer be useful
- Are there feelings associated with someone or something from your past you need to honor, care for, cherish or resolve?

Antlers
- Protection of the divine masculine part of yourself
- Power
- Strength

Ape
- Copying others rather than finding your own truth
- Primitive power

Applause
- Self-acknowledgment
- Needing acknowledgment from yourself or others

Apple
- Healing potential
- Wholesomeness, vitality
- Temptation
- The "apple" of someone's eye

Apron
- What type of apron is it? Is it the apron of a housewife or a baker? What is it being used for in the dream?
- Something used to protect you from the things on the outside while you create or form new ideas

Archer

> • Focusing on a specific target or in a specific direction with clarity and single-mindedness
> • Do you need to be more focused in life? What are you aiming at?

Architect

> • Creating a blueprint for your life or needing to create one.

Arguments

> • Parts of yourself are in conflict. What is the argument about? What is it showing you about yourself?
> • Do you need to clear the air by expressing a grievance?

Ark

> • Provides safety and protection while you are in the deep waters of your feelings.
> • Feeling a need for safety and security

Armor

> • Protection. Do you need to put on your spiritual armor?
> • Are you trying to protect yourself from your feelings?

Arms

> • Open arms symbolize being open and reaching out to life
> • Closed arms are closed to life
> • Can be used as weapons or to be defensive

Army

> • Opposition to be overcome
> • Inner resources

Art/Artist

> • Creative expression in life
> • Your potential and ability

Ascent

- Ascending in life or with your goals
- Your energy level is rising
- If you are too lofty, it may mean you need to come down to earth.
- If it's a difficult ascent, it may be reflecting the uphill struggle you are experiencing in life.

Ashes

- Spiritual purification
- Death
- Absence of life or vitality
- The very essence of something

Asleep

- Unaware of something
- Stagnation
- Not willing to change
- In a state where the ego is out of the way

Asthma

- Feeling constricted to the point of not being able to breathe
- Stress
- Not feeling connected with life
- A need to slow down or be calm

Astronomer

- Reach for the stars in life

Atomic energy

- Great power which can be used positively or negatively

Attic

- Upper levels of consciousness
- Can represent old issues from your past
- Your head

Attorney

> • How you deal with your own forces of law and order
>
> • Perhaps you are only seeing one side of an issue

Aunt

> • A feminine aspect of yourself
>
> • What do the particular qualities associated with this person reflect about you?

Aura

> • Energy field surrounding a person or thing. Is it radiant and clear or do you need to simplify or purify your life? Is it dim and unhealthy or full of life?

Automobile

> • Your physical body or Self
>
> • Specific problems with a car reflect things inside you.
>
> > Examples:
> > Overheating may mean you need to cool down.
> > Bald tires may indicate not getting enough traction in life.
> > Failed brakes may be telling you to slow down.
> > Broken down may indicate you are about to break down or need a break

Avalanche

> • Overwhelming surge of previously frozen feelings
>
> • Feeling overwhelmed

Ax

> • Cutting away unnecessary things
>
> • Splitting wood may mean the separation of something
>
> • Executioner's ax or judgement
>
> • Using power with certainty

• Fear of loss

B

Baby
  • New birth within yourself
  • New beginnings
  • New projects or ideas
  • New spiritual awareness
  • Potential growth
  • A need to be babied, pampered or the center of attention

Back
  • Back up, back off, or back out of a situation
  • Turning your back on someone or something
  • Your support system in life
  • Your physical back, pay attention to its needs
  • Carrying an emotional burden
  • Wanting someone to "get off your back"

Backyard
  • Things going on behind the scenes
  • The things we keep away from the view of others

Baggage
  • Thoughts or attitudes you carry around that are not needed
  • A need to pack your bags and get out of a present situation
  • That into which we put our belongings while traveling
  • What were you doing with the baggage? Do you need to prepare to move to a different place spiritually or emotionally?

Badger

- Aggressiveness
- Seek new levels of expression, staying grounded and centered in the process
- Anger. Remember that all anger stems from anger towards the self only it is misdirected.
- Are you too shy and insecure?

Ball

- Wholeness, completion or unity (because of its round shape)
- "Having a ball" or enjoying yourself
- Do you have the "balls" to get the job done?

Balloon

- Soaring to new heights
- Unrestrained joy
- A breaking balloon may represent shattered illusions.
- A helium balloon floating free may mean you are at the mercy of the winds of change or perhaps need to "lighten up."

Bank

- A bank is a place for keeping the resources for obtaining your desires.
- Do you need to invest or draw from your inner resources?
- Pay attention to your finances.
- A bank may simply mean something you can count or "bank" on.

Basement

- Lower or base energy centers in your physical body
- Deepest parts of your subconscious
- Root of a problem you are struggling with
- Negative feelings you have stuffed deep inside

• Your feet or the ground you are psychologically standing on

Bat

• Rebirth
• Death of old patterns in your life
• Do you need to listen more intently to the subtle messages being given?

Bath

• Cleansing, purification
• Possibly time to wash yourself of a situation, or of old habits or attitudes
• Baptism or rebirth

Bathroom

• Cleansing
• Getting rid of waste
• Where you prepare yourself for the day

Battery

• Storage of energy
• Source of power

Battle

• Inner conflict
• What are you battling inside?

Beach

• The beach is the border between the subconscious or feelings, represented by the water, and earthy physical aspects represented by the shore.
• Balance in life
• Purifying, rejuvenating

Bear

• Do you tend to be bearish, grumpy, overbearing or angry?
• Bears hibernate during the winter. Do you need to pull into yourself, into your more intuitive side?

• Do you need to be silent and calm the inner chatter?

Beaver

• Your tendencies to work hard
• Do you need to be "busy as a beaver" or do you need to slow down?

Bed/Bedroom

• Sexuality and intimacy
• Rejuvenation and relaxation
• Nurturing or comfort
• Safety or security
• The eternal womb
• Connection point between your conscious and subconscious
• Place where you dream
• Perhaps you need more rest
• May indicate a coming illness wherein you will be bedridden
• Repressed feelings associated with past experiences in a bedroom

Bee

• Organized work
• Productive
• Is something bothering you?
• Stings of life
• Gathering the sweet nectar of life
• Perhaps it is time to just "BE."

Beetle

• Minor irritation or annoyances

Bell

• A warning
• During celebrations they represent joyous things
• Personal attunement

• What kind of sound are they making, clear and
   beautiful or muffled?

Birds (*see* specific bird names)
   • Birds represent thoughts. Birds in flight symbolize
   moving and changing thoughts. If the birds in your
   dream are flying free, they may be symbolizing
   spiritual, psychological, or physical freedom.
   • Soaring to new heights
   • Soaring above your problems
   • Flight into spiritual realms
   • Freedom or abandon
   • Messengers from spirit
   • Seeing things from afar
   • Flight of imagination or fancy
   • Unpretentiousness and simplicity

Birth
   • Renewal
   • Rebirth
   • A new phase in your life
   • Spiritual awakening
   • Unleashing powerful creative forces within
   • Fresh start
   • In order to move ahead with the new, old patterns
   or beliefs need to be released

Birthday
   • Celebration of life
   • New beginnings
   • Getting older and/or wiser

Black (*see* under **Colors**)

Blindness
   • Is there something you don't want to see? Have
   you seen too much?

• An issue you are avoiding because you don't want to see it

• Conflict within, that you don't want to look at

Blood

• Your energy

• Life force, dynamic strength or power

• Powerful emotions and passion

• Loss of virginity represents moving into a new phase of life

• Renewal of life

• Bleeding is a draining of vital life force or energy

• Pain, suffering or injury

• The blood of Christ is a holy sacrifice

Blue (*see* under **Colors**)

Bluebird

• Happy thoughts

Boat

• Being in a boat may indicate an endeavor that is usually spiritual in nature.

• It can represent your emotional body

• Water usually represents feelings and emotions therefore, the way the boat is traveling shows how you are dealing with your feelings and emotions. Ask yourself: Is it on course or not? Is it smooth sailing or are the waters turbulent?

• Leaving a place of stability for new waters and/or distant shores

Body (See specific body parts for more information)

• Each part of the body has specific meaning attached to it. The right side can signify the masculine aspects and outer strength. The left side can represent the feminine, receptive, inner part.

• A naked body can represent vulnerability, being open to the world outside yourself or being unafraid and genuine.
• Clothing represents the parts of yourself you are showing to others and how you are doing so.
• If you are over dressed, you may be hiding something.

Bomb

• Explosive situation in your life
• Failure as in, "it was a complete bomb"
• Emotional power contained inside or being released

Books

• Knowledge
• Wisdom
• Things you learn from, like your lessons in life
• Records of thoughts which reflect your feelings and attitudes

Boss

• Your own authority
• Are you submitting yourself to another's will?
• The aspect of yourself who is running the show

Bottle

• Feelings that may be bottled up
• Is your emotional bottle full or empty?
• That which contains your feelings

Bowels

• Relates to giving and receiving
• Letting go of and releasing that which is no longer needed
• Are you receiving the things that you need to nourish your life?

Box

• Self-imposed limitations

- Things you fear can be like a box in which you are your own prisoner.
- Your feelings and inner feminine aspects
- A square box can have to do with wholeness

Boy

- Masculine aspect or male child within
- Your own childhood if you are male
- A growing aspect of yourself

Bread

- "Bread of life" or just life
- Money or the "bread winner"
- Communion, sacrament and unity of spirit. Christ shared bread with
his twelve disciples.
- That which sustains life, "bread of life"

Break

- Feeling separated from something within yourself or from someone
- Something about to change in your life
- Slow down and be more careful so as not to break things
- Time to break out and set yourself free
- Are you about to have a breakdown?

Breast

- Nourishment, giving and receiving
- Self awareness
- Worthiness/self worth

Bride/Bridegroom

- Joining of masculine and feminine forces within or integrating the male and female
- New beginning through uniting aspects within

Bridge

- Change and transition

B

• If it crosses over water, it may represent an emotional change
• Bridge the gap
• Bringing two ideas together

Brother

• Attitudes of your brother reflected in you
• Universal brotherhood
• Look at the relationship you had with your brother/s while growing up, what feelings need resolving? Are there any feelings associated with not having brothers that need resolving?

Brown (*see* under **Colors**)

Buffalo

• Trying to buffalo somebody
• Are you buffaloing yourself about something?
• Pushing your way
• Honor another's pathway
• Great power

Bugs

• What is "bugging" you?
• Minor irritations
• You are bigger than the little things bothering you.

Building

• The physical body which houses your spirit
• Notice the kind of building. What does it say about your attitudes or health?
• What does it relate to as far as you are concerned? A church, for example, relates to religion, spirituality or adherence to certain beliefs.

Bull

• Strength, force, and power

• In astrology, the bull is equated with the sign Taurus which is tenacious, sensuous, earthy and practical.
• Bull headed
• Quick to anger
• Bullish market means finances are on the upswing.
• Fertility

Burial

• Laying to rest old patterns or thoughts
• Have you buried feelings you need to deal with?
• Let go of old negative feelings.

Butterfly

• Transformation
• The stage the butterfly is in may indicate the stage of your own progression or the stage of an idea of project.
• A need for change in your life
• The outcome of spiritual change

C

Cage

• Do you feel trapped?
• Restrained, restricted, concerned about your personal freedom
• Self-imprisonment through negative feelings
• You may be experiencing inhibition and powerlessness in some areas of your life
• Who or in other words, what part of you holds the key to the cage?

Cake

• The sweet and pleasurable things in life

• The dream may be interpreted according to your interaction with the cake in the dream. Are you eating it or looking at it, something you are internalizing or just observing?

Calculator

• Having to do with numbers, machinery or money
• Do you need to calculate what you are doing more closely?
• If certain numbers are highlighted, look them up under **Numbers**.

Calves

• Choosing
• Do you need to be inventive or conventional
• Signifies the utilizing of experiences to correct mistakes of the past, to become more free

Cancer

• Is something eating away at you emotionally? Express yourself.
• May represent a variety of unprocessed psychological and emotional materials, all of those things that bother, disturb, anger, or hurt that have never been directly dealt with or released.
• You may be experiencing anxiety and fear as a result of a bad habit or a certain situation in your daily life.
• Remember, dreams are usually "symbolic." It probably has nothing to do with actual physical cancer.

Candle

• Symbol of light and connection to the Great Spirit
• Where there is light, there is hope
• Spiritual life force within you or within all things, or your true inner light

• A lit candle may suggest that you are unconsciously seeking comfort and some sort of spiritual enlightenment.

• An unlit candle may suggest that you may be feeling rejection and disappointment or perhaps that you can't see anything positive or "light" in a situation or in yourself.

• If you watch the candle burn down to nothing, it may suggest fears of getting old and of dying.

Cane

• Do you feel a need for support in your life?

• It can also be used for cruel punishment. Do you feel that you are being harshly judged of punished by someone or something? Are you doing it to yourself?

• Sugar cane is a natural source of sweet. Do you need to extract the sweetness from your life?

Cannibalism

• Do you feel like you are being eaten up by a situation?

• Taking the energy of another instead of using your own

• Can also represent extreme possessiveness. Is there someone or something in your life you want to devour? Maybe someone wants to consume you.

• May reflect dark, destructive and forbidden desires or obsessions, possibly compensating for your identification with one sided ideas of "goodness"

• Consider those things which consistently drain you and take away from your enthusiasm and the general quality of your life.

• May be warning you to stay away from things that are destructive and less than honorable.

• Do you need to love your humanness more, "eat it up?"

Canyon

• A vast opening of unconsciousness
• A seemingly impassable chasm
• Remember there is always a way to cross the canyon in life. You can either fly over what it represents or walk through it.

Car

• May symbolize the physical body or Self
• The way you travel through life. Are you doing it with class (fancy car) or hardly getting along (old beat up car)?
• Recurring car dreams usually deal with life's major themes that may include issues of control and/or sensibility.
• Consider all of the details in the dream, including its emotional content (e.g. difficulty of the road, identity of the driver, direction of the incline).
• If the car is having problems, notice the specifics, for example:

Bald tires may indicate that you are not getting the traction you need in life
A failed brake may mean that you need to put on the brakes in your life
Constant window fogging might point to something you are not willing to see

Cards

• Life is a game and can even be a gamble. Put your attention on the process rather than the end result.
• Tarot cards or any other cards used for fortune-telling may relate to a sense of fate. The cards hold your future.

Cartoons

• The way you perceive the world. Cartoon people, or cartoon characters, may suggest that you perceive yourself and those around you as comical or as not having much validity or seriousness. What does this reflect about you?

• If your world is full of stress and your dream made you laugh, it may be compensating for the intense, uptight feelings caused by your daily experiences.

Cat

• Cattiness

• Independence of action

• Does the cat have your tongue?

• Can represent the female side of yourself or your feminine essence

• Your deep intuitive Self

• The cat can be a symbol of sexuality, femininity, prosperity and power

• Historically black cats have been symbols of evil and bad luck as well as good luck depending on your heritage and culture. If you are a cat lover and have one as a pet, the bad symbolism may not apply to your dream.

Caterpillar

• Unharnessed potential

• It may represent a stage in your own personal growth and development

• The butterfly is a symbol of transformation; it represents a level of individual achievement. The caterpillar, on the other hand, may indicate that you are on your way but have not reached your goal. You may be in earlier stages of accomplishing a real-life goal, a relationship goal, or even a spiritual goal.

Cave

• This is a powerful symbol for the unconscious, an entrance to the subconscious, inner realms of the Self, the unexplored parts of yourself.

• Ancient wisdom is stored in the caves of the subconscious.

• A place of spiritual retreat, renewal, and rebirth

• It may represent the security of the womb, as it is literally a cavity in Mother Earth. It can also represent a place of conception and rebirth. Maybe it is time to incubate your plans in life.

• Can represent new life, creativity, warmth and safety

• If you are experiencing much anxiety in daily life, in your dream state you may retreat to a warm cave where you cannot be disturbed by worldly demands.

• Your personal associations and experiences with caves, as well as the details and the associated feelings need to be carefully considered while making an interpretation.

Cellar

• The level of the unconscious mind

Cemetery

• A cemetery is a collection of dead organic matter. Is there something you have released or do you need to release something?

• Dreaming about cemeteries may be a reflection of unresolved grief.

• A cemetery may represent sadness that comes from losing someone you love.

• Past experiences

Chain

• Constraints in your waking world, forged by dependencies

• Are you feeling chained to a situation or person?
• A chain consists of many links joined together to create strength. All links must be of equal strength or there will be a point of weakness compromising the whole chain. Is there a situation in your life requiring linking together for a common goal?
• Do you feel chained up in some way?

Chalice

• Points toward that which is sacred and holy
• The Holy Grail
• The Christ within

Chameleon

• Adaptability and flexibility
• Ever changing
• Not showing one's true colors

Chaos

• If everything around you is in chaos, you may be in a process of renewing your life.
• Do you need to eliminate that which is not truly necessary in your life?

Chase

• Running away from or trying to escape those things that are frightening and unpleasant (possibly your own habits and behaviors), things of which you are presently unaware.
• If you are doing the chasing, it may be that you are expressing some aggressive feelings toward others or are pursuing a very difficult goal.
• If a stranger is chasing you it may represent you chasing a part of yourself. The unconscious attempts to catch up with the conscious.

Chest

• Inner treasures, the potential that exists within you, perhaps still uncovered

• It may relate to your heart. Do you need to open to love in an area in your life?

Chewing gum

• Were you trying to get rid of chewing gum . . . but the more you attempted to remove it, the larger and more unmanageable it became? Are you experiencing frustration in daily life due to an unsolvable problem which leaves you feeling powerless?

• Chewing gum in dreams may be a sign of childlike behaviors, vulnerability, powerlessness or a need for nourishment.

• Consider why you chew gum and what it represents to you.

Chicken

• Fear, cowardice, lack of self-esteem or timidity

• Are you feeling henpecked or dominated by another person or situation?

• Do you find yourself scratching like a chicken to make it in life?

• Chicken hearted, cowardliness, gossip, excessive talking, and powerlessness. They are not known for their intelligence or beauty, and their presence in your dream could be an invitation to be more serious and better focused.

• Chickens lay eggs. Eggs are symbolic of something new and fragile. They represent life and development in its earliest forms and therefore, their possibilities are limitless.

• When we say someone is "chicken," we are referring to fear, cowardice, lack of self-esteem, or timidity. Is there something you are afraid of?

• To count your chickens before they are hatched means to count on something prematurely.

• When you feel henpecked, you are feeling dominated by another person.

Child

• The child within, where the inner aspects of yourself such as playfulness, joy, spontaneity and openness reside.
• May represent the child part of you that isn't being acknowledged
• Old unresolved issues from childhood
• May symbolize a need and an eagerness to learn
• Simplicity, intuition, new endeavors and other positive attributes of childhood
• Your own childish ways

Choking (see also **Smothering/Strangling**)

• Feeling smothered by something
• Are you choking on something in life?

Christ

• Powerful sign of the God force within you
• Unconditional love
• Forgiveness
• Healing
• Spiritual attunement to higher energies
• Sacrifice or martyrdom. Are you sacrificing yourself for others? Doing this at the expense of following your heart, benefits no one in the long run. Do you feel like a martyr in your life?

Church

• Dreaming about churches, cathedrals, synagogues, or any other place of worship may represent your childhood associations with religion.
• A need for greater spirituality in your life

• It may express religious beliefs, everyday occurrences, issues of safety, security and strength through community and religious expression.
• Faith, hope and love
• A sanctuary, spiritual haven, safety
• Temple of the soul
• Can represent the dogma and/or restrictions of religion
• Structures in your life

Cigarette/Cigar

• Interpretation depends on your relationship with cigarettes. If you are a smoker or are surrounded by smokers, cigarettes may be a regular part of your daily life.
• Cigarettes can represent anything from symbols of pleasure to tools of destruction
• An object which carries social and emotional significance. When we are teenagers, we associate them with being "cool," daring, and defiant. As adults cigarettes become more dreadful objects, and smoking becomes a terrible burden. Ask yourself what cigarettes mean to you.

Cinema

• Amplification of life

Circle

• Infinity, the circle of life and the eternal unknown
• Harmony, beauty and balance
• Completeness, wholeness and unity of the Self
• Mandala's are circular images. It represents the psychic center of the personality.
• Are you "going around in circles?"

Circus

• Do you need to walk into childlike joy?
• Is your life like a circus?

City

> • How you perceive the city is usually a reflection of what is occurring within you. What does the city represent to you?
> • Center of activity or ideas

Clam

> • Are you clamming up and not speaking your truth?
> • Are you concerned about something that must be kept secret?

Clay

> • You can mold your life how you want it to be.
> • Is someone trying to mold you in a way you don't like?

Cliff

> • Standing on the edge of a cliff could indicate that you have come to a point of heightened understanding and awareness or increased consciousness.
> • Have you reached a vantage or plateau of understanding?

Climbing

> • Going upward, ascending or moving in the right direction with your business or personal goals
> • If the climb is difficult, it may be pointing to obstacles you need to overcome before reaching your goals.
> • A sign of entering into a high level of consciousness
> • Climbing out of a difficult situation
> • Climbing down can mean the opposite of ascending. It can also refer to the exploration of your subconscious or feelings.

Clock

• It represents the psychic center of personality, symbolic of wholeness, completeness, and unity of the Self. The clock is a circle that revolves and may represent eternal life.

• Are you experiencing anxiety in regard to a time-sensitive situation? It may be a reminder that you need to speed up or slow down in your life.

• What is your relationship to time? The mystic's perception of time is entirely different from that of an ordinary person. The more you reach into your center and touch the divine within, the less you are bound to the constraints of time.

Closet

• Closing yourself off from feelings or others

• Coming "out of the closet"

• Are there skeletons in your closet? Face them and free yourself.

• Closets are used to store things that are needed as well as those things that are useless. Emotionally, closets hold memories, secrets, precious feelings and valuable thoughts. Do you need to clean out your spiritual closet or share the things that you have stored in it with others?

Clothing

• Your outer persona and protection from the elements

• Your worldly appearance or status

• Your public self

• Your attitudes toward yourself and others

• Roles that one plays in life

Clouds

• Clear clouds may represent being spiritually uplifted or experiencing inner peace

• Stormy clouds may indicate spiritual questioning. A storm is brewing or maybe the air is being cleared. Storm clouds can also represent personal purification.
• Are your head in the clouds?
• Thoughts that are hanging over you

Clown

• Laugh and be happy. Don't worry. Enjoy life.
• Are you clowning around when you should be serious in life?

Cobra

• A symbol of the kundalini, which is the life force energy at the base of the spine.
• Transformation and power
• Caution and fear

Cobwebs

• Memories
• Unused talents
• Caught in a web of the mind or someone else's web
• The center of the web may represent your center within. How does the dream relate to your being centered . . . or not?

Cockroaches

• Do you need to reevaluate and reassess a part of your life?
• There are always more than one cockroach. Are there areas in your life that need much cleansing and renewal?
• May be associated with uncleanliness

Cocoon

• Incredible potential awaiting transformation
• Is it a time to isolate yourself for renewal and rejuvenation?

• Are you isolating yourself from others or from what you really feel?

Coffin (*see* also **Burial, Death**)

• May indicate completion, the end of a situation, or perhaps the end of a relationship

• Lack of energy or vitality

• The death of one stage of life and movement into another . . . not physical death!

• Feelings of confinement or lack of freedom

Cold

• Having a cold or being cold may indicate that you are shutting down your feelings and withdrawing into yourself.

Colon (*see* **Large intestine**)

Colors

• Colors are symbolic and their symbolism is part of culture. We communicate and relate ideas with color. Each Color also has a unique energy. The meaning of the colors in your dreams is often associated with the meaning that you give to those colors in daily life. For more information on the meaning of each color read *"Cashing in on the 'Simple Magic' of Color."*

❊ **Black**

• Space

• Night, comforting cover of night

• For some people, black represents strength or authority

• Unknown aspects of yourself, your shadow or mysteries of your subconscious mind

• Depression and despair. Are you suppressing your emotions?

• Mourning

❀ Black velvet
• Like black holes in space, doorways to other realities

❀ Blue
• The most powerful signs of blue are the sea and sky. The sea can represent the subconscious, the feminine, the Great Mother and your deep secrets. The sky can represent the conscious mind, the masculine, the Great Father, and the open, expansive part of yourself.
• Soothing
• Emotionally healing
• Peace
• Relaxation
• Travel, freedom
• Truth
• Depression is often referred to as "the blues." Is there something in your life causing you to feel this way?
• A bruised body turns black and blue. Are you feeling bruised from a recent situation?

❀ Brown
• Earth, ground. Do you need to be grounded?
• The leaves turn brown in autumn, indicating the tree is pulling in its resources. Do you need to pull back or pull in yours as well?
• Wood
• Comfort
• Strength

❀ Gold
• A high vibration

C

• Increases mental and spiritual powers and physical strength

❀ **Gray**

• Negativity

• It is the union of the most rapid vibration with the slowest

• Gray in costume or interior decoration has a very useful place. The continual use of the intense rays of light would be too stimulating.

• In the aura, gray is weakness, sickness, negativeness which should be lifted up at once. A gray soul is the lack of life..

• Death.

❀ **Green**

• Healing

• Renewing of cells

• Fertility

• Abundance of nature

• New growth in your personal development, life

• Money

• Calmness

• Envy, greed

❀ **Indigo**

• Patience

• Rational use of intuitions

❀ **Lavender**

• Spirit

❀ **Maroon**

• Moving into one's task

❀ **Orange**

• Creativity

• Warm and stimulating but lighter and higher in vibration than red
• Happy, social color. Used by clowns all over the world
• Stimulates optimism, expansiveness, emotional balance, confidence, change, striving, self-motivation, changeability, enthusiasm, and a sense of community.
• Tolerant and sociable
• Autumn
• Fire
• Entering an outward social time in your life
• The color orange corresponds to the second chakra and, at times, may be associated with your reproductive system. The second chakra is said to be responsible for your reproductive health and has something to do with your sexual expression.

❀ **Pink**
• Romantic, affection, sensuality
• Pure and divine love
• Pink usually symbolizes good feelings
• Pink is soft and fuzzy, like girls

❀ **Purple**
• Royalty, dignity
• Transmutation power, the vibration of this color transmutes negative vibrations when you come in contact with them

❀ **Red**
• Passion
• Physical strength
• Anger
• Sexuality, sensuality

- Aggression
- Anger
- The color of blood, life and creation
- Love
- Excitement
- Warmth
- Energy

❀ Silver

- Communication

❀ White

- White contains all colors. It is the pure white light of the spirit.
- It can symbolize spiritual advancement
- Openness to the realm of the divine
- Purity, peace, perfection
- Cleanliness, that which is pristine, unsullied and virgin
- It can also represent isolation, starkness, and sterile environments

❀ Yellow

- Light, purity, understanding
- Consciousness directed outward, extroversion
- Wisdom
- Intuition on the high plane
- Understanding
- Spiritual perfection
- Gold of the Spirit and mind
- Sunshine
- Gladness
- Youth
- Trust

Coloring hair
> • Changing your thoughts or at least how you show them to others

Couch
> • Could you use some rest and relaxation?
> • May represent your memories in relation to the couch.

Cow
> • Peace
> • Patience and passive endurance
> • Earth, moon and mothering
> • Regenerating forces of the universe
> • In some cultures the cow is a sacred symbol, representing divine qualities of fertility, nourishment and motherhood.
> • Passivity, docility and general contentment with life

Crab (*see* also **Cancer**)
> • "Crabby" or unpleasant
> • The claws could be symbolic of a clingy or hurtful person . . . or that side of yourself
> • Is there too much dependence, clinging or forcefulness in your life?
> • It may represent your inability to effectively move forward and address difficulties. The crab often moves sideways or backwards. How was it moving in your dream?
> • In some areas of metaphysics, the crab is a representative of the sea and the sky and could therefore represent your thoughts and feelings and if they are in sync.

• Intellectual nourishment which can be obtained from the "sea" within. As with all water dwellers, the crab can represent something in the unconscious.

Crack

• A situation about to break through
• A situation that appears sturdy but actually has some cracks in it
• "Cracking up"or experiencing a mental breakdown. Are you cracking up?
• Amusement. "It really cracks me up."

Cradle

• Caring and nurturing
• Do you feel a need to be cared for and nurtured?

Crash

• Slow down!
• A car crash represents your physical body; a boat crash, your emotional body; an airplane crash, your spiritual body.

Crisis

• A crossroad in life
• Where are you going in life?

Crocodile

• Viciousness and fury
• Power and wisdom. Egyptians show their dead transformed into crocodiles of knowledge.
• Trouble and danger beneath the surface
• False feeling or dishonesty, such as when someone cries crocodile tears
• "It's a crock" indicates hypocrisy

Cross

• Mystical symbol representing the balance of opposites, the celestial and the earthly.
• In Christianity it is equated with infinite love, sacrifice and suffering

• Are you sacrificing yourself for someone or something? Giving freely of yourself and your possessions increases your energy, sacrificing yourself lowers your energy.

• Sometimes used to ward off evil. Do you feel the need to protect yourself?

Crossroads

• Time of decision

• Carl Jung believed that crossroads were a symbol for the mother aspects

Crow

• To crow means to exult loudly or boast. Do you have something to crow about?

• To express pleasure or delight. Do you have something to crow about?

• "As the crow flies" means traveling in a straight line.

• In some traditions they are associated with death, the void or the unknown inner realms.

• In other traditions crow represents things like mystical powers and the creator of the visible world.

• The eye of the crow may represent the entrance to the super-natural realms and the inner mysteries of life.

• Bringer of messages from the spirit realm.

• Considered a powerful sign in many cultures

> Chinese: Isolation of individual living in a superior realm

> Native Americans: Crow represents mystical powers and is the creator of the visible world

> The Celts and Siberians had similar meanings: Crow is a bringer of messages from spirit

- Dwells beyond space and time
- Sometimes associated with death or your inner darkness
- Walk your talk

Crowd

- Feeling a part of something
- Sometimes when in a crowd, there is a sense of anonymity and even secrecy. Is there a part of yourself you want to keep anonymous?
- If it is filled with strangers, you may be feeling like a stranger in you life or perhaps you are becoming aware of unknown parts of yourself.
- A sense of having your individual identity (ego) smothered or overwhelmed by the external world of others thoughts and expectations. May represent your own expectations of yourself.

Crown

- A crowning pinnacle of accomplishment
- A crown made of gold and jewels symbolizes power, honor, and status
- A passage into higher levels of consciousness or spiritual awareness
- What kind of crown is it and who is wearing it? Different types of crowns may
  have varying meanings (Jesus had a crown of thorns and was a martyr).
- Do you need to be congratulated for something?
- All crowns are circular and may therefore represent issues of completeness and wholeness and point to the center of the Self
- The majesty of the inner (or higher) Self

Crucifixion

- The Ego's fear of being sacrificed or murdered
- To allow the birth of the whole, realized Self

• A significant step in moving to the next level of awareness

Crying

• Releasing negative feelings

• Tears of joy. Due to repression or denial, we are sometimes unable to express our feelings. In the dream state, your defense mechanisms relax and emotional releases can occur more easily.

• The resolution of a difficulty

• The release of an attitude that is not serving you any longer

• If others are crying and you don't feel sad, this may indicate that you are grieving about something deep inside.

Crystal

• Transmitter and receiver

• Magnifier

• A powerful symbol of clarity and spiritual energy

Cutting

• Cutting away undesired opinions, attitudes, beliefs or habits

• A desire to cut away from a situation or person

• If you are cut and bleeding, you are losing your life force or energy

• In tribal traditions, cutting is done to signify initiation into a new rank or into manhood or womanhood

• "Cutting someone down" refers to being ridiculed

Daffodil
> • An indication of spring, a time of new beginnings
> • New potential, renewal, or new life

Dagger
> • Could represent significant feelings of anger toward yourself or others
> • If you kill or wound a perceived enemy in your dream, your unconscious mind may be encouraging you to conquer the fears or negative feelings represented by the enemy within.
> • Daggers are often thrust with repressed anger. Do you have deep anger that needs to be resolved?

Dam
> • Pent-up feelings. Perhaps they are about to be released.

Dancing
> • Dancing freely as in free-form may suggest a need to allow spontaneous movement and flow into your life. Follow the promptings you receive.
> • Structured dance, such as a ballet may indicate that you need to be willing to move forward in life taking care to keep form, structure, and discipline as your companions.
> • If you are in a good mood as you dance, you are probably feeling joy, happiness, and a sense of triumph at some level.
> • Dancing while in a bad mood may be compensatory in nature. It may be trying to balance negativity and stress that you feel in daily life.

Danger

- If you are in a dangerous situation, this may be a sign from your unconscious. There could be internal conflict that needs attention.
- If you *faced* the danger in your dream, it may be a positive sign and an indication that you are capable of overcoming current obstacles.

Darkness

- The unknown
- Your subconscious mind
- An area of yourself that is not understood or you are "in the dark" about
- Your fears
- Do you need to shed some light on a situation?
- The womb-like power of the deepest parts of yourself
- The dark is your ancient inner wisdom

Daughter

- A sign of the feminine-child part of you
- Your own daughter and the characteristics she represents about you
- May be reflecting something about your role as a daughter and how you feel about it

Dawn

- Awakening
- Illumination and seeing the light
- Time to make a fresh start

Deaf

- What is it that you don't want to hear about yourself or life?

Death

- Death is usually a symbol of some type of closure or end. It implies an end to one thing and the beginning of another.

• Very rarely does this sign indicate the death of someone you know or your own death! It usually symbolizes transformation, the death of old patterns and programming and making way for rebirth.
• Letting go of the old parts of yourself that no longer serve you
• Releasing the fears the dying person represents about you
• A change in relationship with the person who dies in the dream and the aspect of yourself they represent

Decapitation
• Under normal circumstances the mind controls and directs the body. This may suggest that you are under the control of your bodily drives and may be separated from rational thoughts (head) and/or feelings (heart or lower half of the body).
• Do you need to change your current thinking?
• Disassociation may be occurring in regard to some behavior or issue in life.

Deer
• Gentle aspects of yourself
• Feeling victimized, defenseless or fearful
• Sensitivity

Defecation
• Cleansing and emotional release

Desert
• It may represent the unconscious and your sense of separation from it
• Stagnation and periods of little growth in your life
• Loneliness and feelings of isolation
• If you live close to the desert or love the desert, this may be a positive symbol. For some, the desert

may be a place to commune with nature and feel a
sense of peace.

Devil (*see* also **Satan**)

• Can signal the internal struggle between the part of
you that you have labeled "good" and the part you
have labeled "bad." Look toward becoming whole
by integrating the things you consider "bad."

• The devil does not generally represent something
outside of you. It usually symbolizes the most
negative and least developed part of you.

• It may be that part of you that is ignorant and
destructive.

• All dreams are good dreams in that they bring
unconscious materials to the conscious mind. Only
then can you begin to effectively cope with the more
unpleasant sides of your personality. Carl Jung
called this negative side the "shadow." The devil
could be representing your personal or collective
shadow.

Diamond

• It takes coal being under great pressure to create
diamonds. The areas in your life which seem to
produce great pressure may be the very things
helping you achieve the crystal clarity of a diamond.

• The many facets of pure being

• Something that is valuable, timeless and very
precious

• Love

• Money

• Universal truths and spiritual consciousness

• We all are in constant pursuit of those things that
we have not obtained but want and need in order to
feel complete. Your dream may help you to decipher

what is most valuable and then give you clues where to find it.

Diarrhea
• Usually caused by fear. What are you afraid of?
• Maybe you are not assimilating what you need in life.

Digging

• Digging is generally considered to be difficult work or hard labor.
• You could be "digging" around for the truth or trying to get to the bottom of things, perhaps digging to uncover the truth of who you are. Was the digging being done in hard ground or fertile soil?
• You could be "digging your own grave."

Dinosaurs
• Something from your past or a personal characteristic which you changed and no longer use.
• A part of your subconscious trying to get your attention. More than likely it represents negative feelings that have gone unresolved, having been put behind you, buried in the past (or so you thought). We eventually have to face our dinosaurs.

Dirt/Earth
• Your connection with the Mother Earth
• Are you feeling grounded?
• Something in your life that needs to be cleaned up
• Rich soil indicates fertility and the potential for growth. Is it time to plant the seeds of a new beginning?
• Dry, barren soil may be a reflection of negative feelings. Are you feeling like dirt?

Disasters (Look up a specific disasters by name. *see* **Flood, Earthquake, Tornado**)

• These types of dreams usually indicate that you are experiencing many changes in your life or will soon experience such.

• Most people resist change, sometimes even positive change. Therefore, quick shifts in life style or some kind of crisis may bring about dreams of natural disasters.

Disease

• The word disease literally means "out of ease," disharmony or "dis-ease."

• Disease brings internal issues to the surface. Negative feelings manifest in physical forms such as disease or illnesses. Notice how the disease manifests itself and the feelings you have regarding the disease. Look up the specific part of the body that is affected and see if you can identify the negative feelings causing dis- ease in your body and/or life. This may help you uncover the feelings associated with the disease so you can resolve them and begin healing.

Diving

• Diving in a dream suggests that you are trying to "get to the bottom" of a current situation.

• Water symbolizes feelings and the inner world, thus, another interpretation for this dream may be that you are delving into your unconscious, spirit, or feelings. It can represent getting in touch with your deep fears, or the deep wisdom that dwells within you.

Doctor

• Your inner healer

• A need for physical, emotional, or spiritual healing
• Doctors are respected authority figures and many people follow their advice and guidance in regard to their well being. Depending on your belief system, the doctor in your dream could represent your Higher Self or inner guidance.
• If you are currently experiencing a health problem and doctors are a part of your daily life, this dream may be symbolic of real life difficulties.

Dog

• Faithfulness and loyalty
• Are you loyal to others or are you taking advantage of a loyal friend?
• Are you loyal to your true mission in life?
• Protection
• Friendship
• Service
• If you are being treated like a dog, you are most likely being abused in some way.
• On the metaphysical level, dogs are consider to be the guardians of the underworld.
• Dogs could represent the more basic or "animal" parts of your nature and some think that they specifically represent male energy.

Doll

• Dolls are lifeless images of real people, suggestive of a person that is not genuine and does not express their feelings. Have you been less than "real" in any way?
• They may represent the way you relate and interact with your internal and external environments.
• Dolls may represent feelings of detachment or phoniness.

• Maybe you had a doll in your youth. How were you with your doll/s? It may be reflecting that same characteristic now. Were you motherly or did you take your feelings out on the doll? Pay attention to your emotional response to the doll.

Dolphin

• Unharnessed joy, playfulness, spontaneity
• Spiritual enlightenment
• Are you like the Dolphins, experiencing joy and harmony in your relationships?
• Dolphins represent positive messages from your unconscious mind.
• May represent a positive connection between your consciousness and those parts of the psyche that are a mystery and largely unconscious.
• Dolphins are water dwelling and therefore represent your willingness and ability to navigate through emotions.

Donkey

• Humility, honor and "royalty" in disguise.
• A donkey may also symbolize stubbornness and an unyielding personality.
• It may represent a person who has many burdens and carries a "heavy load." The donkey has the qualities of ruggedness, endurance, and loyalty.

Door

• Passageway
• Going through a door may represent going from one state of consciousness to another, or from one inner plane to another.
• Locked or closed doors may represent obstacles or opportunities that are not currently available to you.
• Many doors may represent your current choices.

Dove
- Peace
- Love
- Purity

Dragon
- In the Far-East it is believed that the dragons are spiritual creatures that navigate through the air and through the sky.
- In the West dragons are considered to be dangerous and need to be destroyed.
- The dragon may represent the enormous power in your unconscious.
- Perhaps it represents large and mystical forces inside of you.
- Life force
- Great potency
- It could symbolize repressed negative feelings such as fear.
- The dragon may represent a period of time when you will confront your fears and empower yourself to effectively cope with negative emotions, extreme materialism, and be able to obtain greater inner and outer freedom.

Drowning
- Drowning may suggest being overwhelmed by unresolved feelings, old issues, or a current crisis. Perhaps you need to release the old in order to emerge and begin anew.
- Do you feel overwhelmed by your feelings or life events?
- It can also be a symbol of death and rebirth, as in a baptism.

Drugs

• The interpretation of drugs in your dreams depends on the relationship you have with them in daily life and if they are doctor prescribed or not.

• Drugs can represent a need to escape from daily stress or a desire to get quick relief.

• Your unconscious mind may be suggesting outrageous things in hopes that you get the message to "have fun, dream dreams, and get out of your own head!"

• Keep in mind that the purpose of dreams is to raise your consciousness and to assist you in having a better life. The message about drug use is most likely not encouraging you to use drugs, rather, it represents a need to feel better or get better.

Duck

• Ducks usually convey a positive message

• They are able to survive on land and in the water. Ducks are flexible and multi-talented, able to swim, walk, and fly. Dreaming about this bird suggests that you are very flexible and can competently deal with emotional issues at hand.

Dust

• Whatever is covered by dust hasn't been used or has been forgotten. Is there something inside that hasn't been touched or is a forgotten part of you?

Dwarf

• Dwarfs represent, or allude to, the childlike creative powers in the unconscious. Think of a dwarf as a "worker" in your unconscious.

• A childlike condition which has the potential and power to influence your life

• It suggests possibilities for learning and brings to the conscious mind messages from the unconscious

• Are you feeling dwarfed by a situation?
• Are you limiting your potential?

ε

Eagle

• To Native Americans, the Eagle symbolizes the Creator
• The Egyptians saw it as a symbol of illumination
• In Northern Europe, it was associated with strength, power and war.
• A messenger from heaven
• Freedom
• Seeing life from new heights
• An eagle is a powerful bird and the unconscious message may be prosperity, success, and liberation.
• If the eagle is on the attack, reflect on your own aggressive and predatory thoughts and tendencies.

Ear

• Do you need to be more attentive and aware of internal and external stimuli?
• Listen!
• Is there something that you are afraid to hear?

Earth

• Mother Earth is female, receptive, rejuvenating . . . the earthy, sensual part of yourself.
• Do you need to be more down to earth?
• The physical part of you. That which is created by spirit.

Earthquake

• Earthquakes can be more symbolic of your physical reality rather than your emotional life.

• Earthquakes may represent problems that occur in daily life . . . something that is "shaking" you up, and changing your daily life.

• Are you afraid of the change you are undergoing? Even though change is often uncomfortable, it brings with it new experiences and growth.

East

• The east is where the sun rises. It may represent new beginnings.

• Spiritual awakening

• Eastern philosophies, focusing more inward

Eating

• Consider all of its details including what type of food you were eating, if you were eating alone, with strangers, or with familiar people. Eating usually symbolizes comfort, pleasure and love.

• Eating can represent taking in spiritual nourishment or a need for physical or psychological food.

• If you are on a perpetual diet and are depriving yourself of food, then this dream may be compensatory in nature.

Eggs

• Something new and fragile

• They represent life and development in its earliest forms.

• Eggs can represent captivity or entrapment. The egg in a dream may very well represent you in the most profound sense. Are you trapped in a shell or did you break?

• In ancient traditions, the egg represented immortality.

• Perhaps you are about to become aware of your potential.

Eight (*see* under **Numbers**)
Elastic

- Stretching yourself into new things in life.
- Are you flexible?

Electricity

- It can represent the life force
- Blown fuses may represent that you are blowing your own inner fuses.
- Your electrical field will often go through a change when beginning a spiritual quest. This may be represented in a dream by electricity.

Elephant

- Gentle loving power
- Destructive power
- Remover of obstacles
- Reminder to have thick skin as an Elephant and let things roll off your back.
- Elephants may also represent knowledge.
- They are also associated with long memory. Is there something in your life that you need to remember? Maybe it is a reminder not to forget.
- Depending on the dream's details, the elephant may be a symbol of a large burden.

Elevator

- Moving from one state of consciousness to another
- The elevator may simply represent the "ups and downs" of life. If you are ascending, then you may perceive your current situation as optimistic and moving upward. If you are descending, you may be experiencing some negativity and helplessness or perhaps you are delving into your feelings.

Eleven (*see* under **Numbers**)

Elf

> • Perhaps you need to be more mischievous or childlike in life.
> • Have fun. Enjoy yourself and your inner magic.

Elk

> • Power
> • Beauty
> • Stamina
> • Dignity
> • They are known to crash through obstacles

Emerald

> • The emerald may signify the magnificent healing power within you.
> • Do you need to enter into your own inner magic?

Emotions

> • Any emotions you see in others usually reflects your emotional state. If it is an emotion you don't recognize in yourself, it is usually because it has been repressed.
> • Emotions are a combination of your thoughts and feelings.

Emptiness

> • Do you need to simplify your life? Perhaps you need to empty yourself of thoughts, patterns or ideals. Often we need to let go of things so other things may "fill us up."
> • Are you feeling empty and alone? Take time to replenish yourself. Do the things you love doing.

Enemy

> • This can represent a war going on inside with your inner enemy, the aspect of yourself which you deny or disown.

Envelope

> • Having to do with receiving news, information, or messages from someone specific or from the world at large.
>
> • If you look forward to mail, the meaning may be positive. However, if you dread the envelopes which typically hold the monthly bills, then it may have negative and anxiety provoking symbolism.
>
> • You may be coming into awareness about some aspect of your life where you make new realizations.

Escalator

> • May represent changing levels of consciousness
>
> • Moving forward with less effort than usual

Ex-boy/girl friend

> • It is very common for people to dream about ex-partners. Those who have been a part of our lives often continue taking up a part of our mind and heart. Just because the relationship ended doesn't mean that everything is finished. You will continue to dream about your ex-girlfriend or boyfriend until you "let go" of them on an emotional level, or until you have learned your lessons from that relationship. Dreaming about your ex-romance does not predict future involvement. It usually has to do with working out old issues.
>
> • Other people in dreams usually represent characteristics about yourself.
>
> • Your teachers in life

Exam/Examination

> • Is it time for a self-examination?
>
> • Are you being tested in some way in your life? What are you being tested for or about?
>
> • Do you feel that you need to prove yourself to others?

• Are you fearing failure? Trust your Self.

Excrement

• Perhaps there is a need to release the waste products of your life such as fear, guilt or shame . . . the things you no longer need.

• This may also indicate that there is something poisoning you from within.

• Is there something within yourself or reflected in others that you disapprove of or despise?

• Are you feeling like you are being dumped on?

• This dream may represent healthy psychological progress. It may indicate that you are cleansing yourself of unnecessary and possibly hurtful attitudes, ideas and feelings.

• Feces could represent a contaminated area of your life, mind or spirit. Look at the details and consider if it has to do with something you have been trying to clean or if it brings up stress provoking thoughts, confusion, and unresolved issues in your life.

Eyeglasses

• To people who normally wears eyeglasses, glasses improve seeing. Is there something you are not seeing as good as you could?

• To those who do not wear glasses, or where glasses are the focal point in the dream, several interpretations could be made. You may need to do a "reality check" and ask yourself if you are seeing the world through "rose colored glasses."

• You may need to see things more clearly, take a close look

• If you need glasses, it may indicate that your thoughts and feelings are not working together.

Eyes

- Windows of the soul
- Sometimes the ego
- Your inner or outer sight
- Be willing to see with clarity and truth.
- Is there something in your life you don't want to see?
- It can refer to the ego "I"
- The third eye is your connection to the spiritual realms.
- Eyes symbolize perceptiveness, personal outlook, clairvoyance, curiosity, and knowledge.
- Eyes reveal information about your personal identity, things you should pay attention to.
- Closed eyes are said to represent fear and an unwillingness to see clearly.

Face/Faces

- What do you need to face? Is it time to face up to a situation?
- May represent different parts of your personality or psyche. Remember that all parts of your dreams are reflections of different parts of yourself. These are parts of you that come from the unconscious.
- Faces may appear in numerous ways. For example: Featureless faces suggest that you may feel unnoticed and unappreciated. On the other hand, some believe that the blank or unclear face represents a teacher. That is someone who is there to show and teach you a lesson but you are

unprepared for it and the face is blank. Smiling faces are representative of happy thoughts and feelings and possibly anticipation of a joyful event in the near future. A young face may reflect your more pure or youthful self.

• Always remember the compensatory nature of dreams and their ability to point to the opposite of what you experience in daily life.

• Are you being "two-faced?"

Failure

• Are you feeling like a failure? Take a good look at your life. Failures can be turning points.

• Represents a feeling of failure that has been buried inside. Face the feeling of being a failure, let go of it and replace it with feeling successful and capable.

Falling

• You may be in a time of personal growth and are unsure of yourself. Remember that we often risk and fail before we succeed at something.

• Feeling a loss of control or out of control in your life.

• It may represent underlying fears and feelings of inadequacy and helplessness.

• Is there a situation in your life that seems to be on a downward spiral or out of control?

• Do any of these familiar sayings relate to you? "Falling in love," "falling on your face," or "a fallen woman?"

• Fall is a synonym for autumn. It may therefore be a sign of completion.

• It may also represent falling into awareness or consciousness

Fast

> • Sometimes you can go too fast. If you are feeling out of control, you may need to slow down.
> • Are you living life in the "fast lane?" Are you happy in your current accelerated pace?
> • Perhaps you need to "fast"(do without food) for purification and cleansing.

7

Fat

> • There are common sayings which indicate fat to mean abundance like having a "fat" wallet, or "living on the fat of the land."
> • It can also have to do with inactivity or suppressing of feelings.
> • Do you have an excess of something in your life which you need to let go?

Father

> • You may be dreaming about your father and the attributes in yourself which he represents or your father aspect within.
> • Authority and power
> • The image of the father could also represent the "collective consciousness," the traditional spirit, and the yang
> • May represent your Father in Heaven, God or Divine Father
> • Your Father aspect within
> • It can also represent a protector or provider. Do you need to protect yourself?
> • For men, it may represent their own fathering skills

Fear

> • If you have repressed issues, they may be coming to the surface. Is there anything in your life which causes you fear? "There is nothing to fear, but fear itself." Face your fears.

Feathers

- The connection between man and God, representing the flight to spirit and to the heavens above.
- To the ancient Egyptians, feathers represented the winds and the gods Ptah, Hathor, Osiris, and Amon.
- Faith and contemplation
- The quill signifies the Word. Finding a feather can indicate a message from the Creator.
- "Light as a feather." Do you need lighten up or perhaps enter into a receptive state of softness?
- Have you done a good job and just need to congratulate yourself or put a "feather in your cap?"

Feces (*see* Excrement)
Feet

- Your foundation or connection to the earth
- Your understanding of your own nature and what life presents to you
- The feet implement your purpose and represent the knowledge and faith necessary to carry out your reason for being here.
- Feet can represent your ability to move forward in life.
- Feet indicate how well you are balanced and grounded.

Fences

- May represent your level of self control. Maybe you need more or less of it.
- Do you have a need for privacy?
- Do you feel trapped or fenced in? Remember that it is self created and can be changed. Take a look at the situation from a higher perspective.

• Do you need boundaries in life? Are there too many boundaries?

• Have you been "sitting on the fence?" Is it time to make up your mind and move forward?

Fighting

• Usually a sign of inner conflict, even if the fight is with strangers. They represent different aspects of yourself. It may be between what you want to do and what you think you should do. Is it time to discover your true path? Listen to your heart and after you make your choice, follow it whole heartedly.

• Fighting can be a sign of suppressed feelings.

• Are you willing to fight for what you believe in?

• Fighting may symbolize anger and confusion that comes during times of change. If nothing is changing in your life, it may be a clue that a change is needed or that you want to change internally.

Fingers

• Pointing a finger at something or someone can represent something within yourself, perhaps a characteristic you need to be aware of for some reason.

• Individual fingers have definite meanings in different cultures. Here is a list of feelings and areas of the body that coincide with each finger. These were shared with me by my friend Karol K. Truman.

Thumb: worry, spleen, stomach
Index: fear, kidney, bladder
Middle: anger, liver, gall bladder
Ring: grief, lungs, large intestine
Little: pretense, heart, small intestine

Fire

- This is a sign of the life force within you.
- It can represent potency, power, psychic energy or enlightenment
- Fired up or filled with energy and ready to go
- It is associated with initiation and opening to spiritual communication and energy. In many traditions, initiates go through symbolic purification by fire.
- An agent of transmutation
- Fire can represent sexual passion just as when someone is "burning with desire"
- Anger, pain or fear
- Is the fire in your dream destroying something or simply warming you?

Fish

- Spiritual symbol of Christianity
- Spiritual food, renewal and rebirth
- They travel in the water and water usually represents emotions, feelings, intuition, psychic perceptions and the subconscious mind, as well as the mysterious realms of the archetypal female energy, so how they are moving through the water has a lot to say about how you are traveling through your feelings and intuition.
- Psychic realizations from the deepest levels of the subconscious
- A sign of fertility
- Does something seem "fishy" to you?
- Associated with the astrological sign of Pisces which has to do with being sensitive, receptive and intuitive.
- Fish may be a desire for acknowledgments as in "fishing for compliments."

Five (*see* under **Numbers**)
Flies

    • Things that are annoying in daily life
    • They could symbolize people and things that get in your way or they could mean that you are currently experiencing frustration. Notice whether or not you were successful in getting rid of the flies in your dream or if they were overwhelming. This may give you a clue as to how well you are coping with the distractions and frustrations in your life.
    • Maybe you just need to "fly"

Floating

    • Floating in water can be symbolic of floating on top of your emotions and being in harmony with your intuition and feelings.
    • Floating through the air has the same symbolism as flying. (*see* also Flying)
    • A sign of liberation and letting go of problems and restrictions
    • Current feelings of peacefulness and general freedom
    • Floating can also be symbolic of aloofness, lack of connection or a need to become more grounded.
    • Floating above a situation can be a way of removing yourself from a traumatic experience.
    • You may also be feeling directionless in life as if you are just drifting.

Flood

    • Water in any form symbolizes your inner world, emotions and feelings. Dreaming about being in a flood is an indication that the dreamer is currently experiencing powerful emotions that may be overwhelming.

• It could represent a very powerful, or even violent, emotionally cleansing
• Water at times represents the flow of life and may represent the feelings of being overwhelmed by the way things are flowing.

Floor

• Your foundation or support, what you stand on
• Notice the details of the floor. If it is wet and slippery so that you are unable to move surely and quickly, it may represent your feelings of insecurity in moving forward with what you are doing in life.
• Are you overwhelmed? ("floored" so to speak)

Flowers

• Flowers are usually signs of beauty, unfoldment and vitality.
• In dreams they can represent the simplest feelings of contentment to the deepest feelings of spiritual completeness.
• A circular flower is a sign which could represent the "mandala" symbol or the symbol of wholeness or "psychic center of the personality." Additionally, the colors could symbolize the energy centers in your bodies called chakras. Each chakra is related to a different color. See individual colors under Colors.
• Flowers also represent hope and positive growth, along with simplicity and innocence.

Flying

• Dreams of flying are common. Some people believe that flying in dreams can be an actual out of body experience, that we go to places on this physical plane as well as into the inner planes (the Astral).
• Your desire to break free of restrictions and limitations

• Reminding you of your unlimited potential
• Are you up in the air about something?
• The way you are dealing with life or how a project is progressing

Fog

• The setting of the dream may give clues about the area of life that it is referring to. Is the fog over water or land, are you in familiar or unfamiliar surroundings? Are you journeying into the unconscious, where things are obscure and mysterious, or into a part of life that is unclear and challenging? Remember, the fog will lift.
• Emotional or mental confusion
• Are there areas of your life or obstacles that you can't quite see?
• Fog may represent your subconscious mind.

Food

• Different foods have different meanings, often having to do with your association with them. What are your feelings about the food in your dream?
• Food represents nourishment of all kinds; spiritual, mental, physical and emotional.
• Pleasure and indulgence
• To the perpetual dieter, the dream could have a "compensatory" function where the food that is denied to the individual during the day shows up in the dream state.

Forest

• Often associated with the female principle and the Great Mother
• Abundance, growth and strength
• A place of protection, refuge or safety. Do you need to take refuge?

• It may represent your "mental space." If you are lost in the woods, it may be reflecting feelings of confusion or a lack of clear direction. The dark and threatening woods may represent the dark and unexplored areas of the psyche.

• Maybe you can't see the forest for the trees . . . feeling overwhelmed.

Forgetting

• Are you feeling forgotten?

• Are you too preoccupied with something?

Fork

• Have you reached a fork in the road?

• How is it being used . . . for eating or something totally different?

• Are you speaking with "forked tongue?"

Fountain

• A clear fountain is a symbol of intuition, free flowing feelings and spiritual rejuvenation

• Your spiritual wellspring

• The "fountain of youth"

Four (*see* under **Numbers**)

Friends

• Friends represent attributes about yourself. In a dream, they rarely have anything to do with the actual person. We learn about ourselves through other people.

• What are the main characteristics of the friends? How are they like you? What character traits, represented by the friend, are you in denial about?

Frog

• Frogs may be considered symbols of the unconscious because they live in the water.

• Frogs can represent positive transformation.

• Frogs may symbolize stillness, patience and focus.
• In some cultures frogs represent purification and cleansing.
• In some places the frog is a symbol of fertility, creation and resurrection.
• Inconsistency . . . hopping from one place to another
• Are you trying to find your prince? Can you see the beauty beneath the surface of ugliness?

Frozen

• Feelings that are stuck inside and immovable at present. Perhaps you need to warm them up a bit (or pay attention to those feelings) so they can be released.
• Are you closing yourself off emotionally?
• Do you need to share your feelings more readily?

Fruit

• This is a sign of reaping the rewards of your labors. The condition of the fruit reflects the condition of that which you will harvest or receive.
• Fruit represents abundance and prosperity.
• As a result of the seeds they carry, fruit may also represent new beginnings.
• According to biblical stories, mythology and literature in general, fruits represent sexual desires and the search for wealth and immortality. In order to understand the meaning of the fruit, consider what it is you are striving for.

Funeral

• It is important to note that dreaming about funerals does not necessarily symbolize physical death for you or anyone else. It usually symbolizes an ending of a different kind. You may be burying or letting go of relationships, conditions or negative feelings you no longer need. Maybe you're just moving on to the next phase of life.

• A funeral may symbolize the burying of sensitivities and feelings that are too difficult to cope with.

• Funerals can reflect numbness or a feeling that is the opposite of aliveness, such as depression and emptiness.

• Burying a person that is alive suggests emotional turmoil.

• What is it you need to let go?

Galaxy

• The expansive part of yourself
• Unlimited possibilities

Gallbladder

• Anger
• The gallbladder can indicate feelings of bitterness or wanting to force things.
• "He had a lot of gall" is a statement that can be a sign of gumption.

Game

• It could have something to do with "the game of life"
• Perhaps it represents the challenges in your life, your competitive nature, or your childishness
• Games may point out goals you are trying to achieve.
• If you are playing a game with people from your daily life, consider your interactions with them and

the role that each individual plays. This may give you insights into what is going on within yourself on a deeper level.

Garbage

• Are there things in you life that need to be thrown out or is there something you need to release? Letting go of clutter frees the mind and makes room for other things. The things from your past or in your life today that are not worth keeping are literally rubbish. Removing "garbage" from the mind, spirit, and body is a necessary step in moving forward. At times it is accomplished in your dreams.

Garden

• Gardens signify beauty, peace, creative activity and growth.

• Each plant in the garden represents a different aspect of yourself.

• Aspects of yourself being cultivated

• A well tended garden may represent the way you are taking care of your creative endeavors.

• A weedy garden may indicate a need to weed out unwanted things in your life. Pay attention to what you are doing in relation to the garden in your dreams. Are you planting seeds (new ideas or thoughts), or harvesting (receiving the fruits of your labors)?

• Do you need to take time and enjoy the beautiful things springing up in the garden of life?

Gas

• Are you running out of gas in your life? Are you feeling tired?

• Gas represents that which is necessary to propel you through life.

• Are the events in your life difficult to assimilate, giving you "gas" so to speak?

Gate

• To help determine what is going on in your life in relation to passing from one place, phase or project to another, ask these or similar questions: Is the gate open or closed, new or old? What is it made of?
• An entrance between one realm and another
• New opportunities

Genitals

• Having to do with your attitudes and concerns in regard to your sexuality. If you are feeling guilty, stressed or concerned about your sexual activities (or a lack of them), they may be reinforced in dreams containing sexual organs.
• Dreaming about the sexual organs of other people is still a reflection of your own attitudes and feelings. What does the other person represent about you?
• Are you holding onto negative sexual feelings that need to be resolved?
• Willful desire
• Conflicts generated by sexual frustration

Ghosts

• A ghost usually represents a part of you that is unclear and that you do not understand, something undefined.
• Things that unattainable or fleeting
• Demonic types of ghost images may represent your negative tendencies, the unpleasant parts of your personality or your "shadow."
• Do you have a ghost in your closet that you need to face?

Gift

• Are you accepting the gifts life has to offer?

• Giving and receiving gifts is usually a pleasant occasion and both parties benefit from the exchange. Dreaming about gift giving may be a reflection on positive exchanges that are occurring in your daily life.

• Giving and receiving are the same thing . . . energy in motion.

• The most valuable gifts may be emotional and spiritual. Perhaps your dream may be trying to make you aware of such gifts.

Giraffe

• This may represent stretching for what you want

• Do you want to stand above the crowd?

• Do you feel like you stick out when you would rather fit in?

• Accept yourself and your unique talents.

Glacier

• Frozen feelings

Glass

• Glass can be a sign of seeing from one realm to another.

• Windows allow sunshine into our homes. Do you need to allow more light inside? Is the dream making you aware of the light that is coming through?

• Glass makes our lives more comfortable, especially when used to help us see more clearly. Do you need to see things more clearly?

• If glass is shattered in your dream, it could symbolize shattered illusions. It could also represent the shattering of dreams or hopes.

Glider

• Going with the flow

• Gliding on the winds of change in life

Glove

- Gloves protect you from the elements as well as shield you from direct contact with others. Do you need to protect yourself?
- Maybe you need to put your gloves on and get to work.
- Do you need to protect yourself while you carry out your ideas, plans or projects?
- May represent what you reveal outwardly (to others) about the things you are doing

Glue

- Stick-to-itiveness
- Are you "coming unglued?"

Goat

- We think of them as being sturdy and tenacious.
- When we place undo blame on an individual we may call him a "scapegoat."
- In pagan mythology goats are considered to be symbols of sexual vitality.
- It is the animal associated with the astrological sign Capricorn. Those born under this sign are often single-minded, determined, and sometimes solitary in their pursuits. Are these characteristics you have or maybe need to develop?

God/Goddess

- Whether or not we believe in a God, all of us have been exposed to the idea of a supreme and omnipresent being. The dilemma over the existence of God is probably the most common dilemma of them all. Everyone from time to time will have a dream about "God." What it means depends on the dreamer.
- God/Goddess usually represents truth, purity, and love.

• God/Goddess can represent the creative energy which is abundant in all of us (whether we know it or not).

• God may have negative connotations for some people. Because of their experiences in life and strict religious environment, God could represent eternal punishment, damnation and invoke massive amounts of guilt.

• To many God/Goddess represents unity oneness and total acceptance.

Gold (as in the mineral) (*see* also under **Colors**)

• Gold is a symbol of the sun. It represents the spirit and life.

• The Latin word for gold is the same as the Hebrew word for light.

• The golden light of inner peace

• Dreaming about gold could represent the concerns you have about your most precious valuables or reference the "alchemist's gold" which is spiritual in nature.

• Are you chasing an elusive treasure such as the pot of gold at the end of the rainbow?

• Do you have a heart of gold? Do you need to acquire one?

• Losing gold may express your anxieties over a missed opportunity.

Grandfather

• Wise old man

• The mature aspect of yourself

• To the American Indian, it is a name for the sun and the Beings above.

• If you are a Grandfather, it could represent your feelings as a grandfather.

Grandmother
- Wise old woman
- The mature aspect of yourself.
- To the American Indian, Grandmother Earth is the loving name given to the earth.
- If you are a Grandmother, it could represent your feelings as a grandmother.

Grasshopper
- Are you hopping from one place or thing to another? Is it serving you well or not?
- This may remind you of the parable of the grasshopper and the ant. If so, the grasshopper represents living for the moment and having fun at the expense of being prepared for the future. How are you living your life in relation to this story?

Graveyard (*see* Cemetery)
Gray (*see* under Colors)
Green (*see* under Colors)
Guilt
- Guilt is a way of denying responsibility. What are you not taking responsibility for in your life?
- Do you need to forgive yourself for something?

Guns
- Do you feel a need to protect or defend yourself either emotionally, physically or both?
- What was the gun used for in the dream? If you were using it to shoot something, it could represent something you need to get rid of in your life or even that you need to shoot for. Maybe it was being used against you. What part of yourself is overtaking you? What feelings did you experience in relation to the gun?

• Your unconscious mind may be telling you not to harbor your negative feelings but express them more freely before they become explosive.

Guru

• One who gives you guidance
• Your inner teacher

H

Hair

• That which comes out of your head . . . thoughts, knowledge and reasoning
• It is symbol of vanity, security, sensuality, sexual appeal, and youth.
• It represents physical and spiritual strength. Samson's hair was the source of his strength. Losing hair may therefore indicate a loss of strength.
• White or gray hair represents age and wisdom while body hair may symbolize protection and warmth.
• Because it grows out of the head which is the energy center that connects us to spirit, it can represent spiritual power flowing out and connecting you to the universe.

Halo

• A halo is the visual image of the energy field around angels and holy people.
• A connection to your inner, Divine Self.

Hands

• What you do with your hands shows what you are doing with your thoughts.

• You express yourself with your hands. The hands may reveal information about emotions, intentions, and overt behaviors. For example, if in you dream you see clenched fists you may have much repressed anger. Sometimes extended hands suggest a need to develop close friendships.

Happiness

• If you are currently experiencing sadness, this dream may be an attempt to compensate.
• Life is good

Hats

•There are many different kinds of hats. Notice the characteristics of the hat. If it is a hat of a particular profession, it represents the attributes a person would have in that line of work. The type and quality of the hat may also represent the degree of authority and respect that your unconscious mind is giving to the person wearing it and the part of yourself that the person represents.
• Hats are usually symbolic of power and authority.
• The type of hat worn can stereotype the person who is wearing it. Generally the person wearing the hat is representing a part of you. What is the hat saying about your position in life and your attitude toward it?

Hawk

• Symbol of the soul
• Victory
• View your life from a higher perspective seeing new possibilities.

Head

• Your "I Am"

• This is where one experiences the conflict between centering oneself with genuine awareness as opposed to ego-tripping.

Heart

• Love
• The heart relates to feelings such as resentment and/or hurt, compassion or rejection, feeling or not feeling approval from others.

Heaven

• All of those things for which most people hope. Some of us may not be convinced of its existence, but all of us have definite ideas about what heaven should be like. Pay particular attention to your own views of heaven.
• Enlightenment, understanding
• Bliss, peace, happiness
• Union between God and man
• Some people work for a "Heaven on Earth." Others believe there are many different heavens and in dreams, some people visit those places through soul travel.

Heel

• To heel can mean to come to attention, pay attention or submit to another person's authority.
• "Heel" can also be a homophone for "heal."
• Are you being a real heel?

Hell

• Hell may be a sign of the difficulties you are going through.
• If you grew up learning about "hell fire" or the place you go if you are "bad," it may have similar applications in your dream.
• Unexplored realms within yourself

Hide

> • In daily life we hide from things that we don't want to deal with or from danger. As children we played the game of "hide and go seek." What is it you are hiding from? What things don't you want others to know about you? When brought into the light, these things are not as bad as they may seem but may diminish your energy when kept within.
>
> • If you are hiding to be out of danger, you may consider those things in your life that propose a threat to you. Are there associated feelings needing a resolution?
>
> • We often try to hide our own negativity and mistakes. This dream may call for an honest reflection on personal characteristics and an evaluation of how much fear influences your life.

Hills

> • Rounded hills may represent female sensuality. Do you need to step into your sensuality?
>
> • Small issues that seem big. Are you making a mountain out of a molehill?

Hippopotamus

> • In nature the mother hippo gives birth in the water. Are you about to give birth to a new idea or project? It may have to do with spiritual endeavors.
>
> • Is there something that is weighty in your life?

Hips

> • A sign of support and power. Is there something you are doing that you really need to throw your hip into?
>
> • Celebration as in "Hip, hip, hurray!"
>
> • A damaged or immobilized hip may have to do with your fear of moving forward.

Hog

• Overindulgence
• Selfishness. Are you not getting your share or not giving your share? Are you hogging something?
• May be a sign of uncleanliness
• Hogs are intelligent and powerful, yet humans usually them a negative connotation. Perhaps there is something in your life that is positive and valuable which you only see as undesirable.

Hole

• A dark part within yourself that you are not acknowledging
• Holes in things such as socks may represent feelings of faultiness or depravation. It may be bringing your attention to the fact that there is something missing or in need of repair in your life.
• Dark holes can symbolize the great "unknown" or the entrance to the unconscious
• Holes can represent the feminine
• If the hole is in the shape of a circle, it can represent wholeness or completeness.

Home

• Your physical body, spiritual self or both
• What happens inside the house usually represents what is going on in your life or inside of you.
• Each room in the house symbolizes different aspects of yourself. For example, the kitchen may represent nourishment, sustenance, or creativity. Liken whatever you usually do in the room to yourself and the things you do inside yourself. The attic usually represents your super conscious and the basement your subconscious.

• Is the house cluttered? Perhaps it represents an area in your life which needs to be taken care of, discarded or cleaned.

Homosexuality

• Sexual dreams are usually about power, control, identity and other non-sexual issues of life.

• If you are homosexual, dreams regarding this particular sexual orientation are not atypical. They are simply the extension of your thoughts and feelings in the form that is the most familiar and meaningful to you.

• If a heterosexual person is having a homosexual dream, it may be about loving their Self.

• A dream of homosexuality may be about integrating ideas and attitudes.

Honey

• Sweet experiences and good health

• The food of the gods, the life force in all things,"the land of milk and honey"

Hook

• Are you being hooked by or on something or someone?

• It may represent a "Captain Hook" in your life e.g., someone who is feared or dishonest. Is it you?

• Was the hook used to hang things? It may represent a need to organize.

• A fishing hook may have to do with fishing for feelings in the subconscious that need to be looked at or resolved.

Horn/Horns

• The horn was used in ancient times as a cup.

• The abundance in all things

• Some cultures used horns to issue warnings.

• They were used to call the forces for the Holy War

• They can represent the power of music
• Horns also represent evil or the destructive forces within

Horse

• The horse represents a powerful aspect of yourself. It can represent your feelings or physical body. A symbol of power.
• Is it wild and free or tame and controlled? This may represent how you are feeling about a situation in your life.

• At times, horses can also be considered messengers, relaying information from the unconscious to the conscious, from the spiritual to the physical.
• If you are riding the horse and in control, it suggests that you are self assured and feel a sense of control in your daily life.
• The color of the horse is also significant. See the meaning of specific colors under Color for ideas.

Hospital

• Most of us need some kind of healing either physically, psychologically, emotionally or spiritually. By paying attention to what happens in dreams, you may be able to identify the source of pain and where and how the healing needs to take place.
• What are your feelings with regard to your experiences with hospitals? They may indicate what the dream symbol is trying to portray

Hostage

• Feelings of victimization or entrapment. May have to do with feelings of powerlessness, not being able to see your way out of a difficult situation

• Because a hostage is taken against his will, perhaps your will has been taken away by another or by circumstances.

• It may be a part of your personality that is not being expressed, perhaps your creativity, intellect, or inner freedom. This dream may be to make you more aware of the limiting conditions in your life.

• Maybe you need to look for new ways out of your present situation.

Hotel

• All dwelling places generally represent the dreamer's psychological, emotional, or spiritual condition.

• A hotel is a transitory dwelling and therefore suggests a time away from responsibilities or routine.

• If the hotel is luxurious it suggests prosperity and positive decision making. If the hotel is rundown and inadequate, it may reflect a time of uneasiness and depravation.

• Does it represent a retreat or a place to escape?

House (*see* Home)
Hug

• Love and tenderness
• Comfort and protection

Hummingbird

• Are you too busy in life, needing to slow down
• Absolute energy and joy in retrieving the nectar of life
• Put your joyous energy in all directions

Hunting

• Is there an unknown part of yourself you need to hunt for? What you are hunting for in the dream and

its characteristics may indicate what aspects of yourself you need to find or cultivate.
• What are you looking for in life?
• Is there a part of yourself which you are trying to do away with? Is this a good thing to do or not?

Hurricane
• Sudden and unpleasant changes in life
• An emotional storm is either in your life or on the horizon

Hyena
• Hyena may be a sign of noise and merriment out of proportion or perhaps not appropriate to the situation. Have you been acting like a hyena?
• They are ferocious and have powerful jaws. How does this relate to what is going on in your life right now?

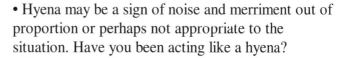

Ice
• Water in the solid form, is associated with the feelings that are frozen or not readily accessible to you. These feelings may be negative such as fear and anxiety.
• Things that are frozen are generally not usable.
• Things that do not change or grow.
• Are there feelings or thoughts that are inaccessible to you or is there a part of you that is inaccessible to others?
• Frigidity

Ice-cream
• Taking in the pleasures of life

• Eating, making, selling or serving ice cream suggests that you are feeling contentment and satisfaction in your life.

• Are you needing to compensate in a dream for a lack of enjoyable and sweet things in daily life?

Ice-skating

• There may be feelings inside in a stagnant or inaccessible form. You may be functioning in your daily life without paying attention to larger issues which you are in denial about. (Skating on top of the frozen feelings within.)

• Take a look at those parts of your life that you are most reluctant to address.

Illness

• Every illness corresponds to negative feelings which are ultimately the cause

• Illness is good in the sense that it brings to your awareness the buried feelings you may be avoiding. What are the feelings you need to deal with?

• Sometimes illness is a sign that you just need to slow down, be still and quiet within yourself.

Incest

• A sign that you need to integrate the adult attributes of yourself with the child attributes

• May be a sign of a forgotten childhood abuse that is surfacing

• However disturbing this dream is, more than likely it has nothing to do with sex. It is reflecting feelings within you.

Indigo (*see* under **Colors**)

Infidelity

• These types of dreams may be connected to feelings of inadequacy or dissatisfaction.

• It could be telling you something about the relationship that you have with yourself, giving you clues about the nature of your inner world.

• Are you being true to yourself?

• Do you need to love yourself more?

Insects

• What is it that has you annoyed or "bugged" in life

• Minor irritations

Intercourse

• This is a complex and complicated dream symbol because the interpretations vary with each dreamer and with the situation in the dream. A sexual dream may be about physical pleasure but it may also be about power, control, manipulation and effectiveness.

• It shows to you your relationship with your True Self as represented by the characteristics and attitudes of those involved.

Intruder

• An unconscious part of you trying to get your attention

• The intruder may be a symbol of your guilt and self-indulgent attitudes or behaviors

• If you had a fearful experience with an intruder in real-life, you may be reliving that experience and hopefully letting go of the fears or perhaps you are dealing with other resulting feelings from the experience.

• Are there attitudes or beliefs that are intruding which keep you from doing what you really desire to do?

Iris

• The Goddess of the rainbow. She is a messenger that represents the link between heaven and earth and between gods and men.
• Beauty
• The center of the eye or center of what we see
• Because the iris in the eye is round, it can represent wholeness, completeness or eternity.

Island

• Consider your feelings and mood in this dream. Was the island a place of rest, peace and solitude? If the answer is yes, it suggests that you may need time to yourself for restoration and renewal.
• The sea or the ocean generally symbolizes your inner world.
• If you were very lonely or fearful of the waters around you, it may be an indication that you are unwilling to look deeply into yourself. Perhaps you are afraid of that which is buried beneath your conscious thoughts and feelings.

J

Jail

• Are you feeling confined or controlled in your life? Perhaps you need to control or contain yourself in your everyday activities.
• Are you feeling a need to punish yourself? Forgive yourself and move on.
• Do you feel a fear of being trapped emotionally or physically?

• If you are the jailer in a dream, you may have an unconscious desire to exert control over others or over a particular situation.

• Obstacles in your life that may be hard to overcome

Jaw

• A sign of communication

• If the jaw is tightly closed, you may need to be more open in your communication.

• Are your communications concise and to the point, or are they sometimes too verbose as denoted by "jawing" which is being boring and long-winded?

• A square jaw indicates strength and toughness. Do you need to be stronger in your life?

Jealousy

• Being unaware of your jealousies during the day may cause you to dream about them.

• Jealousy is usually a result of insecurity. Analyze some of your feelings of insecurity or inadequacy and begin dealing with these issues.

Jesus

• Powerful sign of the God force within

• Unconditional love

• Forgiveness

• Healing

• Spiritual attunement to higher energies

• Can also represent sacrifice or martyrdom. Are you sacrificing yourself for others? Doing this at the expense of following your heart benefits no one in the long run. Do you feel like a martyr in your life?

Jewelry

• That which is precious, abundant and brilliant

• A possible sign of riches either spiritually or physically. Look for the jewels in life.

• Materialistic values

• For a man this dream may symbolize material wealth and for a woman, love

• What type of jewelry it is? Is it genuine or costume? How did you react to it and in which way was it important in the dream?

Journey

• A time of self-exploration and growth

• It represents your path in life or a part of your life's journey.

• Notice the mode of transportation you are using. This will give greater insights into the meaning of your journey.

• Do you need to take a journey?

Judge

• Self judgement

• Guidance from your Higher Self

Jungle

• The wild, intuitive part of yourself

• "It's a jungle out there" is a common saying. Perhaps it represents your difficult, confusing and overwhelming feelings regarding daily life.

• If it is an impenetrable jungle, your unconscious may be revealing the anxiety you have about a particular situation, a current difficulty, or the future.

• If you find yourself freely exploring the jungle, it might be encouraging you to discover unexplored areas of your own psyche.

Jupiter (Zeus)

• Greek god Zeus and the Roman god Jupiter are one and the same. Zeus is the god of gods. He is the creator of day, thunder and lightning, the seasons

and is the "sky god." He represents external order and authority. Jupiter, or Zeus, is a "good father" that provides the opportunity for growth, development, prosperity and health.
• Jupiter, as a planet, has a central position among the other planets in the solar system.
• Astrologically, Jupiter represents balance, organization, abundance and optimism.
• If things are not going too well or if you feel disorganized, this dream may be calling for awareness of supportive internal and external forces.
• Jupiter is a reminder that there is an order to the universe that provides us with an opportunity to have a prosperous, balanced and joyful life.

Kangaroo

• The kangaroo is a strong and powerful animal. It has huge feet that it uses for mobility and self-protection. Your dream may have to with issues of strength, freedom to move, and grounding.
• A sign for great leaps forward in your life
• Mobility

Key

• Are you trying to figure out or unlock a mystery? Perhaps the key to the solution is at hand.
• Keys are about opening doors for yourself on the spiritual and physical plane. You are probably going through or will go through a new door of perception.

• Are you locking something up or are you opening the door?

Kidnaping

• The main theme in abduction dreams is fear, feeling out of control in a situation or feeling victimized. Are you feeling like a victim? Are you sabotaging yourself? Consider the details of your dream and try to isolate or identify the fear that created the dream. Are you afraid of leaving home, childhood, a familiar support group, or long standing ideas? These type of dreams may be most prevalent during times of psychological or physical transition and during stressful times of life when the future is somewhat uncertain.

Killing

• What feelings do you have in association with this sign?

• Most generally it means that you are releasing or need to release attitudes or beliefs that aren't serving your highest good at the present time.

• It could represent hostile feelings surfacing. Consider this as an opportunity to look at your negative feelings and decide what would be the best and the least destructive way to address them.

• If you witness a killing, you are probably being shown the changes going on inside of yourself.

• Are you feeling a loss of life and energy?

• Do you have a subconscious death wish?

King

• Power and majesty. Do you need to step into your own majesty?

• God, the King of kings

• A sign of authority, self-responsibility, and taking charge of your own life

• Archetypal man, the male expression of the ruling or governing principle.

• The coronation of the king is a high honor, hence the king may represent the essential male within us all.

Kiss

• Warmth, affection or love

• It can also represent a deep communion with yourself

• You may be expressing feelings that are difficult to express during the day

• If you don't receive enough love and affection in your daily life, then this could be a compensatory dream, where you are comforting or loving yourself.

• If you are kissing the object of your affection, the dream could represent your acceptance and love for the part of yourself symbolized by the object

Kitchen

• Houses in dreams generally represent the dreamer. The kitchen is the heart of the house. For most families, the kitchen is a place of warmth and nourishment both emotionally and physically. Pay attention to the conditions of your dream kitchen to become aware of emotional needs and feelings toward yourself or others.

• A need for spiritual food

Kite

• A symbol of spiritual soaring which is grounded and anchored

• Childlike freedom

Knees

• Flexibility

• Is your attachment to worldly possessions a burden to the point your knees can't bend properly?

• Knees can represent fear as when they shake or buckle in certain situations
• Being in awe of something or kneeling to worship. Do you need to worship your creator?

Knife

• Knives may represent a fear of being penetrated emotionally, physically or sexually.
• Are you feeling knifed in the back?
• They are used to cut things? Is there something in your life that needs to be cut out, such as old patterns of thinking?
• Knives can also be a sign of either creative or destructive forces.

Knock

• A new awareness or part of yourself trying to make itself known to you
• Opportunity knocking at the door

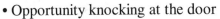

Ladder

• Attaining a higher awareness. Reaching new heights in life.
• Movement toward a goal
• It suggests hard work and an exertion of energy
• Symbolic of the "way to heaven," as in Jacob's ladder . . . perhaps the heaven within.
• Are you climbing up the ladder of success or descending into the subconscious and the feelings contained deep inside?
• If you are going down the ladder perhaps your fortunes are diminishing.

• Missing rungs may represent missing elements or hardships and handicaps you are or have been encountering on your way to bigger and better things in life.

Ladybug

• A sign of good luck
• Because of the familiar rhyme, "Ladybug, ladybug, fly away home, your house is on fire..." it may indicate that you need to tend to your personal affairs at home.
• Perhaps the colors of the ladybug have a message for you. See the meaning of specific colors under Colors.

Lake

• Your Self with the surface (consciousness) and depths (the unconscious)
• Water represents your feelings and inner world. Therefore, a still clear lake represents intuition, deep inner wisdom and emotional balance. Choppy water may indicate emotional turmoil. A murky lake can represent stagnant feelings.
•Anything on the water represents a part of your unconscious showing you some unseen issue or problem. See also **Water** for more information.

Lamb

• Purity, gentleness, warmth, love, innocence, and for the spiritually-minded, the Lamb of God. Is it time for you to be more like all or one of these characteristics?
• Another interpretation of this symbol would be that the lamb in your dream is a "sacrificial" lamb, or "lamb going to the slaughter." Are you being made a sacrificial lamb? Let out your inner lion.

• Scriptures talk of the "lamb and lion lying down together." This has to do with balancing your good and bad attributes, bringing all opposites together in harmony within yourself.

Lameness

• What self imposed things are keeping you from stepping forward in life?

• Are you feeling ineffective? Perhaps you can change the way you feel.

• Are you afraid to move forward in life? Do you fear change?

Lamp/Lantern

• Your inner light

• Are you allowing your light to shine forth?

Land

• A solid foundation. Being grounded and down to earth.

• Are you on solid ground in your life?

• Do you need to create supportive structures in your life?

Large intestine/Colon

• The large intestine allows the release of toxic matter. Maybe it is time to release that which you do not need or use.

• The colon sends nutrients to your body. Are you assimilating spiritual food and information in your life effectively?

• Do you have the guts to move forward?

Lateness

• Perhaps you need to be more perceptive and use more foresight when making plans

• Lateness suggests that you may be feeling unprepared and distracted in a particular situation in daily life or in regard to long term goals.

Laughter

> • Genuine laughter is very healing. Are you willing to laugh at yourself and the things that happen in life?
> • Do you take yourself or life too seriously?

Laundry

> • Do you need to clean up your act? Does your personal life need some cleaning up?
> • What is your association with laundry and how does it represent an aspect of yourself or something you need to do?

Lava

> • Something that has been suppressed for a long time, usually negative feelings such as anger. Do you need to constructively release your anger or other negative feelings?

Lavender (*see* also **Colors**)

> • A sweet smell
> • Lavender essential oil is good for nearly any kind of ailment. Do you need a cure all?

Leak

> • Any type of a leak is usually a waste of energy and resources. Where are you wasting energy and resources (be it in your daily life, emotional life or thinking)?
> • Is information being "leaked" from the unconscious to the conscious? The leaking water may represent emotions, thoughts, or insights entering slowly into your conscious experience.

Leather

> • A sign of strength
> • Is there a situation in your life that requires you to be as tough as leather?

• May represent how you deal with all that goes on around you. Is your "hide" tough enough to take it?

Leaves

• A sign of growth and abundance
• If the leaves are green, healthy and vibrant, it could represent an achievement.
• Are you getting ready to "leave" someone? Is someone about to leave you?
• Autumn leaves may represent things you are releasing because it is time to do so.

Leech

• Parasites that drain your energy and your resources
• What are the things in your life that are draining from you?
• They may represent your habits, thoughts, and negative emotions.
• In some places they are harvested and used for infection or other physical conditions where a poisonous or harmful substance needed to be removed from the body. Maybe the leeches are in your dream to suck out the negativity that you acquire throughout your day or in a particular situation.

Left

• The receptive forces of the universe. Do you need to be more receptive and open in your life?
• Do you feel "left out?"

Legs

• Your foundation
• Weak legs could mean a lack of a firm foundation or a lack of feeling centered.
• Strong legs suggest being well supported and on a firm foundation.
• Do you feel like you don't have a leg to stand on?

Lemon

• Lemons are a cleansing and purifying agent. They not only cleanse your body but your feelings as well.

• Sometimes things are "real lemons," meaning that something is poorly constructed.

Leopard

• A sign of prowess, cunning and stealth

• It is also a sign of ferocity, valor and power

• Do you need to incorporate the strengths of the Leopard into your life?

Letter

• A letter usually represents receiving news, information, or messages from someone specific, from your unconscious, or from the world at large.

• If you look forward to mail, the letter may have a positive meaning for you. However, if you dread the envelops which typically hold the monthly bills, then this dream may have a negative and anxiety provoking meaning.

• You may be coming into greater awareness about some aspect of your life, having new realizations, increasing self- understanding, or getting to the truth of things that concern you.

Letters of the Alphabet (*see* also **Names**)

• The list below has two parts. The first part has to do with possible character traits of people in your dream or life. To determine what another persons name may reflect about you, first look up the letter that begins their first name. The characteristics of this letter has the most significance. Add these to the characteristics from the last letter of their last name. This will give you a more complete picture of what certain people represent about you in your dreams.

You can also look up all the letters in their name to see if other characteristics apply to you. The last letter of the first name and beginning letter of the last name are also significant letters to pay attention to. For fun, look at the beginning letter of your own first name now and see if the characteristics apply.

The second part has to do with the *shape and/or direction each letter is facing.* This can also have symbolic meaning. After reading the ideas below for the letter/s in question, pay particular attention to the ideas that come to your mind. Don't limit yourself to the ideas listed, rather let them be your jumping off place.

A . . . action, activity; shaped like a pyramid with a ladder rung in the middle

B . . . beauty, brains, strong sense of color; male energy on the left (line) and female energy on the right (two half circles).

C . . . cautious, curious, courageous; incomplete circle on the right

D . . . domestic, dramatic; a pillar, male on the left and half circle or feminine energy on the right

E . . . expressive in an artistic way; a pillar with three lines facing right, outward

F . . . friendly and forthright; a pillar with two lines facing right, outward

G . . . go getter in a friendly; incomplete circle with horizontal line cutting it off on the right, outward side

H . . . hope, health, heart; a ladder, two
  pillars, standing firm and balanced

I . . . insatiable; pillar, strength

J . . . justice; a pillar with a hook on the left
  bottom side

K . . . power; a pillar with lines of energy
  connecting from the center (heart) up
  to heaven and down to earth

L . . . learn, love, a good heart; a pillar with
  line extending from the base or
  ground level toward the right,
  outward physical side

M . . . motherly, manipulation, management;
  moving up and down, up and down,
  vibration or two pillars with arms
  open to receive from above

N . . . neat, nice, nasty; moving up and
  down, vibration

O . . . obsessive, obstinate; circle,
  completeness, wholeness

P . . . pensive, pretty; a pillar with half circle
  on the upper half facing right,
  thoughts connected to feelings

Q . . . quick, quiet, quirky; circle,
  completeness, wholeness with line
  going out or coming in from the
  bottom or ground level or grounded
  wholeness

R . . . reason and rhyme, everything has to
  make sense; pillar with lines going
  out from the center, connecting
  feelings (heart) with the thoughts
  (top part of the R) and being

grounded (bottom extension of the R).

S . . . Self (concerned with), success, leadership; snake, flowing, transformation

T . . . lack of trust in Self, doubt; a pillar with line on top perhaps stopping the flow of an upward movement of energy, strong thoughts

U . . . universal understanding, sensitivity; cup, container, receiving

V . . . vitality, vivacious, victory; up stretched arms, receiving

W . . . wise, wilful, stubborn; two sets of arms upraised receiving from above, up and down motion, vibration

X . . . anything in excess; coming to the center from four directions, going out in four directions or being x'd out

Y . . . yin, yang, thinks in two ways; a pillar with up stretched arms receiving from above, strength in receiving

Z . . . zigzag, can do two things at once; moving back and forth from right to left, back and forth between thinking to feeling, moving back and forth between the outer world and inner world

Library
- Your inner knowledge and resources
- Are you trying to assimilate some new information or idea?

• A place of learning suggesting that you may be close to solving a problem or discovering something new and exciting

Light

• The Spirit or God
• The spiritual light within you
• Hope. There's "light at the end of the tunnel."
• Enlightenment
• Lifting of shadows
• The acquisition of understanding and knowledge
• A positive force
• It may represent a well-lit journey through life
• A solution to a current problem
• Consciousness

Lightning

• Great power
• A break-through may be on its way
• Energy
• An altering force
• The "awakened" state of consciousness
• Try to connect it to important and highly charged events from your daily life which have suddenly occurred or come into your awareness.

Lion

• Feelings that you have not dealt with or dangers (hurtful and negative things) being "swallowed" by the unconscious.
• The lion is a symbol of social distinction and leadership.

Lips

• Symbols of communication
•Can be symbols of sexuality and sensuality

Liver

• Anger

Lizard

• Because they stay in the shadows during the heat of the day, they are considered to be keepers of the shadow lands and dream time, as well as keepers of dreams. Therefore, they represent your subconscious mind and your inner shadow lands.

• What are your fears and recurring negative feelings?

Lock

• If things are locked up and we don't have the key, then it is impossible for us to get to it. Are you the one that is locked up inside, or are opportunities closed to you? Are you shutting yourself away from the realities of the world?

• Things that are currently inaccessible to you

• May be a symbol of security

Lost

• Are you unsure of who you are or where you are going?

• Do you need to pay more attention to your inner guidance?

Lotus

• Spiritual awakening

Love

• There is nothing more important to your emotional, psychological, or spiritual well-being than love. It is a vital part of any growth process. We need to have a healthy dose of self-love so that we can, in turn, love the world.

• It is about acceptance and belonging. To be loved is to feel accepted and have a sense of belonging.

• The dream may be wish-fulfilling or compensatory in nature. Perhaps you aren't feeling loved in your life.

• Love is ultimately who you are, your divine nature.

Lungs

• The breath of life
• Taking in life and taking charge of your life
• Are you living life to the fullest?
• Sometimes associated with grief. Are you grieving over something?
• Do you need more space to breathe?

Magic

• Mystical powers
• Do you need to listen to your inner magic?

Magician

• Someone who channels power from the inner to the outer realms
• Transformation and manifestation
• The magician creates illusions. Is there something in your life that appears real but is in fact an illusion?
• Sage or wise man

Mail (*see* **Letter**)

Man/Male

• The male part of yourself. Females have a male side as well as a female side.
• The focused, conscious part of you
• You may dream about your father, son, husband, or friend. These should therefore be interpreted according to the details of the dream, remembering that they reflect aspects of yourself.

• A father figure may represent collective consciousness and the traditional human spirit. He is the Yang and his energy creates the earthly realities.

• The masculine figure could be interpreted as the Creator or Destroyer.

• At times, women dream about men that are strangers to them. These men may represent the women's unconscious psychic energy. They play a vital role in obtaining a deeper understanding of the Self.

• At times, a strange and ominous man in men's dreams represents their "shadow" or the negative and darker sides of their personality.

Mandala

• A mandala is a circle or a square surrounding a central point, with spiritual geometric forms or sacred paintings within it.

• Mandalas represent the whole Self and the entire universe

• A symbol of harmony, beauty and balance

Map

• Do you need to plan your inner and outer journeys?

• The interpretation depends on whether you are following a map to a particular destination and you feel good about it, or whether you are trying to follow a confusing chart. A confusing chart may indicate that you lack a clear sense of direction in your everyday life or that you are in the midst of changing long term plans. Following a good map in your dreams suggest that you are feeling confident in your current path and pursuits.

Maroon (*see* under **Colors**)

Marriage

- Uniting of the male and female parts within yourself
- Integrating the various parts of yourself
- Your conscious and unconscious elements are becoming more familiar and are embracing one another
- It can also represent a coming together of ideas
- Having to do with commitment
- What are your views about marriage?

Mars (Ares)

- It is named after the Greek god Ares and Roman god Mars. He was originally the god of farming, fertility and prosperity of the harvest. Later, after the Romans came into contact with Greek culture, he became the god of war, spring and youth.
- Mars represents energy, aggression, violence, desire, male sexual organs and sometimes the symbol of life and death

- Frustrations that lead to aggressive thoughts and feelings
- Mars can represent small disharmony in your life
- It may be a sign to focus and direct your power toward prosperity.

Masks

- Different aspects of yourself, your persona and how you appear to others. The roles that you play in life such as parent, student, or worker.
- On the other hand, masks can be a symbol of pretentiousness. If you are wearing a mask, look inside and check if you are being sincere in your presentations, or if you are hiding and pretending to be something you are not.

• If other people are wearing masks, remember that they represent aspects of you as well. What are you hiding that you don't recognize as being a part of yourself?

• Are you in need of transformation? During initiations in native cultures, they wore masks to hide themselves because the rituals of transformation were so mysterious and awesome.

Maze

•Your current mental outlook

• If in your dream you are trapped in a maze and are having difficulty getting to the end, perhaps you need to stop and consider your current emotional and psychological status. Are you often confused and unsure of which way to go? Listen to the voice within.

• This could be a homophone for "maize," the staff of life for the early Native Americans

• If you are facing many hard decisions, perhaps this is a sign that you need to step back and look at the whole picture.

• Are you emotionally disorganized?

Meadow

• A place of beauty, spiritual harmony and balance. It is also a place of rest that is very nurturing and healing.

Meat

• The edible part of an animal or fruit; nourishment

• The essence, substance or gist of something

• A homophone for "meet."

Medicine

• Used to restore one's health and balance. Your unconscious mind may be encouraging you to take measures to insure your health. Consider all of the details of your dream and decide if the medication taken was helpful or hurtful. Try to connect these thoughts to your situations in daily life.

• Are you getting a "taste of your own medicine?"

Meditation

• Perhaps your Higher Self would like to communicate with you. Be silent and listen.

Melody/Song (*see* also **Music**)

• Nice sounds are usually positive symbols. What kind of melody was it?

• More than likely, the song that you are dreaming about has messages in it that will assist you in solving a problem or will help you to feel better.

Melting

• Perhaps you are melting the barriers between yourself and other people or between the various parts of yourself.

• Are you melting old structures to create room for new understandings?

• Melting may indicate the advent of a dramatic inner change because you are letting go of personal form and structure.

• Melting ice may represent repressed feelings that are being freed.

• Metal melting by fire may symbolize form being transformed into spirit.

Menstruation

• Releasing the old and embracing a new beginning

• Connected to the female cycles of the earth and the moon. Are you tuning in to your own inner cycles?

• A time for introspection and stillness, a time to go within and tap into your inner resources.

Mercury (Hermes)

> • As a metal, mercury is a universal alchemical symbol representing the yin. It is the symbol of the passive state which may be found deep within.
>
> • It is quick, changeable in temperament and volatile. Are you like this?
>
> • Mercury was the messenger of the gods and the bearer of messages. Perhaps you will be receiving a good message. It may represent your need for communication, adaptation and movement.
>
> • This symbol may be calling your attention to more personal matters, suggesting a need to look carefully into your internal world.

Mermaid/Merman

> • These symbols can represent spiritual and magical communion with your feelings and the depths of your being.
>
> • Is there a conflict between your thought and your feelings?

Milk

> • Milk is a symbol of nourishment and it suggests, depending on the details, that you are giving or receiving an adequate amount of support and consideration from your environment.
>
> • Fresh milk can represent the milk of human kindness.
>
> • Sour milk represents something that went sour.
>
> • Are you taking time to nurture yourself?

Mirror

> • A reflection of yourself. What is it you see?
>
> • If you see a clear image, you may be getting a glimpse of your True Self.

• Broken mirrors always seem to be a sign of bad luck, or, at least, represent distortions in the way you see things.

• Do you need to reflect on what is really going on in your life and who you really are?

• Confront yourself and see yourself as you really are.

Miscarriage

• Your plans may need to be aborted or perhaps they won't be fulfilled.

• A miscarriage of a fetus could represent bringing unresolved feelings to the surface to be healed and released.

Missing the Boat/Plane/Train

• Are you feeling a lack of progress or feeling left out in your life?

• A missed opportunity

• Do you need to put forth more effort to complete your plans or projects? What is most important to you?

Mist

• The mystical inner realms

• Mist may represent your subconscious mind and something with which you are not coming to terms.

• Homophone for "missed." What have you missed out on? Are you missing something or being missed?

Mole

• Something beneath the surface in your life that you are unwilling to let others see or that you deny about yourself.

Money

• Whatever money means to you in your waking state is reflected in your dreams.

• Money is a symbol of power and wealth. It represents those things that are most valuable to you and not necessarily cash. What is it that you place the most value in?

• Coins can represent a change coming in your life.

• Finding money may be telling you that you are in the process of acquiring valuable character traits.

Monkey

• Playfulness

• "Monkeying around"

• Do you take life too seriously?

Monster

• We have to include this symbol. Dreaming about monsters and demons is very common. They may represent negative forces inside of yourself and in your life.

• Most of the monsters are representing your own negative characteristics and tendencies or hidden fears.

• The way that you deal with the monster is generally symbolic of the way you are dealing with the corresponding negativity in your daily life.

• If you wake up frightened by monsters, just remember that their purpose is to teach you something about yourself.

• It has often been my experience that my children have bad dreams of monsters on occasion right before they get sick. Therefore, they may represent the negative feelings that are being released by way of illness which is often a cleansing of the body.

Moon

• Feminine energy

• The moon is associated with the irrational and the intuitive.

M

• The moon could represent romance and your earthly impulses and passions.

• It could reveal things about the nature of soul and the unconscious.

• Sometimes the moon is a sign of poetry and inspiration.

• The phases of the moon indicate different states of mind or being. A full moon represents wholeness and creativity. A new moon or crescent moon may indicate a time of reflection.

• Fertility

Moose

• A moose may represent how you feel about yourself; your self-esteem.

• Moose appear to be very awkward and yet they are very capable. Do you need to give yourself more credit for what you are doing?

Moth

• Moths will beat themselves against a light until they die. Do you have perseverance beyond reason? Are you working at something without ever achieving your desired results?

• Moths eat holes in clothes in dark closets. Is something eating away at you with or without your awareness?

Mother

• The relationship that you have with your mother is the most psychologically significant relationship of all.

• The general image of mother in a dream symbolizes a variety of feelings and ideas: caring, nurturing, love, acceptance, hard work, sacrifice, etc.

• The mother in your dream could also represent the "collective unconscious," the source of the "water of life," and the yin.

• The woman is that force, or current, inside of you that nudges you on and inspires you. It is your intuition and the knowledge that is not necessarily attached to words.

• The mother can be the wise woman who dwells inside of you.

Mountain

• A mountain is an attainable goal or opportunity whether spiritual, emotional, or material.

• Going up the mountain means you are progressing toward your goal.

• Going down the mountain means that you are either moving away from the goal or are now enjoying some easy sailing after your hard trip up the mountain.

• A mountain may represent spirituality or mental development and self-awareness.

• Do you feel like you are struggling to attain insurmountable heights? You can do it!

• Are you making a mountain out of a molehill?

Mountain lion

• Leadership, responsibility

• Strength and courage

• Your pride or tendency to be regal or fit for a king

Mouse

• Timidity or fear

• Do you feel a need to be quiet as a mouse, to quiet the inner chatter?

• Scrutiny, paying attention to details

• Every detail carries weight, look at yourself carefully and listen for what message is being sent.

• See what is right before your eyes and take action accordingly.
• Are you putting off something that needs to be done right now?

Mouth

• A sign of communication and verbal expression
• Power of speech
• Are you speaking your truth? Are you willing to express yourself freely and openly?
• "Mouthing off" is speaking with a lack of respect. Are you guilty of this or do you need to speak up more?
• Someone with a "big mouth" is perhaps a gossip
• May represent sensuality, sexuality and kissing or expressing these things.

Movies

• Observing life instead of participating in it
• Are you being caught up in the drama of life?
• The different roles you play in life
• Perhaps it's time to make a "move"
• Entertainment

Mud

• Are you stuck in the mud of life?
• Are things muddy and unclear?
• Negative feelings
• Are you willing to roll up your sleeves, really live life and get dirty?
• A union of the most basic aspect of earth with the transformative energy of water.

Mule

• Being stubborn
• A mule has the ability to carry a heavy load. Are you carrying too heavy of a burden?

Murder (*see* **Killing**)
Music

    • Music is healing to the soul, and as you are listening to it in your dream, you may be connected to the wonderful, creative spirit or flow of life suggesting a degree of inner harmony and emotional expression.

    • Notice the way you react to the music. Are you in rhythm with your life?

    • Music that is out of tune may be showing that you are feeling at odds with your life.

    • Music reflects your inner state.

    • The words of the music may contain messages for you. Sometimes the name of the song carries a powerful message.

Musical Instruments

    • Each instrument symbolizes something different:

        Drums . . . staying with the beat, marching to a different drummer

        Harmonica . . . the wandering minstrel, time with friends, delight

        Harp . . . angels, celestial alignment

        Piano . . . keys of life or balance of black and white, good and bad

𝑛

Nail

    • The small things that support larger structures. They hold the components of projects or ideas together. Do you have the details in place for what you are doing?

• How is your aim in life? Are you "Hitting the nail on the head?" Are you getting to the main part of your problem?

• Have you been "nailed," or caught doing something you ought not to be?

• "Spitting nails" refers to being extremely angry.

• Biting your finger*nails* has to do with anxiety or feeling spiteful.

Nakedness

• Nakedness is a sign of total freedom and honesty.

• Childlike freedom and exhilaration

• Nakedness can represent extreme vulnerability or feeling exposed.

• For some, nakedness is associated with shame because of the repression or personal trauma experienced regarding the body.

• Exposing a situation

• Baring your soul. Being open and frank.

• Sensuality or reveling in your passions and in your body

Names

• Pay attention to the names of the people in your dreams. Names can carry important messages. If a person's name is highlighted it may be a symbol for the name of a city or location. Does the name rhyme with something else in the dream? What does the name bring to mind? Don't lock yourself into the idea of it only being the name of a person. Free association can be very helpful in determining the meaning of a name.

• There is power and meaning in the letters in a name. Each letter and the unique combination of them creates a unique frequency in the universe.

You may want to look at the meanings of each letter. (*see* **Letters of the Alphabet**)

Narrow

- Having to do with feeling limited or restricted
- Focused attention and the discipline necessary to reach your goals
- Do you need to see a bigger picture?
- Perhaps you need to narrow down your options or something else in regard to what you are doing?

Nausea

- What is it that is making you sick? What is it that you don't like seeing in your life? What is it you can't stomach?
- Perhaps you are taking in information that is not for your highest good.
- Are there things in your life that aren't needed?

Navel

- It may be about your relationship to the mother aspect of yourself.
- A symbol of the center of the universe or of yourself.

Neck

- Willfulness
- Are you being willfully constructive or not?
- Taking a risk by "sticking your neck out."
- There is an energy center in your neck connected to communication. Are you speaking your truth?
- Is there something in your life that is a "pain in the neck?"
- The neck is the connection between the head (intellect) and the heart (feelings). Do you need to balance your feelings with your intellect or vice versa?

• A sign of flexibility, being willing to see both sides of an issue.

• Being "stiff necked" has to do with being immovable. Do you need to loosen up?

Nest

• A nest can represent incubating an idea or project.

• It may be a symbol for pulling inward and for rejuvenation such as when one is "nesting" which refers to creating a warm, cozy, safe place within your home.

Net

• Perhaps you are caught in a web or net.

• A fishing net may be a symbol of catching that which is represented by a fish. (*see* **Fish**) Apply this idea to the type of net in your dream and what you were trying to catch or do with it.

• Are you doing things that require a safety net?

Night

• Night represents the realms of the feminine principle, the place of dreams, mysteries and the subconscious mind.

• Night time and darkness precede the creation of all things, it is therefore a symbol of germination and fertility.

• Night sometimes represents not being in touch with your inner knowing.

• If the stars are visible or the moon is shining, it can represent your intuition and your inner realms.

• Extreme darkness suggests that you are hiding something or are unwilling to see things clearly. The darkness may represent a lack of awareness and illumination.

• Are there areas of your life or personal experience that need warmth, light, and airing?

Nightmare

(Imagine...finding "nightmares" in this list. *Just adding a bit of "lightness" to this "nightmare."* It reminds me of the joke: "Do you know how to get rid of your night*mares*?" Feed them.)

• Nightmares bring important messages to us. They help us become aware of the unresolved issues in our waking life that we are not allowing into our consciousness. The nightmare is a way of healing these unresolved issues. Be grateful for your nightmares!

• If you have a recurring nightmare, listen to the messages. Identify any negative feelings and resolve them. Doing so will end the nightmare.

• Nightmares may suggest that you are holding on to traumatic or guilt based conflicts. You may have powerful negative feelings that require reconciliation. Nightmares are often a direct result of overwhelming feelings of fear and helplessness, or a result of an unprocessed traumatic experience.

Nine (*see* under **Numbers**)

North

• That which is above (*see* also Above)

• To North American Native Americans, the north was the realm of the ancestors, death and rebirth. To those living in the Southern Hemisphere, north was a sign of warmth and light.

• If you live in the Northern Hemisphere, the north can represent cold and darkness.

Nose

• Are you or is someone else being "nosy?"

- Is someone "nosing" into your business?
- Are you being honest with yourself or are you a "Pinocchio?"
- The nose is the most prominent protruding feature on the face. Are you wanting some recognition?

Nudity (*see* also **Nakedness**)

- Being naked in a dream suggests vulnerability and exposure
- It could be a compensation for what is going on in daily life. Are you very guarded and unwilling to let people see the "real" you or are you feeling embarrassment as a result of a mistake or emotional reaction?
- Perhaps you need to become more open with your feelings and more accessible emotionally.
- If you see yourself naked in inappropriate places, your rebellious side may be coming through and with it some fear that people may not accept you for who you really are.

Numb

- Not feeling. Are you being numb to your feelings?
- Are you suppressing something that you are afraid of?

Numbers

Since the beginning of time, numbers have had great mystical significance. There are many systems used for interpreting them. Numerology is the study of numbers prior to their use in mathematics. It is an ancient science. In this system, a number of more than one digit is first reduced to a single digit number. The main meaning of the more complex number is then taken from this single digit number. To reduce a number, you add the digits together. You continue doing this until they reduce to one single digit. For example, the number 376 would reduce to 7 by first adding 3 + 7 + 6 which equals 16. Because 16 is still two digits, you then add 1 and 6 together which equals 7. The main meaning of the original number (376 in this case) is derived from the reduced number (7). The individual digits in the number may also be considered to provide additional meaning.

It is important to remember, however, that above and beyond the meanings given to any number by any system, you first need to consider your own feelings and any associations you have with each number.

Here are a few things to keep in mind when considering the meaning of a number:

- If a number keeps appearing for you in various forms, it has stronger significance.
- Every zero after a number gives greater power to that number. For example; if you see the number 2 by itself, it will not be as powerful as 20, 200 or 2000 etc., each one increasing the significance and meaning of 2 more powerful to you.
- Sometimes when a zero appears in the middle of the number, such as in 205, you may want to treat it as two separate numbers, 2 and 5, rather than adding the 2 and 5 and using the resulting number 7 as being the most significant number to look at.
- Even numbers represent the feminine while odd numbers represent the masculine.

Remember . . . the ideas below are *only* suggestions. The most accurate meaning is the one you connect with emotionally.

❀ Zero

> • Zero can have the same meaning as a circle. The circle symbolizes infinity, completeness, and wholeness, the circle of life and the eternal unknown.
> • Perhaps you have come to a greater degree of spiritual awareness.
> • There is a possibility that you are "going in circles."

❀ One

> • Unity
> • Independence
> • Beginning or origin place
> • Individuality
> • Strength
> • Ego

❀ Two

> • The first division which can be strong if the two parts are working together or weak if they are in opposition. You need two elements in order to create.
> • Balance of the yin and yang energies (the polarities) of the universe
> • Self surrender, putting others before yourself

❀ Three

> • Three is the result of creation. It is the idea or concept which has the strength off 1 and the weaker sort of 2. It can either be manifested or changed.

• The trinity; mind, body and spirit
• Expansion, expression, communication, fun and self-expression
• Third time's the charm
• Three is an active or a process number (Something is going on in the psyche).

❀ Four

• Taking the idea or concept that has been created and bringing it into material manifestation. It is the number of the material world where things tend to be four-square.
• Security and foundations
• It is the four elements and the four directions
• Productivity, organization, wholeness and unity
• Completion and femininity

❀ Five

• This is where you begin to explore the material world further and thereby develop the ability to change and adapt to the circumstances in the material world.
• Five is the number of change, but also has to do with stability because it is the middle number in the single digit spectrum. Remember, the only thing permanent is change.
• Freedom
• Sometimes considered the Christ number.

❀ Six

• Six is the number of balance between the mental and physical aspects of an individual.
• A number of some power because of the harmony and balance that the individual has been able to achieve both within and without.

- Compassion, love, service, social responsibility, beauty, the arts, generosity, concern and caring
- It also may relate to children and community service.

❀ Seven

- Seven is the number of spiritual awareness.
- The things you learn in your spiritual advancement
- The inner life and inner wisdom
- A mystical number symbolizing wisdom and the seven chakras or energy centers in the body, and the seven heavens.
- A symbol of birth, and rebirth, religious strength, the path of solitude and contemplation.
- A sacred number in Christianity and Judaism; the highest stage of illumination and spirituality.

❀ Eight

- Another number of power and weakness
- It symbolizes the ability to balance the spiritual knowledge gained at the 7 with material and mental understanding. When these are in balance they represent true power.
- Sometimes associated with money
- Integration

❀ Nine

- It is the number of completion in which the individual has achieved a balancing and a functioning at all levels . . . physical, mental and spiritual and emotional.
- Humanitarianism, selflessness, and dedication of your life to others

• It is a symbol or universal compassion, tolerance and wisdom

❀ Ten

• Ten is a new beginning at another level in which the individual is becoming more aware of the meanings behind the universe.

❀ Eleven

• This is the number of increased awareness and is sometimes called the number of physical mastery.

• Developing intuition, clairvoyance, spiritual healing and other metaphysical faculties.

❀ Twelve

• The completion of another cycle which indicates the integration of yourself with the universe as a whole but it goes on to 13.

• Twelve represents time and may mark the most important cycles in life.

❀ Thirteen

• This is where things once again change and a new awareness is given.

❀ Twenty-two

• It is sometimes called the number of mental mastery and certainly involves the ability to make right choices.

• Unlimited potential of mastery in any area, physical, mental, spiritual and emotional.

❀ Thirty-three

• It is sometimes called the number of spiritual mastery and is another number of significant completion.

One of the phenomena occurring these days, is the appearance of three or more of the same number. Have you ever awakened in the middle of the night and the clock read 2:22, 3:33 or 4:44? Maybe during the day, you have glanced at the clock and it read 11:11, or 12:12. Here are some possible meanings for the numbers when they appear to you in this way. Remember the importance of the ideas that come to you.

❀ 000

- Great void
- Experiencing a null zone
- Switching or moving into a new energy field

❀ 111

- Energy flow
- Enhancing whatever level you are presently in

❀ 222

- Resurrection and ascension process

❀ 333

- Decision number
- It either directs you into a phase of 999 completion, or negatively, it puts you in the 666 frequency which throws you back into the third dimension.

❀ 444

- This is an actual resurrection number.
- It means you have just completed an important phase.

❀ 555

- Experiencing the energy or a level of Christ Consciousness

❀ **666**

- Material world
- Third-dimensional frequency
- Denseness

❀ **777**

- Symbolizes an integration of some portion of the four lower bodies with higher spiritual frequencies within the Third-dimensional plane, or at the level in which you are manifesting your physical reality on the Earth Plane.

❀ **888**

- Symbolizes infinity, the unified spiral of the physical merging with the Spiritual, moving toward the completion of the ascension process through the energies of 222 and 444.

❀ **999**

- Symbolizes the three levels of the completion

❀ **10:10**

- Moving into a new beginning(one) and moving into the pattern of the great void (zero) or a much higher resonance or frequency of Spirit.

❀ **11:11**

- Beginning of a whole new level or phase of development
- Another dimension or frequency of experience
- A portal way opening

❀ **12:12**

- A cosmic connection.
- A bridge to the future.
- Signifies a level of completion or graduation.

Nut

• Gathering of nuts for the winter symbolizes harvest and abundance.

• A nut has the potential to create an entire tree, thus it may represent new life and potential yet to unfold.

• Is someone or something driving you nuts?

O

Oak

• The oak is thought to be a world axis in many traditions.

• A symbol of strength, steady progress and solidarity.

Oar

• If you are using the oars, perhaps you are feeling in control amidst emotional imbalance.

• If you are in a boat and don't have an oar, you may be feeling adrift.

Oasis

• An oasis can be a place of refuge and rejuvenation.

• Do you need to find a personal retreat where you can replenish your inner reserves?

Obesity

• Obesity may indicate that you have issues with self-esteem and personal power.

• Fat emotionally insulates us from others and isolates us physically. Why are you feeling a need to protect yourself?

• Are you unable to express your true feelings? Give yourself permission.

• Are you stuffing your feelings? What are those feelings? Perhaps you are feeling frustrated, not good enough, unable to measure up to the expectations of others or are feeling unloved. Find ways to resolve your feelings.

Obituary

• Releasing old ideas, thoughts or beliefs

Obstacles/Obstructions

• Physical obstacles that block your way are indications that perhaps you need to reevaluate your life. What is it that is blocking your progress?

• Are you subconsciously sabotaging yourself?

• Do you need to take a risk and step beyond your own limitations?

• Do you need to leave your comfort zone?

Ocean (*see* also **Water**)

• The sea of life, your subconscious mind and intuitive power. Trust your intuition.

• Unconscious memories, feelings, individual and collective experiences

• The meaning of this symbol varies according to the condition of the water. Is the water clear or murky, calm or turbulent? Are you catching fish, or are you stranded and afraid? A calm ocean represents great inner power and emotional and spiritual balance. A rough or turbulent ocean indicates emotional upheaval.

Octopus

• It has eight legs which invokes the power of eight while propelling to the depths of the subconscious feelings

• A symbol of transformation

• In Cretan art, it represents the mystic center of the universe and the unfolding of creation.

• Are you trying to grasp many concepts at once or trying to do too many things at once?

• The octopus is shy and retiring by nature. Are you shy and afraid to show your true colors?

Office

• An office may be a symbol of production, thought processes or organization

• Is it time to get yourself organized and more structured in your business or personal life?

• Place of work or whatever you use your office for

Officer (*see* also **Police**)

• Perhaps you are feeling the need for protection. Look within for the strength of your inner Self.

• Are you feeling guilty for something you think you could or should be punished for? Perhaps your conscience is bothering you and part of you wants to be punished.

• It may also be that you are accepting authority for your own life or that you need to become aware of your own authority within.

Oil

• If there is a sticky situation in your life, perhaps it needs a little lubricating with love, negotiation or understanding to smooth it out.

• Traditionally, oil is used as a part of many religious rituals. Anointing with oil could represent that you are blessed.

• To oil someone's hand or palm is to offer a bribe or a tip. Are you trying to bribe someone or is someone trying to bribe you. Perhaps you need to give yourself a "tip" or reward for a service well rendered.

• Oil represents wealth for people who own it.

Old man/Old woman

• Carl Jung said that the wise old man is the "archetype of the spirit" and the "speaking fountainhead of the soul." Dreaming about him may attempt to bring the dreamer into awareness of the larger meaning of ones life.

• Old people in dreams represent wisdom and maturity. They may appear in your dreams at times of confusion and lack of direction, or when you need consultation and help in decision-making.

• Your Higher Self

Olive

• A symbol of peace

One (*see* under **Numbers**)

Onion

• Potential sadness

• The many layers of consciousness

Open

• Do you need to be open to life?

• The way will open to you.

• Perhaps you are being too open.

Opossum

• Diversion, playing dead

• Be clever with achieving your desires.

• Drama and surprise

• Don't get caught in the drama of your life.

Orange (*see* under **Colors**)

Orchard

• A symbol for the fruits of your labor or being fruitful in your life.

Orchestra

- Harmony and synergy
- If the orchestra is discordant, perhaps it represents discord within you.

Orgasm

- It can be an indicator of the alignment with your inner male and female energies. It is also a connection to the life force energy.
- It can also be a sign of achieving completion and satisfaction with something you are doing or a phase of your life.
- The meaning depends on your feelings associated with an orgasm and whether or not you have physically experienced one.

Orphan (*see* also **Abandoned**)

- Feeling isolated and alone
- Perhaps you are feeling guilty about abandoning or having abandoned someone or something.
- Needing to connect with other aspects of yourself such as the mother or father aspects

Ostrich

- Do you have your head in the sand so that you cannot see what is going on around you?
- Are you avoiding looking at something in your life?

Otter

- Otters are capricious, playful and fun-loving.
- Are you willing to have a little fun?

Oven

- An idea or project that is incubating within you
- A warm oven is said to have "fruitful,"or positive, connotations while a cold oven has the opposite meaning.

• "A muffin in the oven" can indicate pregnancy.

Owl

• Transformation
• The darkness of the unknown or the unconscious
• Associated with death as well as rebirth
• Wisdom from the inner realms
• Seeing in the darkness what others cannot see
• Dreaming about owls is a powerful dream, which may indicate that changes are on the way.

Oyster

• This symbol can indicate hidden beauty or beauty developing unseen, just as the pearl develops within the oyster.
• Even small irritations, such as the grain of sand within the oyster, can eventually be transformed into something of beauty.

P

Pacing

• Uncertain about your direction in life. Perhaps you need to look more closely at both sides of a situation

Pack/Packing

• Carrying a pack can represent something, someone, or an idea that you are carrying around with you that may or may not be necessary.
• Another meaning for carrying a pack may be that you have all your essential provisions with you.
• Are you preparing for change in your life?
• Are you ready or needing to "pack it in?"

Package

> • If you are sending a package, it can symbolize letting go of an attitude, pattern or belief.
> • Receiving a package may indicate that you are acknowledging a previously unrecognized part of yourself.

Pain

> • Pain is usually God trying to get your attention so that you will address problems or disharmony in your life. It lets you know that there is a problem.

Palace

> • Anciently, the palace was located in the center of the city. It symbolized the origin of creation. It is your true inner, magical kingdom, the fullness of who you are.
> • It can represent your body

Pan

> • A pan or pot can symbolize "cooking up" an idea
> • Panning for gold can mean looking for the true essence of who you are or for something else in your life.
> • Panning with a movie camera means taking in the bigger picture.
> • Does it represent the "Peter Pan" part of you?

Panda

> • Panda's are associated with tranquillity and being cuddly and lovable.

Panic

> • Panic suggests lack of control and confusion.
> • Are you feeling fear or a sense of confused helplessness?
> • Perhaps you feel you don't have what you need in order to deal with a situation at hand and therefore feel out of control.

Pants

    • Clothing generally represents the roles that you play in life and how you perceive yourself.

    • If putting on pants or changing your pants, plays a major part in your dream you may be questioning your role at work, home, or in any other area of life.

    • How the pants look, who is wearing them and your feelings are important elements to consider.

Parachute

    • Let go and enjoy the ride. The means is provided for your safety.

    • Be willing to take a risk

Parade

    • A parade is a community effort.

    • A public show. Are you willing to show yourself or what you are doing to others?

    • Remember that each person or thing in the parade is an aspect of yourself. What exactly did you see in the parade?

Paradise

    • Paradise is a place of perfect peace and love found within yourself.

    • Innocence or the fall from innocence as in Adam and Eve in "The Garden of Eden."

    • Are you facing something that you fear will take you out of your paradise or perhaps already has?

Paralysis

    • The fear that paralyzes you in the dream may be symbolic of the fear that you are experiencing in daily life. Are you feeling unable to change a current situation which was manifest in your dream in a form of paralysis?

    • "Frozen with fear." Feeling completely immobilized in some area of your life.

• This dream may be cautioning you to stay still and do nothing for now in regard to a real-life situation that you are dealing with.

Parasite

• Something draining your energy
• Perhaps there is something inside of you that is eating away at you

Parents

• This dream usually has to do with the male and female aspects of the Self. Women in dreams represent our collective unconscious and men our collective consciousness. Thus, the mother represents the inner realms of intuition, feeling and nurturing. The female aspect is that force, or current, inside of you that urges you on and inspires you. This knowledge is intuitive and unexpressed by words. The father can be a sign of your projecting force and your inner authority. The male aspect of yourself represents the active part that uses the information received to create the physical reality of your life. When the male and female aspects of yourself are working together well you have balance and experience awareness leading to peace and productivity.
• Parents can also have to do with your experience with your parents or your parenting skills.

Parking lot/Garage

• Traveling in a vehicle generally represents your journey through life, or a portion of it. If you find yourself in a garage or a parking lot, the parked car could represent a period of inactivity and indecision. The dream could be pointing out that you have been idle for a period of time and that it may be good time to "get moving." It may also be that the parked car is symbolic of a reflective period or mood.

Parrot

• Possibly a symbol of insincerity and speaking another's words without thinking. Are you expressing your own individuality?

• A symbol of the jungle, of color or expression

Party

• A time to celebrate

• Are you socializing too much?

• A political party is a coming together of people for a common cause.

• Are you being a party to something you shouldn't or should be a party to?

Passenger

• Passengers are along for the ride. They are not the one in control of steering. Is there something in your life of which you are unsure or something you feel is out of your control?

• Do you need to allow another aspect of yourself, or someone else, to take the wheel for awhile?

Passport

• Perhaps a change is just around the corner.

• It has to do with your identity. How do you feel about your identity?

• Perhaps you need to travel to a part of yourself you don't usually visit.

Path

• Your path in life. The condition of the path and the details will represent how you are doing in life. If it is a straight and narrow, it may represent being in alignment with your goals and purposes. A crooked path may indicate that you are somewhat unsure of

your direction. A rough path could be showing you the difficulties you are passing through.
• Whatever your path presents to you, it is perfect for you and for your highest good.

Pattern

• Are you following the same old pattern or creating a new way of doing things? How do you feel about the patterns in your life?
• Perhaps it is time to break out of old habits.

Peach

• Is your life peachy?
• An uplifting symbol. Consider what a peach represents to you.
• Spiritual knowledge

Peacock

• Have you heard the expression "as proud as a peacock." It may have to do with beauty and pride. Perhaps you are being too cocky or are you just extremely confident?
• Do you need to show your true colors?
• In many ancient cultures, the peacock had several meanings. In Persia, two peacocks on either side of the Tree of Life represented the polarity of man being sustained by cosmic unity. In Hindu mythology, it represented the stars and the firmament because of the patterns on the iridescent feathers. In Rome, it symbolized the deification of princesses. In some Christian art forms the peacock is shown as the symbol of immorality. So take your pick. See which meaning resonates with you.

Pearl

• Life's irritations can be transformed into a thing of beauty just like the grain of sand in the oyster.

• A pearl may represent the feminine aspect of yourself because it is associated with the moon, water and the shell which are all feminine symbols.

• Genius in obscurity

• A pearl may signify pregnancy now or in the future.

Pen/Pencil

• Perhaps you need to communicate with yourself or others. Your ability to communicate through written language is a vitally important and necessary part of life.

• A way to think and express your thoughts

• A pen symbolizes expressing yourself fluidly and is more permanent than a pencil.

• Are you feeling penned up?

Pendulum

• A sign of uncertainty or decision in your life. Are you trying to make up your mind about something? Perhaps it is time to come to decision about something.

Penguin

• The penguin is an interesting earth-bound bird that lives in and around the ocean. As a dream symbol it may represent concrete thinking.

• It may also represent feelings of being burdened by unwanted emotions, lethargy, and a need to achieve balance.

Penis

• The male principle, power and potency

• The divine, virile, propagating energy within yourself

• Your gender and sexual orientation play a part when interpreting this dream. Are you dealing with issues of sexual orientation, power, or aggression?

Penny

- Do you need to prepare for a small change in your life?
- Something with little value
- "A penny for your thoughts"

People

- Dreams are usually filled with people. When interpreting dreams with people in them, consider all of the details and your feelings in the dream. If the person is known to you, think about the characteristics of that person and consider what that person represents about you. Other people are your mirrors. What is the occupation of the person? What is the main thing that comes to mind when you think about that person?
- Strangers represent things about yourself that are "strange" or simply unknown.

Pepper

- Spicy, heated or stimulating feelings
- Do you need some spice in your life?

Perfume

- Smell affects the way we perceive everything around us. It usually causes certain feelings. What are your associated memories with the particular scent?

Perspiration

- Are you afraid or nervous about something?
- A symbol for exerting yourself. Have you been doing too much or do you need to do more?

Phone (*see* **Telephone**)

Photograph/Picture

• An objective observation of someone or a particular situation. Do you need to stand back from a situation and see it without being involved?

• Seeing old or even unfamiliar pictures in your dream may be a reflection of how you remember certain parts of your life. These pictures may represent past unresolved feelings as well.

• Dreaming of pictures may mean you have not learned a particular lesson in life. The dream may be calling attention to past events and reminding you that you are making the same errors all over again.

Physician

• A physician may represent the power or "physician" within who is the ultimate healer.

Piano (*see* also **Musical Instruments**)

• Creative expression through sound

• The piano symbolizes music, harmony, and expression. All types of sounds may be symbols of spiritual awareness.

• If the piano is out of tune, it may indicate that you are out of tune with your True Self

• If you play the piano, it may have to do with your creativity or how you feel about playing it. Do you need to spend more time creating joyful music in your life?

Pier

• Water symbolizes the unconscious and your feelings. If you were standing on a pier looking out over the ocean (or other large body of water) perhaps you were waiting for your ship or a boat to come in. If you are waiting for the opportunity to begin a new adventure, it could be reflected in this dream. Or, you may have a desire to get to know yourself better and to grow in an emotional, psychological, or spiritual way.

• Perhaps you are standing on a pier because you need or want to go on a journey in real life or an internal journey to the truth of who you are.

Pig

• In some cultures pigs are considered to be very "dirty" and unfit for human consumption.

• At times, people are referred to as "pigs" for their excessive desires or attitudes.

• They are associated with greed, stubbornness, and gluttony Are you (or someone important to you) being "hoggish" with money, time, food, energy, or personal possessions?

• In some cultures the pig is a symbol of prosperity because the families owning one are assured of food for an entire year.

Pimple

• Bringing things to a head
• Unresolved frustrations
• Hidden anger surfacing
• Perhaps there is something about yourself you don't feel good about.

Pink (*see* under **Colors**)

Pioneer

• You may be about to expand into new areas within yourself.

Pipe

• As a musical instrument, it can mean joy and freedom.
• As a tube for conducting liquids or gases, it can represent the flow of energy within.

• Native Americans use a peace pipe which symbolizes unity with spirit. Is it time to make peace with yourself and with others in your life?

Planets

• Heavenly bodies
• Perhaps you desire to explore your internal world
• Planets could also represent the way you relate to yourself. They can say something about the relationship that exists between your soul and ego. An orbiting planet could represent your ego. It is traveling around the sun (i.e. soul) and the entire thing could be a huge circle representing wholeness or the real you.

Play

• Joy and spontaneity
• Are you playing enough?
• Maybe it represents the play of life in which you are the writer, actor and director.

Pluto (Hades)

• Pluto or Hades are synonymous with hell. Pluto is the brother of Zeus and Poseidon and the ruler of the underworld, or the land of the dead. It is not only the holding place for the eternally damned, but is symbolic of the transition from death to life.
• Pluto may represent the deepest and the oldest part of the psyche. It may be the holding place of your darkest and most negative and disturbing elements or feelings. This part may also hold the greatest amount of transformative energy and power.
• Perhaps you need to explore your inner world; to face your fears and negative traits, to travel inward and thus emerge stronger and more alive than before your soulful journey began.

Pockets

• A place for safekeeping, a place in which something of value is kept.

• Things that you keep just for yourself: your memory, your secrecy, your valuable possessions, or your inner resources.

• If you were hiding your hands in the pockets, perhaps you feel a degree of helplessness in regard to some situation in daily life. It may also mean that you just need to keep your hands in your pockets in regard to a situation and do nothing.

Poison

• Is there something destructive or harmful in your life?

• Is there a fear threatening you?

Police (*see* also **Officer**)

• The police can symbolize protection and guidance.

• If the police are chasing you, it may represent a situation in your life about which you are feeling guilty. Find and face the feeling.

• Perhaps you are feeling that you can't meet all of your obligations and fear repercussions due to an unmet commitment.

• Do you feel safe?

Pond

• Feelings and intuition

• Is the pond clear and calm? If so, it represents good feelings.

• The size of the pond is an indication of the size of the feelings it represents.

Pool

• Intuition and the deep inner realms of yourself

• Swimming pools are associated with things like summer fun, rest, relaxation, vacations and training.

Porcupine

• Innocence
• Being childlike
• If life has recently dealt you a hard blow, begin again by placing your faith in the ability to overcome with joy.
• Be alert to the "quills" of life that could be coming your way.

Pregnancy

• This is a wonderful symbol indicating that you are about to give birth to a new idea, new relationship or a new way of viewing the world.
• Pregnancy may mean that you are going in a new direction.
• Perhaps you are pregnant with ideas.

Priest

• A priest may represent spiritual needs, your conscience, a desire to be virtuous, inner guidance, or your Higher Self.
• This dream could be comforting if it reassures you that there is safety and strength in spiritual things.
• Some people may have had negative experiences with clergy, therefore, a priest may have an entirely different meaning. It may be bringing up the associated feelings that have yet to be resolved.
• Your own spiritual qualities, strengths and abilities, or the spiritual forces around you

Prince

• The divine masculine part of yourself

Princess

• The divine feminine part of yourself

Prison/Prisoner

  • Self-imposed confinement. You are the only one who can imprison your spirit.

Profanity

  • Feelings inside that are unacknowledged or unexpressed

Prostitute

  • Are you prostituting yourself? Are you using your energies inappropriately?

  • This dream may be trying to balance your outwardly sterile life. Maybe you need to loosen up a bit, moving beyond the limitations you place upon yourself.

  • Is it time to revel in your sensuality?

  • Are you being untrue to yourself?

Prune

  • Does your energy feel dried and shriveled up?

  • Do you need something in your life that will allow you to loosen up or let go more easily?

Puppet

  • Are you feeling manipulated or are you manipulating others?

  • Perhaps you are giving your power away to someone or something outside yourself.

Puppy (*see* also **Dog**)

  • Puppies may represent playfulness, dependency, and carefree fun.

Purple (*see* under **Colors**)

Purse

  • A place where money and needed items are kept. What are the valuable things that you need to keep safe with you?

  • Are you tied to someone's purse strings?

Pyramid

• This ancient and powerful symbol represents the coming together of the world of man with that of God; the material with the spiritual.

• The purpose of the pyramids was to bury the dead and to assist them in reaching eternity. In this way, the pyramids were holy places.

• It is a place of initiation, where you move to a new level of awareness and a new level of understanding within yourself

• Being open to guidance from higher energies and from your Higher Self

• If you have accomplished a personal goal and feel a sense of wholeness, this dream symbol may be an affirmation of those feelings.

• The pyramid may represent your deepest desires. Whether they represent fulfilled or incomplete goals, a pyramid is a very positive dream symbol.

Python

• This represents the potent life force within you

2

P
2

Quail

• Fear or recoil in dread

Quarrel

• Inner conflict

• Perhaps it represents your inability to resolve important issues, ideas, or values

• You may be experiencing ongoing difficulty with making decisions, cannot accept authority, or you may have carried an argument from your daily life into your dream.

Quartz

• Clarity and spiritual attunement

• A transmitter and magnifier of energy

• It may also mean that you need to attend to your spiritual path and focus your spiritual energy.

Queen

• Feminine power and authority in both women and men

• Accept that you have a queenly aspect

Quest

• A spiritual journey

Quicksand

• You may be experiencing feelings of fear, helplessness and an inability to get out of a situation in your daily life.

• Do you need to open up your horizons and expand your perspective? There is always more than one way out. Instead of fighting against the situation, become one with it and open yourself to all possibilities.

Quilt

• Something used to cover up with and also for comfort.

• The different parts of a quilt may represent the harmonious coexistence of many aspects of yourself or your life.

• Your unconscious may be comforting you in this dream.

• If you lack comfort and harmony, this dream may be compensatory and is providing you with that which you need more of in daily life.

Rabbit

- Fear. What fearful thing are you putting your attention on? Be aware that the things you fear you draw to yourself.
- Are you frozen in motion? Do you need to burrow into a safe place and resolve your fears before proceeding?
- Timidity
- Rabbits tend to increase and multiplying rapidly. Is there something you need to duplicate quickly? Perhaps you need to increase a quality in yourself. Look at what is happening in your life and see how this symbol might have application.
- Rabbits can represent luck, quickness, fertility, pregnancy, or magic
- They can also symbolize the dreamer's lack of consciousness or awareness. Perhaps you are hopping from one thing to another.
- Do you react too quickly to life's situations sometimes? Perhaps more thought and planning may be needed.
- It is used at Easter reflecting newness of life
- Inner gentleness and softness

Race

- Are you competing or running from or to something?
- Perhaps you need to slow down in your everyday life.

• If you are competing, you need to consider your competitive drive and realistically look at the current challenges.

• If you are running in a race and win, your unconscious may be expressing confidence that you may or may not feel in the wakened state.

• Running in your dreams may also symbolize the energy levels, the strength, or the force that you have to get through life.

• Remember the real race is only against yourself.

Radio

• There is unlimited potential for you. You just need to tune the inner dial to the frequency of all possibilities.

• Communication and guidance from within. Tune in.

Rain

• Water represents feelings. Are you going through an emotionally cleansing experience?

• Unresolved grief

• A resolution to a problem may be arriving.

• You may be entering into a fertile time in your life.

• Dark clouds and a heavy downpour may indicate feelings of isolation and helplessness or unconscious material and emotions attempting to enter your conscious mind.

Rainbow

• A blessing

• A message from spirit indicating that you are going in the right direction.

• Joy, celebration and completion

• Usually a rainbow follows a rainstorm. If so, you have weathered a difficult time that is coming to a close.

• Good luck

Ram

• Symbol for the astrological sign Aries
• As the ram charges forward it represents the pioneering spirit
• Initiation of new projects and ideas
• Masculine thrusting strength. Take life by the horns and charge forward.

Rape

• Because rape is a brutal and deeply personal violation, it suggests that the you may be feeling robbed of options and negated as a human being.
• Rape in a dream is about power, control, anger, and other very destructive emotions. What areas of your life that causes you great anxiety and fear?
• If you were a rape victim, the traumatic nature of this experience may cause you to have a dream like this from time to time as you process the feelings associated with your experience.
• Sometimes when childhood memories of abuse begin to surface, this symbol will appear in dreams.

Rat

• Betrayal. Are you ratting on someone or is someone ratting on you?
• Are you letting something gnaw at you?
• Do you live or work in a rat's nest? Better clean it up.
• Danger, poverty, filth, and illness
• Things in your life that disgust or appall you. These are things that need to be integrated into yourself.

Raven

• Unknown darkest parts of yourself

Red (*see* under **Colors**)

Refrigerator

- Are your feelings frozen or cold?
- Are you feeling closed off from those around you or from your own feelings?
- Spiritual food that has been preserved for you.

Relationships

- Relationships represent the different sides of your personality.

Resurrection

- The word resurrection has positive and miraculous implications. Jesus resurrected on the third day. The theme of resurrection is explored in all cultures and religions. Perhaps you are awakening your own spiritual nature.
- New energy
- Some feel that dreams about resurrection are symbolic of reincarnation.

Right

- The right side of the brain is associated with fluid intelligence, nonverbal reasoning, and creativity.
- Are you concerned with direction or being right?
- Maybe it is telling you that you are on a right path or doing the right thing.
- The right side in dreams can represent the physical, conscious realms.

Ring

- The continuous circle of life.
- Completion, wholeness
- Friendship, engagement and marriage
- Eternal love
- If the ring is a noise, it can be interpreted as an attention seeking message or if it is a pleasant

ringing, it may be a "joyful" noise and the sound of
God.

River

- The river of life or the river of time
- Movement and the rhythm of change
- Go with the flow
- Water sustains life and is the most abundant
compound in all living things
- It may represent the flow of your energies
- Your feelings. Examine the details of your dream
to better understand the feelings and what it
represents about them. Is the water clear or murky?
Is it fast-moving, turbulent, or stagnant? Are you
just floating along its currents or actively controlling
your movements?

Road

- Your direction or a road in your life. It could be
the road to your heart, spirit, or mind.
- The road you take to achieve your goals.
- Consider the kind of road that your are on and see
how it relates to your daily realities. If the road is
straight, well-marked and lit, it may be
reinforcement to you that you are moving in the
right directions. If there are many obstacles and the
road is very hard, you may want to reconsider where
you are traveling.

Robber/Robbery

- Do you feel like a victim? Do you feel like you are
at the mercy of what happens?
- Are you removing things or situations from your
life that are actually for your good?
- Insecurity

Robin

- First sign of spring or new life in the north

• A time for introspection when they are flying south
• Joy

Rocket

• Soaring to spiritual heights

Rocks

• A symbol of strength, permanence, solidity and a firm foundation.
• A rock represents being grounded.
• Rocks can also represent physical obstacles, or difficulties which you may need to overcome.

Roller coaster

• The emotional ups and downs that you are experiencing. Although, this ride can be fun, it can also seem out of control and even be a frightening experience.
• Perhaps you need to achieve greater emotional balance. Sever changes in mood and temperament are draining and unproductive.

Roof

• Your general protection in life
• A roof may have to do with your thoughts or head.
 • If you are dreaming about a leaky roof, new information may be trying to get into your conscious awareness.
• A roof may represent a barrier between states of consciousness.

Room

• An aspect of yourself
• What is the room usually used for?
• Do you need to make room for something in your life?
• Are you giving yourself room to grow spiritually?

Rooster

> • The rooster represents male energy and possibly aggression. They are very aggressive, demanding, and territorial.
>
> • A rooster crowing is a traditional wake-up call on a farm while in literature it is sometimes symbolic of some type of a warning. Do you need a wake-up call?

Rope

> • A rope can symbolize a lifeline.
> • An attachment to a person, place or thing.
> • Are you feeling tied up?

Rose

> • Femininity
> • Beauty
> • Love or romance
> • Roses may have spiritual significance
> • The mystic center of the heart
> • They unfold and can be considered symbols of innocence
> • Pay attention to the color of the rose, as well as the details of the dream when making an interpretation.

Running

> • Running away can be running from something you are not ready to see, running from something you are unsure of or afraid of, or running from a situation you don't want to face.
>
> • Running toward something can mean that you are rapidly moving forward in your life or in a particular situation.
>
> • If you are running in a race and win, your unconscious may be expressing confidence that you may or may not feel in the wakened state. You may also want to consider your current challenges.

• Running with no goal may be an indication that you need to slow down in your every day life

Rust

• Are you using your talents or are they gathering rust? Are you a bit rusty in your skills?
• A sign of deterioration.

S

Sacrifice

• Before you can nourish others, you first need to nourish yourself.
• Making sacrifices is human, but when you do too much for the world and not enough for yourself, you are left feeling neglected and weak. Perhaps you need to prioritize. You may want to consider the fact that whatever is constantly requiring you to make personal sacrifices may not be in your best interest or conducive to your health or happiness.

Saddle

• Are you saddled with a load or burden? Is there a situation from which you would like to be free?
• A saddle enables you to more easily ride an animal. Perhaps you are now better able to deal with some of the negative feelings surfacing.
• Maybe you need to saddle up and get going.

Sailboat

• Navigating through emotional change

Saint

• Messenger from your guardian angel or Higher Self. Listen.

Salt

- Strength and stability
- A medicine, a preservative and a link to the spirit world. It used to be considered so valuable that it was traded ounce for ounce with gold. In early China, salt cakes were even used as currency.
- Salt is used for purification and for dispersing negativity. Do you need to purify your thoughts or body? Are there negative feelings that need to be resolved?
- If someone is truly trustworthy and possessing integrity we refer to them as "the salt of the earth."

Sand

- Sand may symbolize small irritations and annoyances in your life.
- A house built on sand doesn't have a permanent foundation. Nothing is permanent. Are your dreams or is your life built on the shifting sands of time?
- There may be changes coming your way.

Satan

- An aspect of yourself. Carl Jung called such dark figures "the shadow" and said that they represent the negative ego personality and qualities which are painful and regrettable. You may have dark thoughts or have engaged in negative actions and are now experiencing guilt, fear, and anxiety.

Saturn (Cronos)

- Saturn is a Roman deity representing the Golden Age.
- Astrologically, Saturn represents barriers, misfortune, fixation and impotence, as well as loyalty, righteousness, consistency, knowledge and self-denial.

S

• Saturn symbolizes man's ability to recognize the difficulties of life and to confront the impulsive and passion motivated lifestyle.
• It may be an unconscious message regarding self-restrain and a need for a more intellectual, moral and spiritual life.

Saw

• Do you need to be cut down to size?
• Perhaps you are or need to be constructing something new.
• A saw is sometimes used for pruning. Are there areas of your life that need to be thinned out in order for there to be room for the new growth?
• Is there something you "saw" that needs to be addressed?

School

• A place where you learn
• Going to school or attending class in a dream is your unconscious reminder that there is a need for new learning and that you may need to learn an important lesson. What is it you need to learn more about?
• If you were a teacher in your dream, you may be dealing with issues of authority.
• If you had a particularly positive or negative experience while in school, which is a predominant thought whenever you come in contact with the word school, your dream may have to do with the feelings associated with your experience while there.

Scissors

• Scissors can represent cutting away or releasing that which you no longer need in your life.
• Perhaps you are feeling cut of from something or someone.

Scorpion

- A scorpion may be symbolic of something which is hurtful, dangerous and "stinging." It may represent bitter words or negative attitudes.
- A symbol of transformation.

Sea (*see* **Ocean**)

Seed

- Seeds symbolize new opportunities and new beginnings. Great things grow from small beginnings if they have a good environment. Just as a seed is the beginning of a new life or its earliest stage, the seed in your dream may be indicating that the ideas you have planted are beginning to germinate.
- Your past experiences and hard work may be leading to new opportunities or possibilities
- "As you sow, so shall you reap"

Seven (*see* under **Numbers**)

Sex

- There are many possible interpretations for this dream symbol. It is so complex that interpretations vary with each dreamer and situation in the dream.
- It shows to you your relationship with your True Self as represented by the characteristics and attitudes of those involved.
- A sexual dream may be about physical pleasure, but it may also be about power, control, manipulation, virility, and effectiveness.
- It may be a compensation for a lack of sex in daily life.

Shadow

- The unknown parts of yourself
- A sign of fear. Remember that the shadow is an illusion which disappears in the light.

• Your latent potential

Shark

• Omen of danger

• A hidden fear

• Water in your dreams usually represents your emotions and the unconscious. Because sharks dwell in water, they could represent unpleasant emotions or difficult and painful feelings coming up from the unconscious.

• When people are referred to as sharks, it means they are taking advantage of others. Are you taking advantage of others? Or, maybe there is something in you life of which you need to take advantage.

Sheep (*see* also **Lamb**)

• Are you following without using your own judgement?

• Are you listening to your own inner wisdom and judgement?

• Are you being "fleeced" or taken advantage of in some way?

Shell

• If you are pulling into a shell, it represents closing yourself off from the outer world.

• It may symbolize emptiness. Are you feeling empty and unfulfilled in your life?

Shepherd

• The guardian of your spirit and inner path

Shield

• Protection which allows you to stay balanced amidst difficulties and change.

• It is used for defense. Do you feel a need to defend something or someone?

Ship

• Water represents your unconscious, your feelings. The ship could represent you and the ways in which you navigate thought these parts of yourself.

• Consider the kind of voyage and the type of ship. If the voyage is calm you are probably doing well with what is going on in your life. However, if it is a very stormy voyage, you may be in for some stormy feelings rising to the surface.

Shirt

• Shirts generally represent your worldly appearance, status or public self.

• Different professionals have varied types of shirts they wear. The type of shirts being worn will give you clues to the meaning of the dream and to your unconscious ideas about yourself and others.

• Shirts may also represent your attitudes toward yourself and others.

• If you are putting on many shirts, you may be confused about what you want to be or how you want others to see you.

Shoes

• The steps you need to take to reach your goals
• Protection from the elements
• They keep you connected or grounded to the earth
• Don't judge another until you have "walked a mile in their shoes."
• Are you trying to fill too many shoes, playing too many roles?

Shooting

• Shooting at a target has to do with focusing energy on a particular goal in life.

• You may be trying to get rid of an aspect of yourself. If it is something that is not needful any

more, this may be good but it may also be something
you need to integrate into your consciousness.
• Do you feel like you are a victim in life?
• It may reflect aggression, powerlessness, release of
strong and dangerous emotions, and/or symbolize a
conclusive event in a particular situation or
relationship.

Shopping

• Depending on the situation and your feelings about
it, shopping can be a source of pain, pleasure,
recreation, and, at times, "quality time" with family
or friends.
• If shopping in your dream is pleasurable, it may
suggest that those things which you desire are
available to you.
• Do you know what you want? This dream calls
upon you to know yourself and then you will be able
to get what you truly desire.

Shoulders

• Represent the trouble you may have in making up
your mind.
• Are you shouldering your responsibilities?
• Put your "shoulder to the wheel."
• Where you carry burdens. Do you feel like you are
carrying the burdens of the world?

Sibling

• You learn important lessons about yourself
through your brothers and sisters. They are a
reflection of you, and you cannot escape their
presence, love, hate or any other emotion . What
characteristic or attitude do they represent about
you?

Silver (*see* under **Colors**)

Six (*see* under **Numbers**)

Skeleton

> • Bones are symbols of the death of physical structure. Is there a physical structure such as a club or social group from which you need to release yourself?
>
> • Do you need to get to the "bare bones" or essence of something?
>
> • It may be telling you that you need to begin "filling up" with feelings, adventures, work, or general enthusiasm for life. Eat the fruits of life and fatten up!

Skunk

> • Is there something that really "stinks?"
>
> • A skunk walks tall because he has the power of protection. Do you need to be reminded of your power within and with it...walk tall?

Sky

> • The sky is the limit. No limitations.
>
> • That which is above or beyond you

Sleeping

> • Do you need to wake up to what is going on?
>
> • Do you need more sleep?

Slide

> • Perhaps you are feeling out of control in your life, slipping and sliding.
>
> • If it is a water slide, you may be about to plunge into an emotional situation.

Smell

> • What is the smell and what do you associate with it? It could represent that which it brings to mind . . . a memory.

S

• May represent your nose and have to do with sticking your nose into something.

Smoke

• This may be warning you of a situation about to go up in flames

• Is the view or direction of your life unclear?

• To Native Americans, it is a vehicle on which prayers travel to the Creator.

• Are you or someone else just "blowing smoke?"

Smothering/Strangling/Choking

• Dreaming that you are having difficulty breathing and are in danger of dying may have to do with forces either from within your emotional and psychological makeup or circumstances on the outside.

• Do you feel suffocated by the experiences in your life?

• Perhaps you have so many unresolved negative feelings stuffed inside that it is choking your ability to move forward in life. Recognizing that they exist is a big step in releasing them.

Snail

• Are things moving slowly? Maybe you need to get going.

Snake

• This is not something to be feared. It is a symbol for healing.

• A powerful symbol of transformation and resurrection. Just as the snake shed its skin as it grows, this symbol may indicate that you are shedding your old Self, thoughts, feelings, beliefs etc., to embrace the new.

• It may represent a temptation.

Snow
> • Purity and cleansing
> • Time for a fresh start or new outlook on life
> • Snow can also represent frozen or blocked feelings

South
> • Below

Spider
> • A spider weaving a web represents creative forces
> • The web spirals to the center and can represent you and the center within.
> • It can also be a "web of illusion."
> • Entrapment. Are you getting caught in either your own web or someone else's web of manipulation and deception?

Spiral
> • A symbol of transformation or evolution
> • An upward spiraling; progressing in your life and goals
> • Achieving

Spring
> • New growth, new possibilities or new life
> • Do you need to add some spring to your step?

Square (*see* also **Mandala**)
> • A symbol of stability and firmness
> • The four elements; four sacred winds; four directions; four seasons.
> • If someone is square, they are not in touch with what is going on.
> • Do you feel like you are boxed in?

Squirrel
> • Frugality and comfort through patience
> • Do you need to make preparations for leaner times?

S

• Maybe you need to create a reserve of energy within yourself.

Star

• A star represents light, guidance and insight and the spirit within.

Statue

• Immobility
• Frozen feelings
• Feeling lifeless
• Lacking strength or energy

Stomach

• Awareness of the needs of others and your own
• Do you need to give out nourishment or take it in?
• Is there something you just can't stomach?
• The stomach holds nourishment and may represent the attitudes, ideas and feelings you take into yourself.

Stones

• Each stone has its own energy and meaning such as the clarity, brilliance and love represented by a diamond.
• Feeling solid
• Seer stone

Stork

• New arrival of new project in your life
• Birth of a new idea
• Happiness and contentment

Storm

• Internal conflict
• It may indicate that the air is clearing in a particular situation in your life.

Strangling (see **Smothering/Choking**)

Suicide
  • Warning sign
  • Doing away with parts of yourself.
  • This may be an indication that you have things you need to integrate into yourself and feelings that need to be resolved.

Summer
  • Fulfillment
  • Happiness, contentment
  • A season to enjoy

Sun
  • The source from which all things flow
  • A symbol for God, Great Spirit, Christ and the God within
  • Power, strength and clarity
  • Your own inner light
  • Do you need to project your energy forth and just go for it?

Sunflower
  • It is circular, therefore representing wholeness and completeness
  • Embracing the fullness of life
  • Sun

Swamp
  • Feeling bogged down and overwhelmed

Swan
  • White goddess
  • Beauty
  • Gliding into new heights with grace and freedom
  • Balance of female and male energies
  • Apollo, the god of music was associated with the swan

Swimming
  • Moving through feelings

• Are you having trouble staying afloat amidst emotional changes?

Sword

• Power
• Truth
• Honor
• A means of defense
• It is also the means of slaying the ego and cutting through the difficult things in life
• A two edge sword cuts to the truth of an issue

7

Table

• Assimilation, or "coming together" of various parts of yourself
• Do you need to put your cards on the table and let people know how you feel?
• A table may represent nourishment, friendship, and unity
• It could represent emotionally charged events, such as a family dinner or pleasant/unpleasant meetings
• Tables are either round or square which can also indicate partaking of wholeness
• Food is served on tables. They can therefore represent spiritual food or knowledge.

Target

• Your direction in life
• Your goal

Tattoo

• Things that are only "skin deep" but interesting and fun

• They could represent your thinking, your playful ways, and your seemingly unimportant habits
• Passing fads or ideas that have become permanent. Something that we inflict on ourselves and generally carries with it some negativity.

Teacher

• The meaning of this dream depends on your own experiences with teachers or teaching and, of course, the circumstances in your dream.
• Every person in your dreams or in life are your teachers.
• The dream could be addressing your issues with authority and approval.
• Do you have a need for guidance and new learning? The greatest teacher of all is within yourself.

Teeth

• The gate of the tongue
• How you control your speech
• Teeth can symbolize power and/or control
• Animals use their teeth for defense and nourishment and show their teeth when angry. Humans often display similar behaviors. Look and see if you are losing or abusing power and control in any area of your life.
• Decisiveness. Loss of teeth symbolizes loss of the power of decisive action.
• Each tooth can represent different negative feelings which need to be resolved. Pay attention to what you are feeling at the time of the dream.
• Are you talking too much? Do you need to listen?
• A loss of teeth can also symbolize growing up and moving into a new stage of life

Telephone
> • A ringing phone can mean that God is trying to get your attention.
> • If you are afraid to answer the phone, perhaps there are hidden messages within that you are afraid to hear.
> • Expressing a desire to communicate with yourself and with others.

Temple
> • The intersection or division between the heavens and the earth.
> • It represents your own body. To enter the temple is to enter into your inner realms.

Ten (*see* under **Numbers**)

Theater
> • Theaters may be a metaphor for your physical life
> • Where the drama of life takes place
> • Maybe in your dreams you are acting out some of your personal issues and concerns

Thighs
> • Independent movement
> • Out-going and on-going nature
> • Do you need to be more out going or do you need to hold back?

Thread
> • Look for the thread of truth
> • Used for holding clothing and other items together

Three (*see* under **Numbers**)

Throat (*see* also **Neck**)
> • Is there something in your life you just can't swallow?

• A sore throat may indicate that you have been restraining the things you have felt to say or that you have been speaking strong critical words

Thumb (*see* under **Fingers**)
Thunder

• Fire from the heavens
• Creative force of the universe
• An enormous release of suppressed feelings
• Message from God. Pay attention.

Tide

• The ebb and flow of life and of your feelings
• Do you need to project your energies out or pull them in?

Tiger

• Emperor of beasts
• Powerful symbol for integration of the physical
• Strength
• Stalking

Tires

• Your ability to move in life
• A flat tire can mean that you are not balanced.
• A tire without much tread can mean that you are having a hard time getting a grip on things in your life.

Toilet

• Elimination of that which isn't needed

Tomb

• Transformation
• Death
• Resurrection

Tongue

• Communicating, nourishing the body, and giving or receiving physical pleasure

7

• Are you gossiping or do you have a "harsh" tongue? Do you have other concerns in regard to this body part?

• The extended tongue can be a symbol of mockery, lustfulness, exhaustion, or thirst.

Tornado

• A violent storm in nature which may represent violent emotional storms in your life

• If you have reoccurring tornado dreams, consider the emotional changes in your life and also the amount of anger and rage that you may be currently experiencing.

• Disruptions and upsets in your immediate environment or current issues that may be overwhelming

Tower

• Isolation

• Spiritual point of clarity

• Pillar of strength

Toys

• Do you need to play more or be more childlike?

• Are you being toyed with?

Train

• Going on a train ride may be symbolic of your life's journey.

• If you are the engineer, you may be reassuring yourself in the dream state that you are in control of a specific situation or life in general.

• Symbolic of your need to move on and to do things in an orderly and sequential manner

• If you missed the train in your dream, you may be missing important opportunities.

• A train ride represents the way a person moves and behaves like everyone else.

• Moving the same as others

Trash

• Unwanted emotional baggage

Travel

• Traveling is representative of your journey through life.

• Your current movement toward goals

• Difficult traveling conditions such as a dark road, a bad storm, or an accident in a car, or other vehicle may be symbolic of the difficulties that you experience in your daily journey.

• Dreaming about traveling to a fun place and having a great time could be a form of compensation or wish-fulfillment. This type of a dream can be an escape from your daily life and form of transcendence into a beautiful dream world.

• If you are constantly having dreams about traveling, take a closer look at the current situations in your life. Are things going well, or are they more difficult than you would like them to be?

• Do you need a vacation?

Treasure

• Inner gifts and inner wealth from spirit

• A symbol for future attainment of valuable or precious possessions of any kind

Tree

• The tree in your dream is you. The health, size and overall quality of the tree is indicative of how you feel about yourself. Is the tree alive with leaves, flowers or fruit, or is it barren?

• Tree of Life and the Tree of Knowledge from the Bible

• The roots of the tree, which go deep into the ground, can be likened to your earthly life, while the branches rising into the sky symbolize your higher consciousness.

• What kind of tree is it? Each tree has its own properties. Oak trees represent strength. A pine can symbolize spiritual clarity and purification. Is it tall and straight or old and crooked?

• It can represent your Family Tree or heritage

Triangle

• The power of integration through the trinity: of body, mind and spirit; of mother, father and child; of past present and future; of the Holy Trinity

• The power of the pyramids

• The power of protection

• A musical instrument

Tunnel

• Inner passageway to the Self

• Are you seeing a light at the end of the tunnel, or are you trapped in a tunnel unable to determine your location? If it was not an unpleasant experience, it may symbolize a transitional period and a passage into new levels of understanding and/or ways of living.

• Going through tunnels can represent changing levels of consciousness and moving into different realities.

• A tunnel in a dream may also be a symbol representing the archetype of the feminine.

• Do you have tunnel vision?

Turkey

• Spirit of giving

• Gratitude for all you receive

• Gobbling up anything or everything for fear of not having enough.

Turtle
- Steadfastness and caution
- Turtles move and change very slowly. Are you reluctant to forge ahead? It may also represent the need to keep up a slow steady pace.
- The turtles have strong protective shells, which may also be symbolic of your defense mechanisms or real life protection with which you have surrounded yourself.

Twelve (*see* under **Number**s)

Twins
- Twins in astrology represent opposites, suggesting a duality in thoughts, ideas, feelings, or states of consciousness.
- Twins could also represent the balance that is extremely important to your emotional and psychological health.

Two (*see* under **Numbers**)

𝒰

UFO
- It may represent the quest for personal integration and higher intelligence or the fear of the unknown. Do you fear the unknown parts of yourself?
- Their round shape indicates wholeness and completion.

Umbrella
- Protection from life's storms
- A device that the conscious mind uses to protect itself from the unconscious

• Umbrellas may symbolize your unwillingness to deal with negative feelings, psychological baggage, or trauma

Uncle

• Are you being a "monkey's uncle?"
• What does this uncle represent to you? Are there any particular feelings that come to mind?
• People always represent your own characteristics and attitudes.

Underground

• Your subconscious mind

Undertaker

• Are you undertaking an unpleasant task or experience in your life?
• Are you processing feelings that you need to let go? Dealing with beliefs, thoughts or ideas that are no longer useful.

Undressed

• Feeling exposed or vulnerable
• Freeing yourself from inhibitions or your outer persona

Uniform

• Seeing yourself wearing a uniform in a dream suggests that you have identified with a larger group, a movement, or an organization that requires you to conform and carry out its ideology. This may be positive or negative depending on the associations made and the kind of uniform that you are wearing.
• Are you experiencing too much rigidity and inflexibility in your life?
• Uniforms can be a symbol of authority. Do you have problems with authority figures? Perhaps you need to claim your own authority within.

• The unconscious is pointing to the possibility that your individuality has been covered up and is being unnoticed because you are functioning as a member of a group and not as an individual.

Upper lip (*see* also **Lips**)

• Are you keeping a "stiff upper lip?"

Uranus (Ouranos)

• In mythology, Uranus is the sky-god and the personification of Heaven. He represents limitless potential for growth and is symbolic of evolution.

• Astrologically, Uranus represents cosmic power that causes creation, progress, sudden changes and, at times, upheavals and interference.

• The planet Uranus in your dream may represent unexplored possibilities and potential. It may be an unconscious encouragement to create change and to progress.

• If life appears to be a bit out of control and if many unsettling changes are occurring, this may be a positive sign from the unconscious. It suggests that turmoil can be used to create new possibilities and that in the end things will be better off then when they began.

Urination

• Releasing repressed feelings

• Many people dream about the need to urinate which wakes them up and then they realize that they really do need to use the bathroom.

Urn

• Because of the round hollow shape, it can symbolize the female energy

• They are used to contain ashes of the dead. It may therefore be holding the feelings or attitudes that serve you no longer.

𝒱

Vacation
• Do you need a vacation?
• Taking a vacation from your old way of thinking

Vacuum
• Living in a vacuum
• Cleaning or removing that which is no longer needed
• Eliminating the negativity in your life

Vagina
• A symbol of womanliness, openness, acceptance and receptivity
• Inner valley of spirit
• It may represent repressed feelings from negative sexual experiences

Vampire
• Feeling overwhelmed in some areas of your life; struggling with negative thoughts, feelings, and actions.
• The vampire represents personal attributes or negative habits that drain energy and resources or cause emotional exhaustion.
• If you are being attacked by a vampire, you may perceive yourself as a powerless victim. Interpreting this dream's message may help you to identify the source of your negative feelings and helplessness.

Vase

- Something personal that has value and beauty
- It is a holding vessel for water and flowers. Look up these words for further understanding of what the vase represents.
- If you are dreaming about a broken vase, you need to consider the areas of life that seem to be falling apart and need mending.

Vegetables

- Nourishment
- Interpreting the symbolism of vegetables in your dream depends on how you feel about them in daily life: whether you like them for their taste and nutritional value, or find them dull and boring. You may be projecting a need to feed your body or soul or reflecting on a dull and not very satisfying part of life.

Velvet

- Sensuality or desire

Venus (Aphrodite)

- Venus, the planet is known as the Morning Star. It also sets in the west and is the Evening Star. Due to the way this planet travels across the sky, it is often a symbol of death and rebirth. It is associated with the sun and considered to be the sun's messenger and an intermediary between the sun and mankind.
- In Greek mythology, Aphrodite is the goddess of beauty and love. The love that she represents is not of the emotional and fruitful kind, but rather lust, sensual pleasure and raw animal attraction. Aphrodite may represent your basic sexual nature before it is tamed and humanized by emotions and spirit.

• Are you full of lust and/or has your sexuality been ignored?
• If you are feeling drained by life, the planet Venus may be a representation of the ability to regenerate and begin anew.
• It may be a reminder that there is an abundance of internal energy and resources accessible to all that tap into it.

Vineyard

• Time to harvest the fruits of your experience
• The source of wine which can represent the life blood or life energy

Violence

• Confusion and conflict that are experiences in daily life
• Unconscious negative feelings such as fear, anxiety, and anger
• If you are not dealing with these feelings consciously, your dreams may be compensating and bringing into awareness the need for honest reflection and emotional balance in daily life.

Virgin

• Chastity
• Mother Mary
• Female aspect of God
• Newness

Volcano

• Erupting emotions. Feelings that you may be harboring during the day might take the form of a volcanic eruption in a dream state. The unconscious psyche may be releasing positive or negative feelings in a safety of a dream.

Vomit

- Showing you that there are things in life that you don't like seeing
- Things in life that cause you emotional stress, repulse you, and make you ill
- This dream suggests that you are rejecting a thought, idea, feeling, or circumstance and that you need to get rid of quickly.

Waiter/Waitress

- Serving others or being served

Walking

- The way you move in dreams, or the means of transportation, may represent how efficiently you maneuver and progress on your personal journey through life. Is the means of transportation appropriate for the journey?
- If you are walking to no specific destination, it may represent that you are searching for your direction in life. Were you walking around aimlessly or swiftly going to a particular destination?
- Your goals may be met through a slow but steady pace.

Walls

- Walls are generally considered obstacles or blockages in your life.
- Walls can be sources of isolation or confinement.
- Climbing the wall suggests that you are becoming prepared or are able to overcome difficulties and/or challenges.

• Walls are used to define areas of your house. Perhaps it is showing how you have your feelings, life in general or aspects of your Self divided up. Do you need to open up the rooms inside yourself?

Wand

• The ability to change things instantly
• Symbol of transformation

War

• Inner conflict and aggression
• You may be faced with a situation that requires you to be aggressive or assertive and to come to terms with opposition.
• War veterans and others who have experienced war first hand may, from time to time, have such dreams based on memory and trauma. In these cases, it is helpful to identify the feelings associated with the experience and resolve them.

Washing

• Releasing the past or old attitudes and beliefs

Wasp

• Stinging thoughts or words being spoken
• Irritations; unwanted intrusions

Watch

• The passing of time
• Do you feel like you are running out of time?
• Perhaps you need to "watch" for other symbols and be aware as you pass through the hours of your day.
• Watch out! Pay attention.

Water

• The meaning of water varies somewhat from culture to culture but usually has to do with emotions, feelings, intuition, psychic perceptions and

the subconscious mind, as well as the mysterious realms of the archetypal female energy.
• It is considered the source of all life by some and as the holder of the secret of the preservation of life by others
• In some Christian baptismal rites, water represents life, death and resurrection. When one is submerged under water, the old person disappears and a new person emerges.
• Flowing water symbolizes flowing emotions and feelings. If the water is dammed, it means your feelings are blocked.
• Is the water clear or murky? Clear water represents clarity, being in tune with life and connected to the inner feminine energy of receptivity and intuition. Dirty water may represent being full of negative unresolved feelings.
• Water also has to do with spiritual alignment and attunement. It is the "water of life" or the "flow of life."

Waterfall (*see* also **Water**)
• A waterfall is a positive dream symbol that suggests a cleansing of negative emotions or psychological issues. Simply visualizing or a daydreaming of standing in a waterfall makes a person feel energized and refreshed.
• If the waterfall in your dream is overwhelming or too powerful for you to enjoy, it may represent emotional energy and unconscious drives that are very difficult to effectively cope with on the conscious level
• A complete emotional release, healing and recharging

Waves

- Surging forward
- Great emotional strength and power
- The waves may represent emotional fluctuations
- Tidal waves suggest a period of emotional upheaval. Anxiety, stress, and unconscious materials may be coming to the surface and affecting your daily moods. The outcome of your dream may reveal how much strength you have to "ride out" personal storms.
- If you drown or someone else in the dream drowns, it may mean that you are "in it over your head" and should seek assistance

Weasel

- Weasels are very quick with speedy reflexes and are expert hunters. Perhaps there is a situation in your life that needs quick action.
- Is someone weaseling in on your territory or are you pushing someone else out of the way? What would be the best for everyone's highest good?

Weather

- The weather is a good sign of your emotional state
- Stormy weather reflects an inner storm; rain can represent grief or emotional purification; fog could mean not seeing clearly.

Wedding

- A symbol of the union of the conscious and subconscious parts of your mind, of your body and spirit. Uniting the male and female aspects of yourself
- The marriage in your dream may represent the union of the different aspects of your own character.

Weeds

• Weeds represent neglect. Perhaps you have not been regularly tending your physical or psychological environment.

• Weeds are indicative of negativity as well as growth of useless and harmful elements in your life. Just as we need to weed out the garden to have healthy plants, we need to weed out the negativity in our minds.

Well

• A symbol of a depth of wisdom and inspiration

• It contains refreshing, life giving waters

• Deep within yourself

Whale

• Because they use sonar to tune in to the world around them, they can represent perception and intuition. Do you need to use your intuition to tune in to the situations in your own life?

• Perhaps you need to access your inner power and strength as well as the gentleness and love the whale represents.

• The symbol of the whale may be an indication of the size of something as in "a whale of a job." Perhaps the feelings you need to deal with are of major proportions.

• Whales are symbolic of the connection that exists between the unconscious and conscious mind.

Wheel

• References to wheels are many: the "wheel of life," the "wheel of fortune," and the "wheel of karma." The only part of a wheel remaining in the same place is the center. Are you able to remain centered in the face of the outer extremes of the wheel of life such as with the opposites of life and death, mystery and form?

White (*see* under **Colors**)

Wind

- Wind can represent your own spirit or the life force
- The wind may represent changes in your life as in "the winds of change." The greater the force of the wind, the grater the change. A very gusty wind could represent stress and turmoil but also the energy that you need in order to make changes.
- Air is the element that represents thought, intellect, spirit or the celestial breath of God.
- The wind can carry messages from the realm of spirt.
- Changing winds can represent that there are changes in the wind for you.

Window

- A window can represent your personal outlook on life. If you are looking through the window, pay close attention to what you are looking at. Is it familiar to you or from your past or just what?
- Some say that a window may represent a time frame. A closed window suggests an inability to effectively communicate and an opened widow may represent desire for new adventure in life.
- Windows in our houses allow us to see the world on the out side, the windows in our dreams may encourage us to better see the world within ourselves, as well as the world outside.

Wings

- Wings are associated with flying, which in turn is associated with freedom and the heavenly domain.

• Transcendence and liberation. Do you want to transcend the current difficulties and problems? Perhaps you have just been given the wings you need to do so. Is there something that has come into your life which is providing the help you need?

• Wings sometimes carry messages from spirit.

Witch

• A witch can represent power, magic, and goodness.

• The witch may also represent evil and ugliness. The word witch is sometimes used to describe a mean and heartless person, and your dream may be revealing a part of yourself which fits this description.

• Whether good or evil, the witch always tries to defy natural law using a short cut to accomplish a task. Ask yourself questions about the general message in the dream; is it about revealing negative characteristics or about solving your problems and getting what you want out of life by using shortcuts?

• Maybe you should consider solving your difficulties by using creativity and intuition which will bring you closer to finding powerful and magical parts of yourself.

Wolf

• Wolves can represent wisdom. Do you need to share your wisdom with others?

• Seek the wisdom of the voice within

• Have you been howling about something?

Womb

• A symbol of nourishment, safety or protection

• Perhaps you need to pull inside for a period of time.

Worm

• Things going on beneath the surface. Do you need to prepare fertile soil for your ideas or projects?
• A person who is a lowlife; someone with no backbone.

X

X-Ray

• Seeing what is within with more clarity
• This dream suggests that you are ready to look beneath the surface of a current situation or problem.
• X-rays require focused energy and your dream may be a reflection on the energy that you already possess. This energy will assist you in gaining insight and awareness or help you with problem solving.

Xylophone (*see* **Music**)

Y

Yard

• The yard in your dream may be a reflection of how well you have been able to maintain your internal and external environment.
• The backyard points to things that are less obvious and, at times, may be unconscious. It may also represent childhood memories that hold positive and negative feelings and lead to self-awareness.

• If the *yard* in your dream was a measuring unit, think about what you are measuring and if any growth has taken place.

Yawn

• A sign of boredom
• Do you need a good outlet for your creativity?

Yellow (*see* under **Colors**)

Yo-Yo

• Going up and down
• Repeating the same old patterns

Zero (*see* under **Numbers**)

Zombie

• "Walking around like a zombie," usually means that you are emotionally disconnected from things going on around you. You may be experiencing unhealthy detachment and are unable to appropriately feel positive or negative emotions.
• Are you out of touch and outside of the main flow of life?
• Do you need to become more aware of emotional issues and circumstances in daily life that are difficult for you to face?

My Personal List

of Symbols

This section is for recording your own
symbols and their meanings.

Summary

Some of the stepping stones for Knowing and BEing Your "True" Self . . . simplified.

• Desire to know the truth of all things for yourself. Seek knowledge and wisdom by following the direction given to you from within.

• Be willing to face your self with honesty. Look at yourself in the many mirrors available . . . every day. Look with a desire to become aware of the things that are keeping you in the box labeled "less than who you are."

• Resolve any negative feelings and thoughts and false and limiting beliefs which are covering the truth of who you are. Do this on a daily basis.

• Take a few minutes each day to be silent and *listen*. Practice hearing the voice within and become more aware of how the messages are being communicated to you.

• Live in the present moment. Experience what is happening with all of your senses; feel it, hear it, see it, smell it, taste it . . . be one with it.

• Value "your" truth. You are unique for a reason. As you uncover your True Self, have the courage to live that truth. Let go and trust the power within. BE who you really are and live your life with abandon!

• Balance the opposition in your life, peacefully. Accept "what is" without judgement or blame.

Appendix I

Examples of how to state the negative feelings and positive replacements when using the "Painless Tool."

Here are two examples of negative and positive feelings for physical problems. These lists illustrate the negative feelings that can cause **HEADACHES** and **NECK** problems with their appropriate replacements stated in the way you would say them if you were using the *"Painless Tool"* to resolve them. With each one of the feelings listed, you may want to be more specific as to your situation. The more precise you are, the better.

After identifying the negative feelings associated with any part of your body experiencing discomfort or pain, make a similar list. Write down both negative and positive feelings. Use the *"Painless Tool"* as illustrated in Chapter 14 to resolve these feelings.

HEADACHE

Negative Feelings	Positive Replacements
Feeling conflict in where to center myself	I choose being centered in who I am; I feel centered in who I am; I am centered in being who I am.
Feeling pressured	I choose being relieved; I feel relieved; I am relieved.
Feeling anxious	I choose being calm and peaceful; I feel calm and peaceful; I am calm and peaceful.

Negative Feelings	**Positive Replacements**
Feeling stressed out	I choose being peaceful, calm and relaxed; I feel peaceful, calm and relaxed; I am peaceful calm and relaxed.
Feeling unable to express my feelings	I choose expressing my feelings; I feel able to freely express my feelings; I am freely expressing my feelings.
Feeling unable to resolve my emotional upsets	I choose resolving my emotional upsets; I feel able to resolve my emotional upsets; I am resolving my emotional upsets.
Feeling unable to control my circumstances	I choose letting go and allowing things to be as they are; I feel able to let go and allow things to be as they are; I am letting go and allowing things to be as they are.
Feeling unable to express my joy, to sing and laugh	I choose expressing joy, singing and laughing; I feel able to express my joy, to sing and laugh; I am expressing joy, singing and laughing.
Feeling fear	I choose being confident and brave; I feel confident, I feel brave; I am confident, I am brave.
Feeling uptight and tense	I choose being relaxed, serene, flowing and flexible; I feel relaxed, serene, flowing and flexible; I am relaxed, serene, flowing and flexible.

NECK

Negative Feelings	**Positive Replacements**
Feeling bullnecked	I choose being pliable, adaptable and flexible; I feel pliable, adaptable and flexible; I am pliable, adaptable and flexible.
Feeling confused	I choose being clear-headed and understanding; I feel clear-headed and understanding; I am clear-headed and understanding.
Feeling resistant to the will of God	I choose accepting the will of God; I feel able to accept the will of God; I am accepting the will of God.
Feeling restrained anger	I choose releasing my anger appropriately; I give myself permission to release my anger appropriately; I am appropriately releasing my anger. I choose feeling peaceful and calm; I am peaceful and calm. I choose feeling loving and forgiving; I am loving and forgiving.
Feeling fear in speaking my truth	I choose speaking my truth; I give myself permission to speak my truth; I feel to speak my truth; I am speaking my truth.

Negative Feelings	Positive Replacements
Feeling to speak critically of others	I choose accepting others and being allowing and forgiving of others; I feel allowing, accepting and forgiving of others; I am allowing, accepting and forgiving of others.
Feeling to swallow my emotional hurts	I choose releasing and expressing my emotional hurts; I feel able to release and express my emotional hurts; I am releasing and expressing my emotional hurts.

Appendix II

Essential Oils

Essential oils are the subtle, volatile liquids (or the life blood) that are distilled from the plants, shrubs, trees, flowers, roots and seeds. Each oil has its own unique "frequency." Clinical research shows that Essential Oils have the highest frequency of any substance known to man, creating an environment in which disease, bacteria, virus and fungus cannot live.

These healing substances have been used for centuries. In fact, there are 188 references in the Bible to these oils. The ancient Egyptians were known to use them for what they referred to as "cleansing the flesh and the blood." for the purpose of removing from their minds "evil deities." Today they're called "negative feelings" or "bad attitudes." As we go through life we have experiences that leave us with trauma which produces fear and prevents us from reaching our highest potential.

Science is only now rediscovering Essential Oils, thanks in large part to Dr. Gary Young, an Aromatologist and owner of Young Living Essential Oils. Dr. Young has created 25 blends of Oils to deal with emotions. His "Feelings" kit features 12 of them. They deal with feelings ranging from lack of courage, disharmony, anger, lack of love for Self, lack of spirituality, trauma from abuse and others. They are designed to assist you in the release of undesirable feelings and are very easy to use.

There is also a unique blend of oils called "**Dream Catcher**." This oil may help open the mind, enhance dreams, and help one visualize their visions and hang onto them until they become reality. It may even help you sleep more soundly.

Lavender, another Essential Oil mentioned in the book is a universal oil that has traditionally been known to balance the body and work wherever there is a need. It is helpful for alleviating insomnia and by promoting sleep, gives you more dream time. It may help allergies, burns, arthritis, asthma, bronchitis, earaches, high blood pressure, headaches, & PMS, just to name a few.

Combine the Essential Oils with the "Painless Tool"and you'll have powerful help for changing negative feelings to positive and your journey will be enhanced!

For more information regarding these Essential Oils, call 208-847-3129 or go to www.valerieann.com and request a FREE TAPE. The book entitled, "Reference Guide for Essential Oils" is an excellent resource for understanding more about the power of Essential Oils and what they can be used for (*see* Bibliography).

Appendix III

DREAM CATCHERS

These beautifully handcrafted Dream Catchers are for those who would like to tap a little extra help remembering their dreams of the night and catching their dreams in life. Skillfully wrapped in soft swede leather, their design is unparalleled . . . inspired by the cover painting. Each one is made with three hoops, woven together with threads which symbolically tie all parts of your world or Self together, creating a spherical shape of oneness and wholeness. When spinning, a figure eight or symbol of integration appears inside. The feathers are wings that help your desires and dreams take flight and your dreams of the night come to mind upon awakening. The white dove in the center represents peace, love and your True Self.

Each Dream Catcher is handmade especially for you by Kristen Johnson with your choice of size and color—no two exactly alike. They will lift your spirits and who knows the magic they might produce for you as you infuse them with your dreams and desires!

Appendix IV

ABOUT THE COVER PAINTING

On the Spring Equinox of 1997, I had an unparalleled and unexpected experience which still amazes me every time I think about it. As a result of receiving divine direction to do so, I painted twelve paintings in one day at a place in Missouri called Adam-ondi-Ahman. The picture on the cover of this book was painted after I returned home—the culmination of my entire experience.

In this painting, the world is represented as a "sea of glass." This is what the earth becomes to each of us, once we recognize our connection to all that is, learning to see our reflection in everyone and everything—when our world becomes a "World of Mirrors."

This entire experience is found in a book entitled, *"Returning to the Heart,"* (*see* Bibliography) which includes an 8" x 10" high quality art print of the cover painting of this book as well as the twelve paintings created in Missouri.

Bibliography
and Suggested Reading

Carter, Karen Rauch, *Move Your Stuff, Change Your Life*,
   Simon & Schuster, Inc, New York, New York, 2000

Chopra, Deepak, *How to know God,*
   Harmony Books, New York, New York, 2000

Clift, Wallace B., *Jung and Christianity*,
   Crossroad Publishing Company, New York, New York, 1993

Diamond, John, M.D., *Your Body Doesn't Lie*,
   Warner Books, New York, New York, 1979

Green Glenda, *Love Without End*,
   Heartwings Publishing, Fort Worth, Texas, 1995

Higley, Connie & Alan, *Reference Guide for Essential Oils*,
   Abundant Health, Spanish Fork, Utah, 2001

Hilton, Suzan, *The Feng Shui of Abundance*,
   Broadway Books, New York, New York, 2001

Jacob, W. Lindsay, M.D., *Interpreting Your Dreams*,
   St. Martin's Press, New York, New York,1985

Jung, Carl Gustav, *Dreams*,
   Princeton University Press, Princeton, New Jersey, 1974

Jung, Carl Gustav, *Man and His Symbols*,
   Dell Publishing, New York, New York, 1964

Jung, Carl Gustav, *Mandala Symbolism*,
   Princeton University Press, Princeton, New Jersey, 1973

Jung, Carl Gustav, *Memories, Dreams, Reflections*,
   Vintage Books, Inc., New York, New York, 1989

Linn, Denise, *The Secret Language of Signs*,
        Ballantine Books, New York, New York, 1996

Morris, William, Editor, *The American Heritage Dictionary*,
        Houghton Mifflin Company, Boston, Massachusetts, 1978

Orman, Suze, *The Courage to Be Rich*,
        Riverhead Books, New York, New York, 2002

Ponder, Catherine, *The Millionaires of Genesis*,
        DeVorss & Company, Marina del Rey, California, 1976

Prather, Hugh *The Little Book of Letting Go*,
        Conari Press, Berkeley, California, 2000

Sanford, John A., *Dreams - God's Forgotten Language*,
        HarperSanFrancisco, New York, New York, 1989

Sanford, John A., *The Kingdom Within*,
        HarperCollins Publishers, San Francisco, CA 94111, 1979

Skinner, Valerieann J., *Cashing in on the Simple Magic of Color*,
        Inner Light Creations, Georgetown, Idaho, 2000.
        Free copy as an e-book at http://www.valerieann.com.

Skinner, Valerieann J., *Returning to the Heart*,
        Inner Light Creations, Georgetown, Idaho, 2002

Truman, Karol K., *Feelings Buried Alive Never Die . . .*,
        Olympus Distributing, Las Vegas, Nevada, 1975

Truman, Karol K., *Healing Feelings . . . From Your Heart,*
        Olympus Distributing, Las Vegas, Nevada, 2001

Van De Castle, Robert L. PH.D., *Our Dreaming Mind*,
        Ballantine Books, New York, New York, 1994

About the Author . . .

Valerieann J. Skinner

Valerieann was raised on a farm in Georgetown, Idaho. Her close association with animals and nature while growing up has resulted in a close connection to and deep love for all things. Painting and writing are the mediums she uses to process and share her experiences in life, a life that includes her husband Alan and their six children. She has taught art lessons for nineteen years, helping many to better know and express their feelings about themselves, their lives, and the world around them through art.

On the spring equinox of 1997, Valerieann found herself in the heart of America painting 12 paintings in one day, at a place called Adam-ondi-Ahman. Later that same year, during the summer and winter solstices, she painted at one of the ancient Mayan ruins in Palenque, Mexico. Her experiences in these places and others have profoundly affected her life and inspired her to write.

Enjoy traveling with her and her pen. Tap the power of *"Cashing in on the 'Simple Magic of Color,"* discover the magic of knowing your True Self by reading *"The World of Mirrors,"* journey into your heart in a healing way by sharing in her experience at Adam-ondi-Ahman in *"Returning to the Heart,"* then look forward to uncovering the *"Courage to Live Your Truth"* in her upcoming book.

Valerieann also conducts personal seminars where she teaches the concepts presented in this book. To schedule a seminar in your area, call 208-847-3129. For more detailed information on the art classes, oil paintings, greeting cards, and e-books available from Inner Light Creations, visit Valerieann's website at www.valerieann.com or send E-mail to valerieann@valerieann.com.

Index

ORDER FORM

Shipping	Product Description	Price
Per each	**BOOKS**	
4.95	The World Within-A Bridge to Knowing and Being Your "True" Self	17.95
6.50	Returning to the Heart - Includes 13 - 8 x 10 Fine art prints, ready to frame	98.00
4.50	Cashing in on the "Simple Magic" of Color - 8½ x 11, spiral bound	14.95
	DREAM CATCHERS - Handmade	
	Circle color and size: White Blue Purple Natural	
4.95	3" - 19.95 5" - 29.95 7" - 47.95 9" - 64.95 12" - 79.95	
	ART PRINTS	
	Cover Painting - Circle size:	
2.00	5 x 7 - 10.00 8 x 10 - 15.00 11 x 14 - 20.00 12 x 16 - 25.00	
	Filling the Measure of Creation (Pea Pod) - Circle size:	
2.00	5 x 7 - 10.00 8 x 10 - 15.00 11 x 14 - 20.00 12 x 16 - 25.00	
	Poppies - Circle size:	
2.00	5 x 7 - 10.00 8 x 10 - 15.00 11 x 14 - 20.00 12 x 16 - 25.00	
	The World Within is the World We're In	
2.00	5 x 7 - 10.00 8 x 10 - 15.00 11 x 14 - 20.00 12 x 16 - 25.00	
	GREETING CARDS - Size 5 x 7 with white envelopes and poetry inside	
1.00	Cover Painting	2.75
1.00	Filling the Measure of Creation (Pea Pod)	2.75
1.00	Poppies	2.75
1.00	The World Within is the World We're In	2.75
1.00	Returning to Myself (Poetry only)	2.75
1.00	**LAMINATED CARD WITH "PAINLESS TOOL"** - Size: 3½ x 8½	1.00

Call for shipping rates on international and larger orders. For multiple items, take the greatest shipping charge and add $1.00 for each additional item ordered. All prices are subject to change without notice.

Mail to: Abundant Health
478 S. Geneva Rd.
Orem, UT 84058-5801
Phone: 1-866-728-0070
Fax: 1-877-568-1988
E-Mail: orders@abundant-health4u.com
Web Site: www.abundant-health4u.com
Visit our website for more products and monthly internet specials.

BILLING INFORMATION
(as it appears on the credit card statement)

Name:_____

Address:_____

City/State/Zip:_____

Phone #:_____

E-mail Address:_____

SHIP-TO INFORMATION
(to which order will be sent)

Name:_____

Address:_____

City/State/Zip:_____

PAYMENT INFORMATION

☐ Visa ☐ MC   Credit Card Number:_____
☐ Check/Money Order
   (Include with order form)   Exp. Date:_____

                             Signature:_____

Qty	Description	Unit Price	Total

SUBTOTAL:	=
Sales Tax (Utah residents only) x 0.0625 :	+
Shipping/Handling:	+
TOTAL COST:	=